LAPHAM'S
QUARTERLY

One religion is as true as another.
                    —*Robert Burton, 1621*

The archangel Michael weighing souls, from *Last Judgment* (detail), by Rogier van der Weyden, c. 1443–51.

www.laphamsquarterly.org

Volume 3, No. 1. www.laphamsquarterly.org. Lapham's Quarterly (ISSN 1935-7494) is published four times yearly (December, March, June, September) by the American Agora Foundation, 33 Irving Place, 8th Floor, New York, NY 10003. Periodicals postage paid at New York, NY, and additional mailing offices. Copyright © 2008 the American Agora Foundation. Nothing shown may be reproduced in any form without obtaining the permission of the creators and of any other person or company who may have copyright ownership. Printed in Canada.
Newsstand distribution: CMG. Newsstand Consultant: Ellen Sugarman, 617-505-5596.
Subscriber Services. Subscription: 1 year, $60; in Canada, $70; in all other countries, $100. All payments in U.S. Dollars. Direct all inquiries, address changes, subscription orders, etc., to: email: custsvc_laphams@fulcoinc.com; telephone: 877-890-3001; mail: Lapham's Quarterly, PO Box 3000, Denville, NJ 07834. Editorial and Business Office, 33 Irving Place, 8th Floor, New York, NY 10003. Postmaster: Send changes of address to Lapham's Quarterly, PO Box 3000, Denville, NJ 07834.

LAPHAM'S
QUARTERLY

RELIGION

Introductory

Voices in Time

DECLARATIONS OF FAITH

Voices in Time

ACTS OF FAITH

Voices in Time

CRISES OF FAITH

The Tower of Babel, by Pieter Bruegel the Elder, 1563.

Voices in Time

Further Remarks

ESSAYS

DEPARTMENTS

Moses drowning the Egyptians,
proposed Great Seal of the United States, 1776.

Many of the passages in this issue have been abbreviated without the use of ellipses; some punctuation has been modified, and while overt misspellings have been corrected, archaic word and grammar usage remains unchanged. The words in all instances are faithful to the original texts.

ART, PHOTOGRAPHY, AND ILLUSTRATIONS

Among the Contributors

Iris Murdoch (1919–1999) began teaching philosophy at Oxford in 1948, published her first novel in 1954, and won the Booker Prize for *The Sea, The Sea* in 1978. Her struggles with Alzheimer's during the last years of her life she described as "sailing into darkness."

The Greek writer **Plutarch** (c. 46–c. 110) directed a school that specialized in philosophy and also served as chief magistrate of his hometown Chaeronea. An extensive traveler in the Mediterranean, he later earned a lifelong priesthood at Delphi around 95. He is best known for his *Parallel Lives* of famous Greeks and Romans.

Alexis de Tocqueville (1805–1859) was born into an aristocratic Parisian family with a history in politics, and entered the French civil service in 1827. He published *Democracy in America* in two volumes in 1835 and 1840 and won his first election to political office in 1839. He died while writing his history of the French Revolution.

Albert Einstein (1879–1955) wondered in his youth what it was like to run alongside a light beam, later leading him to develop the theory of special relativity and overturn Newtonian physics. While lecturing at Princeton in 1921, the dean introduced him by saying, "We salute the new Columbus of science voyaging through the strange seas of thought."

Confucian thought largely owes its survival to the work of **Xunzi** (c. 300–c. 230 BC), one of the three great Confucian philosophers of China's classical period. His essays make the point that religious fictions, while useful as an emotional outlet, should not be considered true by educated people.

Anna Comnena (1083–c. 1153) was the first woman to write a work of history. Raised in the imperial household of Constantinople, she was a devoted student with a penchant for philosophy and medicine. *The Alexiad*, written between 1143 and 1153, encompasses the First Crusade and the definitive schism between the eastern and western churches.

Descended from two rabbinical families, the novelist and short-story writer **Isaac Bashevis Singer** (1904–1991) won the 1978 Nobel Prize for Literature, claiming in his lecture, "There must be a way for man to attain all possible pleasures, all the powers and knowledge that nature can grant him, and still serve God."

Born in Tunis, **Ibn Khaldun** (1332–1406) belonged to one of Seville's most powerful political families, which left the city right before its fall to the Christian conquests in 1248. He is credited with developing one of the earliest nonreligious philosophies of history.

The novelist **James Baldwin** (1924–1987) was born into poverty in Harlem and spent much of his youth in libraries. Knowing his vocation early on, he said, "I didn't know how I would use my mind, or if I could, but that was the only thing I had to use."

Despite run-ins with authorities for his ridicule of court society, **Voltaire** (1694–1778) was revered during his lifetime as France's greatest writer. In 1758, he retreated in exile to his estate in Switzerland, where he became known as "the innkeeper of Europe," visited by the likes of Boswell, Casanova, and Gibbon.

The Russian poet **Marina Tsvetaeva** (1892–1941) self-financed the publication of her first poetry collection in 1910, which met with high praise from critics and ushered her into the forefront of Moscow's literary world. When she committed suicide in 1941, she was buried in an unmarked grave with no one attending her funeral.

Babur (1483–1530) founded the Mughal dynasty that ruled over northern India for nearly two centuries. He composed a remarkable record of his life, matching his ability as a statesman with literary skill.

A dissenting Augustinian monk, **Martin Luther** (1483–1546) helped instigate the Protestant Reformation in 1517 when he wrote the Ninety-five Theses in order to debate a Dominican friar's support for the sale of Papal indulgences. After Pope Leo X deemed some of Luther's writing "heretical, scandalous, offensive to pious ears," he was excommunicated from the Roman Catholic Church in 1521.

Moved around by his theologian father's ceaseless wanderings, the young **William James** (1842–1910) attended schools in the U.S., France, and Switzerland. He taught psychology at Harvard but later called it "a nasty little subject" and turned his attention toward religion and philosophy, the passions that governed the rest of his life.

The Roman emperor **Julian the Apostate** (331–363) was baptized as a Christian and raised by a bishop, but converted to paganism in 351. When he came to power in 361, he proclaimed religious freedom, but began persecuting Christians shortly thereafter. On his deathbed he said, "I die without remorse, as I have lived without guilt."

Guided by a devotion to Sufism, **Hafiz** (c. 1325–c. 1389) produced some of Persia's finest lyric poetry. A student and teacher of theology, his name means "Qur'an memorizer." Every year in Iran, October 12 is celebrated as Hafiz Day.

At the prompting of friends and family, **Flannery O'Connor** (1925–1964) reluctantly traveled to Lourdes in 1958 to take the waters as a cure for the lupus with which she had been diagnosed eight years earlier. "I prayed there for the novel I was working on," she said, "not for my bones which I care about less."

Friedrich Nietzsche (1844–1900) wrote some of his best-known works, among them *Thus Spoke Zarathustra*, *On the Genealogy of Morals*, and *Twilight of the Idols*, in the decade between 1879 and 1889, when, crushed by debilitating health problems, he lived itinerantly throughout Europe, half-blind and in constant pain.

Sacred Ground

 HOUSES OF THE GODS

1. Canyon de Chelly, Arizona
Residence of Spider Woman, weaver of the world in Navajo myth.

2. Saut d'Eau, Haiti
Waterfall home of the love goddess Ezili, where Voodoo practitioners appeal to her.

3. Koricancha, Cuzco, Peru
Temple of the Inca sun god Inti.

4. Ol Doinyo Lengai, Tanzania
Volcano dwelling of the Maasai creator god Engai.

5. Mt. Olympus, Greece
Realm of the ancient Greek gods.

6. Mt. Kailash, Tibet
Home of Hindu god Shiva, dwelling of the Bön sky goddess Sipaimen, seat of the Buddhist deity Demchok; also where Rishaba, founder of Jainism, attained enlightenment.

7. Mt. Fuji, Japan
Dwelling of the Shinto goddess Konohana Sakuyahime, who floats above the peak.

 CREATION SITES

8. Lake Titicaca, border of Bolivia and Peru
Inca god Viracocha arose out of the lake to create the sun, moon, and stars.

9. Kaneana Cave, Makua Valley, Hawaii
Cave from which, according to native Hawaiian mythology, the first humans emerged.

Map by Doug Chayka

10. Pyramid of the Sun, Teotihuacán, Mexico
Pyramid built by the people of Teotihuacán above the cave in which they believed humans originated.

11. Ife, Nigeria
The Yoruba people originated at this site where the god Oduduwa planted the first palm tree.

12. Uluru (Ayers Rock), Australia
Rock formed by Aboriginal ancestors who roamed the earth during the "dream time" and consequently molded the world.

 ASCENSIONS AND DESCENTS

13. Sacred Grove, New York
God and Jesus appeared to Joseph Smith, founder of the Church of Jesus Christ of Latter-day Saints.

14. Lake Averno, Napoli, Italy
Entrance to hell, as described in Virgil's *Aeneid*.

15. Chogha Zanbil, Dur Untashi, Iran
Ziggurat used by Elamite god Inshushinak to travel between heaven and earth.

16. The Rock, Temple Mount, Jerusalem
Site from which Muhammad ascended to heaven; also site of the aborted sacrifice of Isaac.

17. Bodhi Tree, Bodh Gaya, India
Tree under which the Buddha attained enlightenment while meditating.

18. Mt. Tai, Shandong, China
Daoist link between heaven and earth, scaled via "staircases to heaven" carved into its slope.

MANDATES OF HEAVEN

by Lewis H. Lapham

What preoccupies us, then, is not God as a fact of nature, but as a fabrication useful for a God-fearing society. God himself becomes not a power but an image.

—Daniel J. Boorstin

This issue of *Lapham's Quarterly* doesn't trade in divine revelation, engage in theological dispute, or doubt the existence of God. What is of interest are the ways in which religious belief gives birth to historical event, makes law and prayer and politics, accounts for the death of an army or the life of a saint. Questions about the nature or substance of deity, whether it divides into three parts or seven, speaks Latin to the Romans, in tongues when traveling in Kentucky, I've learned over the last sixty-odd years to leave to sources more reliably informed. My grasp of metaphysics is as imperfect as my knowledge of Aramaic. I came to my early acquaintance with the Bible in company with my first readings of *Grimm's Fairy Tales* and *Bulfinch's Mythology,* but as an unbaptized child raised in a family unaffiliated with the teachings of a church, I missed the explanation as to why the stories about Moses and Jesus were to be taken as true while those about Apollo and Rumpelstiltskin were not.

Four years at Yale College in the 1950s rendered the question moot. It wasn't that I'd missed the explanation; there was no explanation to miss, at least not one accessible by means other than the proverbial leap of faith. Then as now, the college was heavily invested in the proceeds of the Protestant Reformation, the testimony of God's will being done present in the stonework of Harkness Tower and the cautionary ringing of its bells, as well as in the readings from scripture

Priest with a sacrificial bull, Pompeiian fresco, first century.

in Battell Chapel and the petitionings of Providence prior to the Harvard game. The college had been established in 1701 to bring a great light unto the gentiles in the Connecticut wilderness, the mission still extant 250 years later in the assigned study of Jonathan Edwards' sermons (*Connecticut*, page 35) and John Donne's verse (*London*, page 115). Nowhere in the texts did I see anything other than words on paper—very beautiful words but not the living presence to which they alluded in rhyme royal and iambic pentameter. I attributed the failure to the weakness of my imagination and my poor performance at both the pole vault and the long jump.

I brought the same qualities into the apostate lecture halls where it was announced that God was dead. The time and cause of death were variously given in sophomore and senior surveys of western civilization—disemboweled by Machiavelli in sixteenth-century Florence, assassinated in eighteenth-century Paris by agents of the French Enlightenment, lost at sea in 1835 while on a voyage with Charles Darwin to the Galapagos Islands, garroted by Friedrich Nietzsche on a Swiss Alp in the autumn of 1882, disappeared into the nuclear cloud ascending from Hiroshima on August 6, 1945. The assisting coroners attached to one or another of the history faculties submitted densely footnoted autopsy reports, but none of the lab work brought forth a thumbprint of the deceased.

If God did not exist, it would be necessary to invent him. —*Voltaire, 1764*

The fact of God's life apparently as unverifiable as the proof of his death, I reached the conclusion suggested by the French philosopher Michel Onfray (*Caen*, page 21) that "God is neither dead nor dying because he is not mortal"—the story about the blessed Virgin in the manger with the three Magi therefore made of the same cloud-capped stuff as the story about Goldilocks in the forest with the three bears. Onfray observes that "a fiction does not die, an illusion never passes away," situating Yahweh, together with Ulysses, Allah, Lancelot of the Lake, and Gitche Manitou, among the immortals sustained on the life-support systems of poetry and the high approval ratings awarded to magicians pulling rabbits out of hats. Similarly the British essayist William Hazlitt (*England*, page 68), who likens the fabrication of divinity to a little girl's dressing up her favorite doll, a harmless enough occupation until the dolls, turning "deformed and preposterous," prompt their votaries to drench "the earth with tears and blood."

The conclave of historians in New Haven placed a strong emphasis on the tears and blood, posting on a blackboard or a map the long list of religious wars, inquisitions, crusades, massacres, and persecutions visited upon the unfaithful by, among others, Richard the Lionheart, Savonarola, Arnaud Amalric, Philip II, Suleiman the Magnificent, Oliver Cromwell, and Vlad the Impaler. Fortunately, so it was said on the lawn of the Elizabethan Club, the revels now were ended, the dungeons and the burnings at the stake shipped off in disgrace to the land of once upon a time. The authors of the American Constitution had seen fit to separate the ambition of the church from the avarice of the state, with the happy result that God's awful and majestic wrath had been securely housed within the walls of the Yale Art Gallery, restricted to the Christmas performance of Handel's *Messiah* in Woolsey Hall.

The good news brought with it what Warren Breckman (*Secular Revival*, page 203) names as "a master narrative" of mid-twentieth-century American social science, the one that reduces God from a power to an image and makes secularization

"virtually synonymous with modernization." It wasn't that the twentieth century had
lost either the talent or the taste for the projects of mass murder—the autos-da-fé
staged by Joseph Stalin, Mao Zedong, and Adolf Hitler on a scale undreamed of in
the theology of Pope Innocent IV (*Rome*, page 156)—but the miraculous births of
Fat Man and Little Boy in the cradle at Los Alamos had placed the fire of heaven
under the control of the secular authorities, into the hands of wise scientists and
caring statesmen. What had been divine had become human, the hydrogen bomb
revealed as both symbol and freight-forwarding agent for the Day of Judgment.

Religion hadn't lost its capacity to bestow, again according to Breckman, "the
consoling message of cosmic meaning and personal redemption," to comfort countless
numbers of its adherents afraid of death and acquainted with grief, to illuminate the
masterpieces of Chartres Cathedral and the Mass
in B Minor, to introduce Gerard Manley Hopkins
(*England*, page 124) to the power and glory of   *Whatsoever is, is in God.*
"chestnut-falls and finches' wings," to restore in   —*Baruch Spinoza, 1677*
Leo Tolstoy (*Yasnaya Polyana*, page 134) "the joy
of being," but it had been relieved of its character
as a public menace. Henceforth religion was to be understood as a private good,
available in cloaks of many colors; it no longer had anything to do with the day-to-
day operations of a world subject to the laws of physics and the rule of reason.

Thus reassured, the students of my generation and disposition were free to
set foot in Sodom without fear of divine vengeance. The license to dance
to the music of the 1960s sexual revolution, to know ourselves "self-begot,
self-raised" in the manner of John Milton's Satan (page 214), didn't negate the 1952
Supreme Court majority opinion that the Americans "are a religious people whose
institutions presuppose a Supreme Being." Nor did it cancel my membership in
the God-fearing society established on the Biblical foundations of John Winthrop's
seventeenth-century city upon a hill. In the way that Montaigne knew himself to be
a Christian "by the same title that we are Perigordians or Germans," I was Christian,
maybe unbaptized and without the documents required to clear customs in Paradise,
but Christian nonetheless. It didn't matter whether I believed that on the third day
Christ had risen from the dead, or that both God and Cecil B. DeMille had parted
the Red Sea to accommodate Moses on the flight from Egypt. The history of that
belief had been indelibly sequenced into the strands of my metaphysical DNA,
dictating my turns of mind and choices of word, superintending my sense of right
and wrong, accounting for my fears of women and the stock market.

The whole fabric of the American creation is woven with threads of Christian
thought. The language and sanction of the Bible informs the texts of both the
Constitution and the Declaration of Independence. The law of the land rests on
the premise that crimes are sins, acts of a disobedient free will unbeholden to the
early toilet training of the Ten Commandments. The inscription on the Liberty Bell
borrows from Leviticus 25 the instruction given by God to Moses on Mount Sinai:
"Proclaim liberty throughout all the land unto all the inhabitants thereof"—all the
inhabitants understood to be limited (in Philadelphia in 1776 as in Sinai in the
thirteenth century BC) to those whom God had chosen as his own—no Negroes or
Moabites among them. The country's codes of moral and social conduct presuppose

no known connection between the birdsong of the spirit and the dungheap of the flesh. Any citizen who stands for public office is first expected to pledge allegiance to the Lord of hosts in whom the country trusts to back its currency. Cures for the soul prescribe salutary doses of suffering and guilt. The dominant trait in the national character is the longing for transcendence and the belief in what isn't there—the promise of the sweet hereafter that sells subprime mortgages in Florida and corporate skyboxes in heaven.

Not that I encountered, at least not in New York or Washington or Los Angeles, large numbers of people leading lives in accordance with the Sermon on the Mount (*Galilee*, page 23). Poolside in Beverly Hills the name of the Lord seldom came up in conversation unless it was being taken in vain. "The hunger and thirst for righteousness" was notably absent from both the character and policy of the Nixon administration. Neither the poor nor the meek were inheriting estates in Westchester County. None of the Las Vegas hotels listed prompt medical attention as one of the finer amenities available to guests disposing of their right hands and plucking out their right eyes.

God is really only another artist. He invented the giraffe, the elephant, and the cat. He has no real style. He just goes on trying other things.
—Pablo Picasso, 1964

The wanderings away from the road to Damascus I took to be confirmations of the secular narrative bound up in the diploma from Yale, further proofs during the decade of the 1970s that although the Christian pieties remained securely in place on the pediment of the Supreme Court, on the table with the coffee at White House prayer breakfasts, acknowledged in absentia at Hollywood weddings, the spiritual infrastructure was beginning to show signs of disrepair—if not at the Iowa State Fair, certainly at the cineplex in downtown Des Moines. My travels seldom took me anywhere except to California or Europe, but if sometimes in an airport bar I ran across a third-generation Baptist, I avoided the embarrassment of a conversation about the Second Coming in much the same way that I'd learned to withhold comment when asked by an author for an opinion of his unintelligibly avant-garde off-Broadway play.

By the mid 1980s I understood that I had been making a serious mistake. Jesus had risen from the tomb in Tennessee into which he had been carried by Clarence Darrow in 1925. He was now appearing at political rallies with Jerry Falwell's Moral Majority, on campus at Bob Jones University to second the motions against abortion, made an honorary member of the National Association of Evangelicals (thirty million exalted souls) that embodied one seventh of the nation's eligible voters. The resurrected sensibility abroad in the land during the sunshine years of the Reagan Administration led to the publication of the *Left Behind* series of Christian thrillers (sixteen volumes, sixty-five million copies sold), foretelling the marvelous and soon forthcoming day when the saved shall be lifted to heaven and the damned shall writhe in pain. Drawing on the precedents in the Pentateuch, the coauthors of the books, Tim LaHaye and Jerry B. Jenkins, express their love of God by delighting in their hatred of man. They imagine the battle of Armageddon as the wholesale slaughter of apostates in Boston and homosexuals in Brooklyn, "their innards and entrails gushed to the desert floor … their blood pooling and rising in the unforgiving brightness of the glory of Christ."

Increasingly frequent sightings of the great beast of the Book of Revelation in Oklahoma recruited large numbers of congregants similarly ill disposed toward the secularization of America's elementary schools. Their collective suspicion of all things urban or modern congealed during the 1990s into a political constituency that in 2000 sent to the White House the twice-born George W. Bush. The bringing down of the World Trade Center towers on September 11, 2001, caused him to behold a geopolitical vision ("the monumental struggle of good versus evil") not unlike the one vouchsafed to Ezekiel in the desert of Judaea. During the rest of his term in office—as bound as had been the prophets of the Old Testament to render justice, mete out punishment, cleanse the world of its impurities—Bush construed the American purpose as surrogate for the will of the Lord. "The liberty we prize is not America's gift to the world, it is God's gift to man." "Events aren't moved by blind change and chance … but by the hand of a just and faithful God."

The American president wasn't alone in his launching of faith-based initiatives. Together with the rising of militant religious fervor in the United States during the last thirty years, devout and literal-minded readings of the Qur'an have brought forth war in Iraq and Afghanistan, massacre in Africa and the Balkans, suicide bombing in Israel, Pakistan, India, and Palestine, heavy security encircling the presence of President Barack Obama, elected to the White House in his persona as a Messiah come not to govern the country but to redeem it.

The flow of tears and blood on the ground has been accompanied by a torrent of theological and quasi-theological polemic slouching toward the postulate of an apocalypse. Treatises tracking *The Evolution of God* or declaring *The End of Faith*; tracts forecasting *The Clash of Civilizations* or arguing that *Everything You Know about God Is Wrong*; magazine articles, op-ed essays, special broadcasts from CNN and Fox worried, not unreasonably, that the rabbis in Jerusalem might seek a thermonuclear settlement of their doctrinal differences with the mullahs in Tehran.

Creation of Adam (detail), Sistine Chapel Ceiling, by Michelangelo, c. 1508–1512.

More than one essay in this issue of *Lapham's Quarterly* regards the secularization of the old religious festivals as a fait accompli. The toxic levels of fear and superstition lowering the air quality in the news and entertainment media—in the nominally nondenominational sectors of cyberspace as well as those under ecclesiastical obligation—suggest otherwise. If large provinces of meaning have been lost to the mandate of the three wrathful monotheisms, so also the master narrative of mid-twentieth-century American social science has depleted its resources of relevance and romance.

In both the public and private sectors of the American mind at the turn of the third millennium, the delusional was no longer marginal. Myriad varieties of free-form transcendence were being backed with the assumption that the emotional intensity with which one held to one's belief, whether in the existence of witches or the extinction of capitalism, validated its credentials—passion perceived as truth in place of truth pursued with passion, no superstition more deserving or more preposterous than any other as long as it was sincere. The methodologies of magical thinking that informed the debates in Congress (about Saddam Hussein's weapons of mass destruction and the export of democracy to Baghdad and Kabul) were made manifest in the nationwide challenges to the teaching of evolution as well as in the quality of the credit-default swaps sold on Wall Street. Most wonderfully of all, they were revealed in President Bush's apparent assumption that America could rule a world about which it chooses to know as little as possible.

The various modes of religion which prevailed in the Roman world were all considered by the people as equally true, by the philosophers equally false, and by the magistrate as equally useful.
—Edward Gibbon, 1776

The desperate and always popular demand for news from nowhere bears out Michel Onfray's supposition that "the last god will expire with the last man," accords with Alexis de Tocqueville's observation (*United States*, page 29) that "unbelief is an accident," faith "the only permanent state of mankind." Tocqueville relies on his premise that "religion is simply another form of hope … no less natural to the human heart than hope itself," that as long as it is sustained upon the desire for immortality, "it can only be destroyed by another religion."

I see no reason to doubt him, and I take it as a task of the twenty-first century to come forward with the fabrication of an image of the divine more closely allied with the strands in the double helix and the structure of the cell, an image that reburies in the desert sand the murderous fiats of Moses and Muhammad and are therefore more useful to societies destined to remain God-fearing. Accept religion as a work of the human imagination (the God made in man's image one and the same with the man made in God's image) and the means of creation is not a brooding upon the waters or an engineering of the firmament, but the telling of a story. Both the Old and the New Testaments find their metaphors in the facts on the ground, God likened to a mountain or a lion, his kingdom to a fisherman's net, a mustard seed, the yeast "hid in three measures of meal."

Surely we can do likewise; God is the greatest of man's inventions, and we are an inventive people, shaping the tools that in turn shape us, and we have at hand the technology to tell a new story congruent with the picture of the earth as seen from space instead of the one drawn on the maps available to the prophets wandering the roads of the early Roman Empire. In the field of American literature no growth is more fruitful than the contemplations of nature clothed in the raiment of transcendence. The words have been with us since the beginning, in the writings of J. Hector St. John de Crèvecoeur and President Thomas Jefferson, as well as in those of Ralph Waldo Emerson and President Theodore Roosevelt, who, during the first decade of the twentieth century, placed 230 million acres of the American wilderness into a Federal Witness Protection Program, meaning to preserve "all useful and beautiful wild things" for the generations yet unborn in order that they might come to know that the "sunshine in the upper air" is more beautiful and useful than the light filtered through stained-glass windows, that the sight of birds in the sky at noon is like "a gallery of the masterpieces of the artists of all time."

Gathered in the mulch of print over the last three hundred years, the American delvings into nature (those of Audubon, Thoreau, Leopold, Muir, Eiseley, Carson, Berry, Dillard, Lopez, Abbey, Hitt, Matthiessen, Erdrich, et al.) can be likened to the compost heap engendering the science and logos of the polytheism (premodern and post-Christian) that discovers every organism in the cosmos to be made from the

The *ba*, one of the soul's three aspects in ancient Egyptian religion, hovering over a corpse, c. 1440 BC.

wreckage of spent stars. The ancient Greeks assigned trace elements of the divine to trees and winds and stones (a river god sulked and the child drowned; the fertility goddess smiled and the corn ripened); the modern American assigns trace elements of the divine to arctic glaciers and tropical rain forests (the ice melts and cities drown; parrots multiply and the flowers bloom.)

A religion still hidden, like the yeast in the three measures of meal, in the secular disguise of environmentalism. The foundational metaphysics already have been incorporated into rituals of devout observance. The worshipful recyclings of eggshells and orange rinds celebrate the resurrection of the disembodied spirit; the eating of free-range chickens and organic heirloom tomatoes signifies the partaking in a feast of communion. Like the Councils of Nicaea and Trent, international conferences addressed to the problem of climate change seek to certify the existence of the Holy Ghost. The miracle is the rabbit, not the pulling of the rabbit out of a hat.

DECLARATIONS OF FAITH

2005: Caen

MICHEL ONFRAY ANSWERS A QUESTION

Is God dead or not? The question is still undecided. However, such glad tidings would surely have generated cosmic events—which haven't yet transpired. Instead of the fertile field such a death would have opened up, we seem confronted today by nihilism, the cult of nothingness, the passion for nonbeing, a morbid relish for the twilight of waning civilizations, a fascination with the abyss and with bottomless pits where we lose our souls, our bodies, our identity, our being, and all interest in anything whatsoever. A lugubrious picture, a depressing apocalypse …

God's death was an ontological gimmick, a conjuror's trick. It was consubstantial with a twentieth century that saw death everywhere— the death of art, philosophy, metaphysics, the novel, music, politics. So let's announce the death of all these fictional deaths! Tongue-in-cheek obituaries that once served certain thinkers—before they turned their metaphysical coats—as a dramatic setting for the paradoxes they uncovered. The death of philosophy

engendered works of philosophy, the death of the novel generated novels, the death of art produced works of art, etc. As for God's death, it has released an outpouring of the sacred, the divine, the religious. Today we swim in these purgative waters.

Clearly the announcement of God's death was as world shaking as it was false—trumpets blaring, news bellowed from the rooftops, drums thundering in an orgy of premature rejoicing. Our era staggers under the weight of revelations solemnly hailed as the authorized utterances of new oracles. Abundance holds sway, to the detriment of quality and truth— never have so many false tidings been celebrated as so many revealed truths. For God's death to be certified, irrefutable facts, clues, and courtroom exhibits should have been produced. Yet none has emerged.

Who has seen the corpse? Apart from Nietzsche. (And even then …) Like that of the corpus delicti in Ionesco's *Rhinoceros*, we should

Monks climbing to heaven or being pulled to hell, twelfth-century illustration of *The Ladder of Divine Ascent*, a seventh-century guide to ascetic and mystical living, by St. John Climacus.

have felt its presence, its dominion—it would have been all pervading, defiling, malodorous, it would have fallen apart little by little, day by day, and we would have witnessed a process of real decomposition—in the philosophical as well as the physical sense of the term. Instead of which God, invisible while alive, has remained invisible even when dead. And we are still without proof of his death. But who could furnish it? What new lunatic for this impossible task?

For, *pace* Nietzsche and Heine, God is neither dead nor dying, because he is not mortal. A fiction does not die, an illusion never passes away, a fairy tale does not refute itself. Neither

Educate people without religion and you make them but clever devils.
—*Arthur Wellesley, c. 1830*

hippogriff nor centaur is bound by the laws governing mammals. A wildebeest or a horse, yes; an animal from the mythological bestiary, no. And God, too, (listed somewhere between "Gnome" and "Golem") is of that mythological bestiary, like the thousands of other creatures enumerated in dictionaries with numberless entries. The oppressed creature's sigh will endure for as long as the creature itself, in other words, forever.

Besides, where would he have died? In Nietzsche's *The Gay Science*? [*Sils-Maria*, page 142] Murdered at Nietzsche's summer home by an inspired philosopher—tragic and sublime, haunted and haggard—in the second half of the nineteenth century? And what was the weapon? A book, books, a life's work? Imprecations, analyses, proofs, refutations (the cold steel of writers)? Was the killer alone? Did he lurk in ambush? Or was he one of a group, along with Jean Meslier [*Étrépigny*, page 33] and the Marquis de Sade as guardian forebears? If he existed, would God's murderer not himself have been a superior God? And doesn't this noncrime mask an Oedipal urge, an impossible desire, an irrepressible ambition powerless to carry through a task essential to the creation of freedom, identity, and meaning?

You cannot kill a breeze, a wind, a fragrance; you cannot kill a dream or an ambition. God, manufactured by mortals in their own quintessential image, exists only to make daily life bearable, despite the path that every one of us treads toward extinction. As long as men are obliged to die, some of them, unable to endure the prospect, will concoct fond illusions. We cannot assassinate or kill an illusion. In fact, illusion is more likely to kill us—for God puts to death everything that stands up to him, beginning with reason, intelligence, and the critical mind. All the rest follows in a chain reaction.

The last god will expire with the last man. And with him fear, terror, anguish—those devices designed to create divinities. They include horror of death's void, the inability to integrate death as a natural process with which we must come to terms, in whose presence intelligence alone can have any effect. And there is denial, the absence of any meaning beyond what we ourselves have to offer, with absurdity as a starting point. These are the genetic bloodlines of the divine. A dead God would imply a vanquished void. We are light years away from such ontological progress.

Baal and Yahweh, Zeus and Allah, Ra and Odin—but also Gitche Manitou, the Great Spirit of the Algonquin tribes—owe their names to geography and history. In accordance with the metaphysics that made their existence possible, they simply assume different names for one and the same fantasized reality. Yet none of them is truer than another. They all live in a pantheon of fictitious revelers where Ulysses and Zarathustra, Dionysus and Don Quixote, Tristan and Lancelot of the Lake—so many magical figures, just like the Fox of the Dogon or the Loa of voodoo—sit down to feast together.

From Atheist Manifesto. *Having once described himself as a "Nietzschean of the left," Onfray has published over thirty books, of which* Atheist Manifesto *is the first to be translated into English. After two decades as a professor of philosophy in the French national education system, he resigned to help establish a tuition-free People's University, which he funds in part with the proceeds of his books.*

c. 30: Galilee

SERMON ON THE MOUNT

When Jesus saw the crowds, he went up the mountain, and after he sat down, his disciples came to him. Then he began to speak, and taught them, saying, "Blessed are the poor in spirit, for theirs is the kingdom of heaven. Blessed are those who mourn, for they will be comforted. Blessed are the meek, for they will inherit the earth. Blessed are those who hunger and thirst for righteousness, for they will be filled. Blessed are the merciful, for they will receive mercy. Blessed are the pure in heart, for they will see God. Blessed are the peacemakers, for they will be called children of God. Blessed are those who are persecuted for righteousness' sake, for theirs is the kingdom of heaven. Blessed are you when people revile you, persecute you, and utter all kinds of evil against you falsely on my account. Rejoice and be glad, for your reward is great in heaven—for in the same way they persecuted the prophets who were before you.

"You are the salt of the earth, but if salt has lost its taste, how can its saltiness be restored? It is no longer good for anything, but is thrown out and trampled underfoot. You are the light of the world. A city built on a hill cannot be hidden. No one after lighting a lamp puts it under the bushel basket, but on the lamp stand, and it gives light to all in the house. In the same way, let your light shine before others so that they may see your good works and give glory to your Father in heaven.

"Do not think that I have come to abolish the law or the prophets; I have come not to abolish but to fulfill. For truly I tell you, until heaven and earth pass away, not one letter, not one stroke of a letter, will pass from the law until all is accomplished. Therefore, whoever breaks one of the least of these commandments and teaches others to do the same will be called least in the kingdom of heaven—but whoever does them and teaches them will be called great in the kingdom of heaven. For I tell you, unless your righteousness exceeds that of the scribes and Pharisees, you will never enter the kingdom of heaven.

A page from *Aachen Passover Haggadah*, by Zoya Cherkassky, c. 2001–03.

"You have heard that it was said, 'You shall not commit adultery.' But I say to you that everyone who looks at a woman with lust has already committed adultery with her in his heart. If your right eye causes you to sin, tear it out and throw it away—it is better for you to lose one of your members than for your whole body to be thrown into hell. And if your right hand causes you to sin, cut it off and throw it away—it is better for you to lose one of your members than for your whole body to go into hell. It was also said, 'Whoever divorces his wife, let him give her a certificate of divorce.' But I say to

To speak of God, to think of God, is in every respect to show what one is made of. I have always wagered against God, and I regard the little that I have won in this world as simply the outcome of this bet. However paltry may have been the stake (my life), I am conscious of having won to the full. Everything that is doddering, squint eyed, vile, polluted, and grotesque is summoned up for me in that one word: God!
—André Breton, 1928

you that anyone who divorces his wife, except on the ground of unchastity, causes her to commit adultery, and whoever marries a divorced woman commits adultery.

"You have heard that it was said, 'An eye for an eye and a tooth for a tooth.' But I say to you, do not resist an evildoer. But if anyone strikes you on the right cheek, turn the other also, and if anyone wants to sue you and take your coat, give your cloak as well; and if anyone forces you to go one mile, go also the second mile. Give to everyone who begs from you, and do not refuse anyone who wants to borrow from you.

"You have heard that it was said, 'You shall love your neighbor and hate your enemy.' But I say to you, love your enemies and pray for those who persecute you so that you may be children of your Father in heaven—for he makes his sun rise on the evil and on the good and sends rain on the righteous and on the unrighteous. For if you love those who love you, what reward do

you have? Do not even the tax collectors do the same? And if you greet only your brothers and sisters, what more are you doing than others? Do not even the Gentiles do the same? Be perfect, therefore, as your heavenly Father is perfect.

"And whenever you pray, do not be like the hypocrites, for they love to stand and pray in the synagogues and at the street corners so that they may be seen by others. Truly I tell you, they have received their reward. But whenever you pray, go into your room and shut the door and pray to your Father who is in secret, and your Father who sees in secret will reward you. When you are praying, do not heap up empty phrases as the Gentiles do, for they think that they will be heard because of their many words. Do not be like them, for your Father knows what you need before you ask him.

"Pray then in this way: Our Father in heaven, hallowed be your name. Your kingdom come. Your will be done, on earth as it is in heaven. Give us this day our daily bread. And forgive us our debts, as we also have forgiven our debtors. And do not bring us to the time of trial, but rescue us from the evil one. For if you forgive others their trespasses, your heavenly Father will also forgive you, but if you do not forgive others, neither will your Father forgive your trespasses.

"Do not store up for yourselves treasures on earth, where moth and rust consume and where thieves break in and steal, but store up for yourselves treasures in heaven, where neither moth nor rust consumes and where thieves do not break in and steal. For where your treasure is, there your heart will be also. The eye is the lamp of the body. So, if your eye is healthy, your whole body will be full of light—but if your eye is unhealthy, your whole body will be full of darkness. If then the light in you is darkness, how great is the darkness!"

From the Gospel according to Matthew. The Sermon on the Mount contains many of the best-known Christian homilies and sayings, among them the Beatitudes and the Lord's Prayer. It also expresses the notion of Christian pacifism.

Queen Nefertari approaching the god Thoth, who weighs the hearts of the deceased, Egyptian tomb painting, c. 1255 BC.

1939: Princeton

ALBERT EINSTEIN
SOLVES THE EQUATION

It would not be difficult to come to an agreement as to what we understand by science. Science is the century-old endeavor to bring together by means of systematic thought the perceptible phenomena of this world into as thoroughgoing an association as possible. To put it boldly, it is the attempt at the posterior reconstruction of existence by the process of conceptualization. But when asking myself what religion is, I cannot think of the answer so easily. And even after finding an answer which may satisfy me at this particular moment, I still remain convinced that I can never under any circumstances bring together, even to a slight extent, all those who have given this question serious consideration.

At first, then, instead of asking what religion is I should prefer to ask what characterizes the aspirations of a person who has given

me the impression of being religious. A person who is religiously enlightened appears to me to be one who has, to the best of his ability, liberated himself from the fetters of his selfish desires and is preoccupied with thoughts, feelings, and aspirations to which he clings because of their superpersonal value. It seems to me that what is important is the force of this superpersonal content and the depth of the conviction concerning its overpowering meaningfulness—regardless of whether any attempt is made to unite this content with a divine being, for otherwise it would not be possible to count Buddha and Spinoza as religious personalities. Accordingly, a religious person is devout in the sense that he has no doubt of the significance and loftiness of those superpersonal objects and goals which neither require nor are capable of rational foundation. They exist with the same necessity and matter-of-factness as he himself. In this sense religion is the age-old endeavor of mankind to become clearly and completely conscious of these values and goals and constantly to strengthen and extend their effect. If one conceives of religion and science according to these definitions, then a conflict between them appears impossible. For science can only ascertain what *is*, but not what *should be*, and outside of its domain value judgments of all kinds remain necessary. Religion, on the other hand, deals only with evaluations of human thought and action—it cannot justifiably speak of facts and relationships between facts. According to this interpretation, the well-known conflicts between religion and science in the past must all be ascribed to a misapprehension of the situation which has been described.

For example, a conflict arises when a religious community insists on the absolute truthfulness of all statements recorded in the Bible. This means an intervention on the part of religion into the sphere of science; this is where the struggle of the Church against the doctrines of Galileo and Darwin belongs. On the other hand, representatives of science have often made an attempt to arrive at fundamental judgments with respect to values and ends on the basis of scientific method, and in this way have set themselves in opposition to religion. These conflicts have all sprung from fatal errors.

Now, even though the realms of religion and science in themselves are clearly marked off from each other, nevertheless there exist between the two strong, reciprocal relationships

Man receiving a blessing from an elephant at Varadarajaswamy Temple, India.

and dependencies. Though religion may be that which determines the goal, it has nevertheless learned from science—in the broadest sense—what means will contribute to the attainment of the goals it has set up. But science can only be created by those who are thoroughly imbued with the aspiration toward truth and understanding. This source of feeling, however, springs from the sphere of religion. To this there also belongs the faith in the possibility that the regulations valid for the world of existence are rational, that is, comprehensible to reason. I cannot conceive of a genuine scientist without that profound faith. The situation may be expressed by an image: science without religion is lame, religion without science is blind.

Though I have asserted above that in truth a legitimate conflict between religion and science cannot exist, I must nevertheless qualify this assertion once again on an essential point, with reference to the actual content of historical religions. This qualification has to do with the concept of God. During the youthful period of mankind's spiritual evolution, human fantasy created gods in man's own image, who, by the operations of their will were supposed to determine or, at any rate, to influence the phenomenal world. Man sought to alter the disposition of these gods in his own favor by means of magic and prayer. The idea of God in the religions taught at present is a sublimation of that old conception of the gods. Its anthropomorphic character is shown, for instance, by the fact that men appeal to the Divine Being in prayers and plead for the fulfilment of their wishes.

Nobody, certainly, will deny that the idea of the existence of an omnipotent, just, and omnibeneficent personal God is able to accord man solace, help, and guidance—also, by virtue of its simplicity it is accessible to the most undeveloped mind. But, on the other hand, there are decisive weaknesses attached to this idea in itself which have been painfully felt since the beginning of history. That is, if this being is omnipotent then every occurrence, including every human action, every human thought, and every human feeling and aspiration is also His work—how is it possible to think of holding men responsible for their deeds and thoughts before such an almighty Being? In giving out punishment and rewards He would to a certain extent be passing judgment on Himself. How can this be combined with the goodness and righteousness ascribed to Him?

The main source of the present-day conflicts between the spheres of religion and science lies in this concept of a personal God.

The Church says that the earth is flat, but I know that it is round, for I have seen the shadow on the moon, and I have more faith in the shadow than in the Church.
—Ferdinand Magellan, c. 1510

To be sure, the doctrine of a personal God interfering with natural events could never be *refuted*, in the real sense, by science, for this doctrine can always take refuge in those domains in which scientific knowledge has not yet been able to set foot.

But I am persuaded that such behavior on the part of the representatives of religion would not only be unworthy but also fatal. For a doctrine which is able to maintain itself not in clear light but only in the dark will of necessity lose its effect on mankind, with incalculable harm to human progress. In their struggle for the ethical good, teachers of religion must have the stature to give up the doctrine of a personal God, that is, give that source of fear and hope which in the past placed such vast power in the hands of priests. In their labors they will have to avail themselves of those forces which are capable of cultivating the good, the true, and the beautiful in humanity itself. This is, to be sure, a more difficult but incomparably more worthy task. After religious teachers accomplish the refining process indicated, they will surely recognize with joy that true religion has been ennobled and made more profound by scientific knowledge.

If it is one of the goals of religion to liberate mankind as far as possible from the bondage of egocentric cravings, desires, and fears, scientific reasoning can aid religion in yet another

Afterlives

Destination	Mode of Transportation	Amenities	Accommodations	Cost
Paradise	Islam	Date and pomegranate trees, goblets of non-sin-inducing wine served by boy waiters, virgins, everlasting peace	Gardens, brocade-lined couches, green cushions, beautiful carpets	Repentance, righteousness, passing of God's tests, including weighing of soul and judging of deeds
Valhalla	Norse paganism	Freshly slaughtered boar, liquor from goat's udder, daily warrior fights	Shield-roofed palace	Glorious death in battle
Sukhavati	Pure Land Mahayana Buddhism	Music of birds, trees hung with precious jewels and gold bells, rebirth	Purifying lotus buds on a terraced pond in a land of bliss	Belief in Buddha Amitabha, invocation of his name at moment of death
Elysian Fields	Greek polytheism	Eternal sunshine, incense- and fruit-bearing trees, music, drinks, singing, dancing, wrestling	Rose meadows on the banks of the River Oceanus at earth's end	Gaining the favor of the gods, living righteously
Heaven	Roman Catholicism	Eternal life, beatific vision, becoming Godlike	Pearl-gate entrance, God's eternal presence	Baptism, dying in God's grace, penance in purgatory
Fields of Earu	Egyptian polytheism	Feasts, boating, checkers	Fields and canals in the sky	Mummification, being provisioned with spells and amulets

sense. Although it is true that it is the goal of science to discover rules which permit the association and foretelling of facts, this is not its only aim. It also seeks to reduce the connections discovered to the smallest possible number of mutually independent conceptual elements. It is in this striving after the rational unification of the manifold that it encounters its greatest successes, even though it is precisely this attempt which causes it to run the greatest risk of falling prey to illusions. But whoever has undergone the intense experience of successful advances made in this domain is moved by profound reverence for the rationality made manifest in existence. By way of the understanding, he achieves a far-reaching emancipation from the shackles of personal hopes and desires—and thereby attains that humble attitude of mind toward the grandeur of reason incarnate in existence, and which, in its profoundest depths, is inaccessible to man. This attitude, however, appears to me to be religious in the highest sense of the word. And so it seems to me that science not only purifies the religious impulse of the dross of its anthropomorphism but also contributes to a religious spiritualization of our understanding of life.

From "Science and Religion." Son of a featherbed salesman, Einstein wrote that as a child he was deeply influenced by two "wonders": a compass at the age of five and a "sacred little geometry book" at the age of twelve. In 1905 he published four seminal papers on physics, introducing the first experimental proof of atoms, the theory of special relativity, and the equation $E=mc^2$. The Nobel Prize–winner once called nationalism "the measles of mankind."

1835: United States

The philosophers of the eighteenth century explained the gradual decay of religious faith in a very simple manner. Religious zeal, they said, must necessarily fail, the more generally liberty is established and knowledge diffused. Unfortunately, facts are by no means in accordance with their theory.

Upon my arrival in the United States, the religious aspect of the country was the first thing that struck my attention, and the longer I stayed there, the more I did perceive the great political consequences resulting from this state of things, to which I was unaccustomed. In France I had almost always seen the spirit of religion and the spirit of freedom pursuing courses diametrically opposed to each other, but in America I found that they were intimately united and that they reigned in common over the same country. I questioned the members of all the different sects, and I more especially sought the society of the clergy, who are the depositaries of the different persuasions, and who are more especially interested in their duration. As a member of the Roman Catholic Church, I was more particularly brought into contact with several of its priests, with whom I became intimately acquainted. To each of these men I expressed my astonishment and I explained my doubts—I found that they differed upon matters of detail alone and that they mainly attributed the peaceable dominion of religion in their country to the separation of church and state. I do not hesitate to affirm that during my stay in America, I did not meet with a single individual of the clergy or of the laity who was not of the same opinion upon this point.

This led me to examine more attentively than I had hitherto done the station which the American clergy occupy in political society. I learned with surprise that they fill no public appointments—not one of them is to be met with in the administration, and they are not even represented in the legislative assemblies.

In several states the law excludes them from political life, public opinion in all. And when I came to inquire into the prevailing spirit of the clergy, I found that most of its members seemed to retire of their own accord from the exercise of power, and that they made it the pride of their profession to abstain from politics.

I heard them inveigh against ambition and deceit, under whatever political opinions these vices might chance to lurk, but I learned from their discourses that men are not guilty in the eye of God for any opinions concerning political government which they may profess with

To doubt everything or to believe everything are two equally convenient solutions; both dispense with the need for thought.
—*Henri Poincaré, 1903*

sincerity, any more than they are for their mistakes in building a house or in driving a furrow. I perceived that these ministers of the gospel eschewed all parties, with the anxiety attendant upon personal interest. These facts convinced me that what I had been told was true, and it then became my object to investigate their causes and to inquire how it happened that the real authority of religion was increased by a state of things which diminished its apparent force—these causes did not long escape my researches.

The short space of sixty years can never content the imagination of man, nor can the imperfect joys of this world satisfy his heart. Man alone of all created beings displays a natural contempt of existence and yet a boundless desire to exist; he scorns life, but he dreads annihilation. These different feelings incessantly urge his soul to the contemplation of a future state, and religion directs his musings thither. Religion, then, is simply another form of hope, and it is no less natural to the human heart than hope itself. Men cannot abandon their religious faith without a kind of aberration of intellect and a sort of violent distortion of their true natures, but they are invincibly brought back to more pious sentiments—for unbelief is an accident, and faith is the only permanent state of mankind. If we only consider religious institutions in a purely human point of view, they may be said to derive an inexhaustible element of strength from man himself, since they belong to one of the constituent principles of human nature.

I am aware that at certain times religion may strengthen this influence which originates in itself by the artificial power of the laws and by the support of those temporal institutions which direct society. Religions, intimately unit-

I believe in an America where the separation of church and state is absolute, where no Catholic prelate would tell the president (should he be a Catholic) how to act and no Protestant minister would tell his parishioners for whom to vote.
—*John F. Kennedy, 1960*

ed to the governments of the earth, have been known to exercise a sovereign authority derived from the twofold source of terror and of faith, but when a religion contracts an alliance of this nature, I do not hesitate to affirm that it commits the same error as a man who should sacrifice his future to his present welfare. And in obtaining a power to which it has no claim, it risks that authority which is rightfully its own. When a religion founds its empire upon the desire of immortality which lives in every human heart, it may aspire to universal dominion, but when it connects itself with a government, it must necessarily adopt maxims which are only applicable to certain nations. Thus, in forming an alliance with a political power, religion augments its authority over a few and forfeits the hope of reigning over all.

As long as a religion rests upon those sentiments which are the consolation of all affliction, it may attract the affections of mankind. But if it is mixed up with the bitter passions of the world, it may be constrained to defend allies whom its interests, and not the principle of love, have given to it; or to repel as antagonists men who are still attached to its own spirit, however opposed they may be to the powers to which it is allied.

The powers of society are more or less fugitive, like the years which we spend upon the earth; they succeed each other with rapidity like the fleeting cares of life, and no government has ever yet been founded upon an invariable disposition of the human heart or upon an imperishable interest.

As long as religion is sustained by those feelings, propensities, and passions, which are found to occur under the same forms at all the different periods of history, it may defy the efforts of time—or at least it can only be destroyed by another religion. The alliance which religion contracts with political powers must needs be onerous to itself, since it does not require their assistance to live, and by giving them its assistance it may be exposed to decay.

If the Americans, who change the head of the government once in four years, who elect new legislators every two years, and renew the provincial officers every year; if the Americans, who have abandoned the political world to the attempts of innovators, had not placed religion beyond their reach, where could it abide in the ebb and flow of human opinions? Where would that respect which belongs to it be paid, amid the struggles of faction? And what would become of its immortality in the midst of perpetual decay? The American clergy were the first to perceive this truth and to act in conformity with it. They saw that they must renounce their religious influence, if they were to strive for political power, and they chose to give up the support of the state rather than to share in its vicissitudes.

In America, religion is perhaps less powerful than it has been at certain periods in the history of certain peoples, but its influence is more lasting.

From Democracy in America. *Tocqueville and his lifelong friend Gustave de Beaumont spent nine months in the United States, copublishing* On the Penitentiary System in the United States and Its Application in France *in 1833. The success of his examination of the new nation's political structure led to his induction into the Legion of Honor and the French Academy; the royalties allowed him to rebuild his ancestral chateau in Normandy.*

C. 1377: Algeria

THE LAW

The purpose of human beings is not only their worldly welfare. This entire world is trifling and futile. It ends in death and annihilation. The purpose of human beings is their religion, which leads them to happiness in the other world. Therefore, religious laws have as their purpose to cause them to follow such a course in all their dealings with God and their fellow men. This situation also applies to royal authority, which is natural in human social organization. The religious laws guide it along the path of religion, so that everything will be under the supervision of the religious law. Anything done by royal authority that is dictated by force, superiority, or the free play of the power of wrathfulness is tyranny and injustice and considered reprehensible by the religious law—as it is also considered reprehensible by the requirements of political wisdom. Likewise, anything done by royal authority that is dictated by considerations of policy or political decisions without supervision of the religious law is also reprehensible, because it is vision lacking the divine light. At the Resurrection, the actions of human beings—whether they had to do with royal authority or anything else—will all come back to them.

Political laws consider only worldly interests. On the other hand, the intention the Lawgiver has concerning mankind is their welfare in the other world. Therefore, it is necessary, as required by the religious law, to cause the mass to act in accordance with the religious laws in all their affairs touching both this world and the other world. The authority to do so was possessed by the representatives of the religious law, the prophets—then by those who took their place, the caliphs.

This makes it clear what the caliphate means. To exercise natural royal authority means to cause the masses to act as required by purpose and desire. To exercise political royal authority means to cause the masses to act as required by intellectual, rational insight into the means of furthering their worldly interests and avoiding anything that is harmful in that respect. To exercise the caliphate means to cause the masses to act as required by religious insight into their interests in the other world as well as in this world. Worldly interests have bearing upon the interests in the other world, since according to Muhammad all worldly conditions are to be considered in their relation to their value for the other world. Thus, the caliphate in reality is a substitute for Muhammad inasmuch as it serves, like him, to protect the religion and to exercise leadership of the world.

> **Ibn Khaldun,** *from* The Muqaddimah. *The historian was for more than twenty years a diplomat and politician working in, among other places, Granada and Fez. In 1375 he retreated to an Algerian castle, where he began his masterwork, in which he sought to develop "a science of culture." Arnold Toynbee called* The Muqaddimah *"a philosophy of history which is undoubtedly the greatest work of its kind."*

Death of the Blessed Ludovica Albertoni, by Gian Lorenzo Bernini, c. 1671–74.

c. 600 bc: Greece

MOTHER OF THE GODS

Gaia, mother of all,
I shall sing,
the strong foundation, the oldest one.
She feeds everything in the world.

Whoever walks upon her sacred ground
or moves through the sea
or flies in the air, it is she
who nourishes them from her treasure store.

Queen of earth, through you
beautiful children,
beautiful harvests,
come.

It is you who give life to mortals
and who take life away.
Blessed is the one you honor with a willing heart.
He who has this has everything.

His fields thicken with life-giving corn,
his cattle grow heavy in the pastures,
his house brims over with good things.
The men are masters of their city,

the laws are just,
the women are fair,
great riches and fortune follow them.
Their sons delight in the ecstasy of youth,

their daughters play
in dances garlanded with flowers,
they skip happily on the grass
over soft flowers.

It was you who honored them,
sacred goddess, generous spirit.
Farewell, mother of the gods,
bride of starry Heaven.

> From The Homeric Hymns. *Composed in the same meter as* The Iliad *and* The Odyssey, *the set of thirty-four poems addressed to the gods and goddesses of the Greek pantheon were in antiquity attributed to Homer.*

Buddha of Bamiyan, Afghanistan, c. 500, one of two giant buddha statues destroyed by the Taliban in 2001.

c. 1725: Étrépigny

INIQUITY

Don't fool yourselves, my dear friends, open your eyes to everything that your pious morons or mocking, self-interested priests and scholars are eager to tell you and make you believe on the false pretext of the infallible certainty of their so-called holy and divine religion. You're no less seduced or less abused than those who are the most seduced and most abused; you're no less in error than those who are the most deeply plunged. Your religion is no less vain or less superstitious than any other; it's no less false in its principles, no less ridiculous and absurd in its dogma and maxims. You're no less idolatrous than those who you yourselves accuse and condemn of idolatry—the idols of pagans are different from yours only in name and shape. In short, everything that your priests and scholars preach to you with so much eloquence concerning the grandeur, excellence, and sanctity of the mysteries they make you worship, everything they tell you so seriously about the certainty of their so-called miracles and everything they recite with so much zeal and assurance concerning the grandeur of the rewards of heaven and the terrible punishments of hell, are in fact only illusions, errors, lies, fictions, and impostures invented at first by the shrewd and crafty politicians, continued by the seducers and imposters, then received and blindly believed by the ignorant and vulgar people—and finally maintained by the rulers and sovereigns of the earth who encourage the abuses, errors, superstitions, and impostures and even authorize them by their laws in order to keep a tight rein on the community of men and make them do whatever they want.

That, my dear friends, is how those who governed the people and who still govern now presumptuously and with impunity abuse the name and authority of God to make themselves feared, obeyed, and respected rather than to fear and serve the imaginary God whose power they terrify you with. That's how they abuse the specious names of piety and religion to make the weak and ignorant believe whatever they want them to. And finally, that's how they establish everywhere on earth a detestable mystery of lies and iniquity instead of working, as they should, to establish everywhere the reign of peace and justice as well as truth—a reign whose virtues would make all people happy and content on earth.

I say they establish everywhere a mystery of iniquity because all the hidden motives of the shrewdest politicians—as well as the maxims and ceremonies of the most pious of religion—are really only mysteries of iniquity. I say mysteries of iniquity for all the poor people who are the miserable dupes of all the mummeries of religions, as well as the puppets and hapless victims of the power of the rulers. But for those who govern the consciences or who are

Reason is our soul's left hand, faith her right,
By these we reach divinity.
                                    —*John Donne, c. 1607*

provided with good benefices, it's like a gold mine or a golden fleece, like a cornucopia that brings forth all kinds of goods at their pleasure. And this is what leads all the good gentlemen to amuse themselves and have all kinds of good times, while the poor people, abused by the errors and superstitions of religion, groan sadly, needily, and yet peaceably under the oppression of the rulers. And while they patiently suffer their pains, while they vainly enjoy praying to gods and saints who don't hear them, while they enjoy the vain devotions, while they repent their sins, and finally, while these poor people are working and worn out day and night in their jobs, sweating blood and tears to earn a paltry living for themselves and lavishly supply pleasures and satisfactions for those who are making them so unhappy in life.

Ah! My dear friends, if you really knew the vanity and folly of the errors that you support on the pretext of religion, and if you knew how unjustly and how indignantly they abuse the authority they've usurped from you on the pretext of governing you, you'd certainly have nothing but contempt for everything they make you worship and respect, and you'd have nothing but hatred and indignation for everyone who abuses you, who governs you so badly and who treats you so shamefully. I remember the wish of a man a while back who had no culture or education, but who, to all appearances,

didn't lack the common sense to pass sound judgments on all these detestable abuses and tyrannies. In his wish and in his way of expressing his thought it seemed that he saw rather far and penetrated rather deeply into the detestable mystery of iniquity of which I just spoke, and recognized very well the perpetrators and instigators. His wish was: *all the rulers of the earth and all the nobles be hanged and strangled with the guts of priests.*

This expression may seem hard, rude, and shocking, but you must admit that it's candid and simple. It's concise but expressive, and it expresses very well in a few words everything these kinds of men deserve. As for myself, my dear friends, if I could make a wish—and I wouldn't fail to do so, if it could have any effect—I would wish to have the arm, strength, courage, and body of Hercules to purge the world of all vices and iniquities, to have the pleasure of bludgeoning all the monster tyrants with their crowned heads and all the other monsters and ministers of errors and iniquity who make all the people of the earth groan so piteously.

Don't think, my dear friends, that I am driven by any particular desire for vengeance or any motive of animosity or any personal interest. No, my dear friends, it's not at all passion that inspires these sentiments or makes me speak and write in this way. It's really only the inclination and love that I have—on the one hand, for justice and truth, which I see so indignantly oppressed, and on the other hand, the aversion I naturally have of vice and wickedness, which I see so insolently reigning everywhere. We can't have too much hatred or disgust for the people who everywhere cause such detestable evils and who abuse men so universally.

Jean Meslier, *from* Testament. *According to Voltaire, who was deeply influenced by his French predecessor's critique of religion, Meslier while at the seminary "devoted himself to the system of Descartes." The son of a serge weaver, he spent his entire adult life in the priesthood. Meslier's* Testament, *consisting of three manuscripts with 366 pages each, was only discovered upon his death at the age of fifty-five in 1733.*

1741: Connecticut

JONATHAN EDWARDS BENDS THE BOW OF GOD'S WRATH

'Tis plain and manifest that whatever pains a natural man takes in religion, whatever prayers he makes, till he believes in Christ, God is under no manner of obligation to keep him a moment from eternal destruction.

Natural men are held in the hand of God over the pit of hell—they have deserved the fiery pit and are already sentenced to it—and God is dreadfully provoked, his anger is as great toward them as to those that are actually suffering the executions of the fierceness of his wrath in hell, and they have done nothing in the least to appease or abate that anger, neither is God in the least bound by any promise to hold them up one moment. The devil is waiting for them, hell is gaping for them, the flames gather and flash about them, and would fain lay hold on them and swallow them up. The fire pent up in their own hearts is struggling to break out, and they have no interest in any mediator—there are no means within reach that can be any security to them. In short they have no refuge, nothing to take hold of; all that preserves them every moment is the mere arbitrary will and uncovenanted, unobliged forbearance of an incensed God.

The use may be of *awakening* to unconverted persons in this congregation. This that you have heard is the case of every one of you that are out of Christ. That world of misery, that lake of burning brimstone, is extended abroad under you. *There* is the dreadful pit of the glowing flames of the wrath of God; there is hell's wide gaping mouth open; and you have nothing to stand upon, nor anything to take hold of. There is nothing between you and hell but the air; 'tis only the power and mere pleasure of God that holds you up.

You probably are not sensible of this; you find you are kept out of hell, but don't see the hand of God in it, but look at other things as the good state of your bodily constitution, your care of your own life, and the means you use for your own preservation. But indeed these things are nothing; if God should withdraw his hand, they would avail no more to keep you from falling than the thin air to hold up a person that is suspended in it.

Deluge, by Georges Rohner, c. 1960.

Your wickedness makes you as it were heavy as lead, and to tend downward with great weight and pressure toward hell—and if God should let you go, you would immediately sink and swiftly descend and plunge into the bottomless gulf, and your healthy constitution, your own care and prudence, and best contrivance, and all your righteousness, would have no more influence to uphold you and keep you out of hell than a spider's web would have to stop a falling rock. Were it not that such is the sovereign pleasure of God, the earth

Book of Esther, Persian scroll, eighteenth century.

would not bear you one moment—for you are a burden to it; the creation groans with you; the creature is made subject to the bondage of your corruption, not willingly; the sun doesn't willingly shine upon you to give you light to serve sin and Satan; the earth doesn't willingly yield her increase to satisfy your lusts; nor is it willingly a stage for your wickedness to be acted upon; the air doesn't willingly serve you for breath to maintain the flame of life in your vitals, while you spend your life in the service of God's enemies. And the world would spew you out were it not for the sovereign hand of him who hath subjected it in hope. There are

the black clouds of God's wrath now hanging directly over your heads, full of the dreadful storm and big with thunder—and were it not for the restraining hand of God, it would immediately burst forth upon you. The sovereign pleasure of God for the present stays his rough wind; otherwise it would come with fury, and your destruction would come like a whirlwind, and you would be like the chaff of the summer threshing floor.

The wrath of God is like great waters that are dammed for the present; they increase more and more and rise higher and higher till an outlet is given; and the longer the stream is stopped, the more rapid and mighty is its course, when once it is let loose. 'Tis true, that judgment against your evil work has not been executed hitherto; the floods of God's vengeance have been withheld, but your guilt in the meantime is constantly increasing, and you are every day treasuring up more wrath. The waters are continually rising and waxing more and more mighty, and there is nothing but the mere pleasure of God that holds back the waters that are unwilling to be stopped and press hard to go forward. If God should only withdraw his hand from the floodgate, it would immediately fly open, and the fiery floods of the fierceness and wrath of God would rush forth with inconceivable fury and would come upon you with omnipotent power—and if your strength were ten thousand times greater than it is, yea, ten thousand times greater than the strength of the stoutest, sturdiest devil in hell, it would be nothing to withstand or endure it.

The bow of God's wrath is bent, and the arrow made ready on the string, and justice bends the arrow at your heart and strains the bow; and it is nothing but the mere pleasure of God—and that of an angry God without any promise or obligation at all—that keeps the arrow one moment from being made drunk with your blood.

Thus are all you that never passed under a great change of heart by the mighty power of the spirit of God upon your souls; all that were never born again and made new creatures and raised from being dead in sin to a state of new and before altogether unexperienced light and life (however you may have reformed your life in many things, may have had religious affections, and may keep up a form of religion in your families and closets—and in the house of God—and may be strict in it), you are thus in the hands of an angry God; 'tis nothing but his mere pleasure that keeps you from being this moment swallowed up in everlasting destruction.

However unconvinced you may now be of the truth of what you hear, by and by you will be fully convinced of it. Those that are gone from being in the like circumstances with you see that it was so with them; for destruction came suddenly upon most of them when they expected nothing of it and while they were saying peace and safety. Now they see that those things that they depended on for peace and safety were nothing but thin air and empty shadows.

The God that holds you over the pit of hell, much as one holds a spider or some loathsome insect over the fire, abhors you and is dreadfully provoked; his wrath toward you burns like fire. He looks upon you as worthy of nothing else but to be cast into the fire; he is of purer eyes than to bear to have you in his sight; you are ten thousand times so abominable in his eyes, as the most hateful and venomous serpent is in ours. You have offended him infinitely more than ever a stubborn rebel did his prince—and yet it is nothing but his hand that holds you from falling into the fire every moment. 'Tis ascribed to nothing else that you did not go to hell the last night, that you was suffered to awake again in this world after you closed your eyes to sleep—and there is no other reason to be given why you have not dropped into hell since you arose in the morning, but that God's hand has held you up.

From "Sinners in the Hands of an Angry God." Having pored over the writings of John Locke and undergone a religious awakening at the age of seventeen, Edwards in 1726 left Yale University for his grandfather's church in Northampton. As a popular preacher and a leader of the First Great Awakening, he sometimes employed what he called the "preaching of terror."

c. 1250: France

CIRCUMCISION

A beautiful woman will court a man who is uncircumcised in the flesh and lie against his breast with great passion, for he thrusts inside her a long time because of the foreskin, which is a barrier against ejaculation in intercourse. Thus she feels pleasure and reaches an orgasm first. When an uncircumcised man sleeps with her and then resolves to return to his home, she brazenly grasps him, holding on to his genitals and says to him, "Come back, make love to me." This is because of the pleasure that she finds in intercourse with him, from the sinews of his testicles—sinews of iron—and from his ejaculation—that of a horse—which he shoots like an arrow in her womb. They are united without separating, and he makes love twice and three times in one night— yet the appetite is not filled. And so he acts with her night after night. The sexual activity emaciates him of his bodily fat and afflicts his flesh, and he devotes his brain entirely to women, an evil thing.

But when a circumcised man desires the beauty of a woman and cleaves to his wife—or to another woman comely in appearance—he will find himself performing his task quickly, emitting his seed as soon as he inserts the crown. He has an orgasm first; he does not hold back his strength. As soon as he begins intercourse with her, he immediately comes to a climax. She has no pleasure from him when she lies down or when she arises, and it would be better for her if he had not known her, for he arouses her passion to no avail, and she remains in a state of desire for her husband, ashamed and confounded, while the seed is still in her "reservoir." She does not have an orgasm, except on rare occasions because of the great heat and the fire burning within her. Thus he who says, "I am the Lord's" will not empty his brain because of his wife or the wife of his friend. He will find grace and good favor; his heart will be strong to seek out God.

Isaac ben Yedaiah, *from an essay. The Jewish scholar was particularly drawn to commenting on the nonlegalistic passages in the Talmud. His theories on sex and circumcision were impassioned and unusual, building upon but departing from the views of his predecessor Maimonides.*

1913: Kraków

CORPSE-WORSHIPPING

Dear Alexei Maximovich!

Whatever are you up to? It's simply dreadful! Really! Today the newspaper arrived, and it contains a paragraph of your article. This is the paragraph:

> "God-seeking" should be given up for the time being. [Only for the time being?] It is a useless occupation. It is no use seeking something that has not been hidden. Without sowing you cannot reap. You have no God, you have not yet [not yet!] created him. Gods are not sought after—*they are created*; life does not invent, it creates.

It appears then that you are opposed to God-seeking only for the time being! It appears then, that you are opposed to God-seeking *only* in order to substitute God-creating for it!!

Now! Is it not dreadful to think that *you* should reason in this way?

There is as much difference between God-seeking, God-building, God-creating, and God-begetting, etc., as there is between a yellow devil and a blue devil. To speak of God-seeking, not in order to oppose *all* devils and gods, all ideological corpse-worshipping (every little god, even the purest, most ideal, not sought for, but conceived little god, is corpse-worshipping)—but simply to choose between a blue devil and a yellow one—that is a hundred times worse than not speaking about it at all.

In the freest countries, in countries where an appeal "to the democracy, to the people, to public opinion, and to science" is totally out of place—in such countries, America, Switzerland, etc., the minds of the people and of the workers are stultified by precisely this idea of a pure, spiritually conceived little god. That is why all religious ideas, all ideas about any little god, even of flirting with a little god, are an unspeakable abomination and one particularly tolerated (frequently even desired) by the democratic bourgeoisie precisely because it is the most dangerous abomination—the most disgusting contamination. The crowd is much more able to see through millions of physical sins, dirty tricks, violences, and infections which are therefore much less dangerous than is the *subtle*, spiritual idea of the little god arrayed in the smartest of ideological costumes. A Catholic priest who violates young girls (about whom I happened to read just now in a German newspaper) is much less dangerous to democracy than are priests who do not wear surplices, priests without vulgar religion, ideological and democratic priests, who preach the creation and making of little gods. The first type of priest can be easily exposed, condemned, and driven out—but the second cannot be driven out so simply. It is a thousand times more difficult to expose him, since not a single "frail and pitifully weak" philistine will agree to condemn him.

And you, knowing the frailty and pitiful weakness of the Russian philistine soul, bewilder this soul with an attractive looking sweetmeat wrapped in gaudy tinsel which contains at the heart of its sugary hodgepodge a deadly poison.

Really, this is dreadful!

"Enough now of self-castigation, which with us takes the place of self-criticism."

Is not God-building the worst form of self-castigation? Everyone engaged in building *God* castigates himself in the worst possible way, because he contemplates the dirtiest, most stupid, and most servile features of his own ego, glorified by self-love into a god of his own building.

All God-building is the adoring self-contemplation of a dull, frail philistinism—a dreamy self-castigation of the "despondent and weary" philistine and petty bourgeois. Rotten philistinism is disgusting always, but "democratic philistinism," engaged in its ideological corpse-worship, is especially disgusting.

Vladimir Lenin, *from a letter to Maxim Gorky. In his 1902 essay "What Is to Be Done?", Lenin rejected the assumption that workers would inevitably come to revolutionary socialism, proposing a political party that was the "vanguard of the proletariat." The following year, he founded the Bolsheviks. After his November 1917 seizure of power, Lenin at the age of forty-seven confessed, "It makes one's head spin."*

Exodus

Persecuted: approx. 2.5 million Israelites
Persecutors: Pharaoh, Egyptians
Leader of Exodus: Moses
Date of Departure: c. 1447 BC
Route: Land of Goshen to Border of Canaan, by way of the
Wilderness of Sin, Mt. Sinai, Kadash, and the Land of Moab
Time in Transit: 40 years
Obstacles Encountered: Sea of Reeds, bitter waters, hunger,
Amalekites and Canaanites, snake bites, distrustful pilgrims
Details: After God inflicted ten plagues on the people of Egypt, Moses
led the Israelites to the border of the Holy Land, where he died, passing
leadership on to Joshua.

Persecuted: approx. 36,000 Bohemian Brethren families
Persecutors: Jesuits, Holy Roman Emperors,
Prince Lichtenstein
Leader of Exodus: John Amos Comenius
Date of Departure: c. 1628
Route: Brandeis-on-the-Adler to Leszno, Poland
Time in Transit: Unknown
Obstacles Encountered: Government commissioners,
the Giant Mountains
Details: Ordered out of Bohemia for his Protestant beliefs,
Comenius led the last band of the Unity of the Brethren to safety
in Leszno, where they practiced their faith freely.

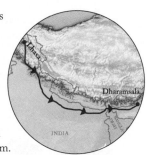

Persecuted: approx. 70,000 Mormons (over 30 years)
Persecutors: Missourians, Illinoisans
Leaders of Exodus: Joseph Smith Jr., Brigham Young
Date of Departure: 1838
Route: Northwest Missouri to Salt Lake Valley,
by way of Nauvoo, Illinois, Fort Laramie, and Fort Bridger
Time in Transit: 9 years
Obstacles Encountered: Governor of Missouri, the *Nauvoo
Expositor*, the winter of 1846–47, scurvy, malaria
Details: After Smith's murder by an angry mob in Nauvoo, Young
led the Mormons across unorganized territory to the Salt Lake
Valley, in what was then Mexico.

Persecuted: approx. 100,000 Tibetans
Persecutors: Communist Party of China
Leader of Exodus: Tenzin Gyatso (Dalai Lama)
Date of Departure: 1959
Route: Lhasa to Dharamsala, by way of Bomdila and Mussoori
Time in Transit: 1 year
Obstacles Encountered: The Himalayas, unfamiliar tropical
climate, diseases of the Indian lowlands
Details: Following the invasion of the Chinese Army, the Dalai Lama
fled his palace under nightfall, armed and wearing a soldier's uniform.

c. 400 BC: Athens

CROWD CONTROL

A time there was when disorder ruled
Human lives, which were then, like lives of beasts,
Enslaved to force; nor was there then reward
For the good, nor for the wicked punishment.
Next, it seems to me, humans established laws
For punishment, that justice might rule
Over the tribe of mortals, and wanton injury be subdued;
And whosoever did wrong was penalized.
Next, as the laws held mortals back from deeds
Of open violence, but still such deeds
Were done in secret—then, I think,
Some shrewd man first, a man in judgment wise,
Found for mortals the fear of gods,
Thereby to frighten the wicked should they

The Pipes of Pan and a Donkey, by Pablo Picasso, 1961.

Even act or speak or scheme in secret.
Hence it was that he introduced the divine
Telling how the divinity enjoys endless life,
Hears and sees, and takes thought
And attends to things, and his nature is divine,
So that everything which mortals say is heard
And everything done is visible.
Even if you plan in silence some evil deed
It will not be hidden from the gods—for discernment
Lies in them. So, speaking words like these,
The sweetest teaching did he introduce,
Concealing truth under untrue speech.
The place he spoke of as the gods' abode
Was that by which he might awe humans most—
The place from which, he knew, terrors came to mortals
And things advantageous in their wearisome life—
The revolving heaven above, in which dwell
The lightnings, and awesome claps
Of thunder, and the starry face of heaven,
Beautiful and intricate by that wise craftsman Time—
From which, too, the meteor's glowing mass speeds
And wet thunderstorm pours forth upon the earth.
Such were the fears with which he surrounded mortals,
And to the divinity he gave a fitting home,
By this his speech, and in a fitting place,
And thus extinguished lawlessness by laws.

The Critias fragment, recorded by Sextus Empiricus in his Against the Dogmatists. *Believed to have come from a play called* Sisyphus, *whose authorship is now debated, the fragment is one of the earliest known naturalist critiques of religion. Sextus Empiricus attributed the work to Plato's uncle Critias, who was among the leaders of the reign of the Thirty Tyrants in Athens from 404 to 403 BC.*

1553: Como

In Como, a little city of Lombardy not very far from Milan, there once dwelled a citizen named Andrigetto da Sabbia, whose immense possessions—surpassing those of any other individual—did not, however, prevent him from adding to them by every means in his power. Being perfectly secure against the attacks of conscience in all his dealings, he was never known to suffer remorse for the most unjustifiable actions. He was in the habit of disposing of the produce of his large estates to the poorer citizens and peasantry, instead of selling

Talk to me about the truth of religion and I'll listen gladly. Talk to me about the duty of religion and I'll listen submissively. But don't come talking to me about the consolations of religion or I shall suspect that you don't understand. —C. S. Lewis, 1961

it to merchants and others, who could command ready money—not from any charitable motives, but in order to obtain possession of their little remaining property, still uniting field after field to the great possessions he had already acquired. It happened that so great a scarcity began to prevail in the city and its vicinity, that many persons actually perished of want, while numbers had recourse to our old usurer for assistance, to whom, from the urgent pressure of circumstances, they were compelled to make over, in return for the necessaries of life, such interest as they might possess either in houses or lands. The concourse of people in his neighborhood was so great as almost to resemble a jubilee or a public fair.

Now there was a certain notary, Tonisto Raspante by name, a most notorious and wily practitioner of his art, and more successful than any other of his brethren in emptying the pockets of the poor villagers. He had still, however, so much regard for an ancient law in Como re-

lating to usurious contracts, which required the money lent to be counted in the presence of proper witnesses, as to refuse to draw up such instruments as Andrigetto often directed him to prepare, observing that they were altogether against the form of the statute, and he would not venture to risk the penalty. But such were the overbearing manners of the old miser, and so great was his authority in the city, that sometimes threatening him with ruin and at other times bribing him to his purpose, he compelled the attorney to obey his commands.

The time for confessing himself being at hand, before presenting himself at the confessional, Andrigetto took care to send to the priest an excellent dinner, with as much of the finest cloth as would make a pair of hose for himself and his servant, announcing at the same time his intention to confess on the ensuing day, when he thought that he was sure of meeting with a favorable hearing. The priest undertook with pleasure the task of absolving from his sins so eminent and rich a citizen, and received his penitent with the utmost cordiality. Andrigetto fell on his knees before his spiritual father, accusing himself with very little ceremony of various sins and errors, not forgetting his usurious and illegal contracts, all which he recounted in the most minute manner. The priest, who had sense enough to perceive the enormous nature of his offenses, conceiving himself bound to make some representations on the subject, ventured certain gentle hints on the impropriety of their repetition, and in the meanwhile strongly recommended restitution to the injured parties. Instead of taking this in good part, Andrigetto turned very sharply round upon his confessor, observing that he was at a loss to understand what he meant and that he had better go and return no more until he had learned how to confess persons in a more rational manner. The priest, owing his preferment in a great measure to Andrigetto—and fearful lest he might lose his favor altogether—began to retract as well as he could, gave him absolution, and then imposing as slight a penance as possible, received a florin for his reward, after which Andrigetto took his leave in very excellent spirits.

Not long after this interview, our old usurer, while rejoicing in this absolution from all his sins, fell ill of a mortal distemper, and the physicians shortly despaired of his life. His friends and relatives having gathered round his bed, took the liberty of suggesting that it was now time to think of a sincere confession, to receive his last spiritual consolation, and make a final arrangement of his affairs like a good Catholic and Christian. After long entreaties and persuasions, he was at last prevailed upon to comply with their request, and agreed to summon to his assistance his old agent, Tonisto Raspante the notary, and Father Neofito, his confessor.

On the arrival of these personages, they addressed the patient with a cheerful countenance, telling him to keep up his spirits, for that with God's help he would soon be a sound man again. Andrigetto only replied that he feared he was too far gone for that, and that he had perhaps better lose no time in first settling his worldly affairs and then arranging his ghostly concerns with his confessor. But the good priest, exhorting and comforting him to the best of his ability, advised him first of all to place his sole trust in the Lord, humbly submitting himself to His will, as the safest means of obtaining a restoration to health. To this, however, Andrigetto replied only by ordering seven respectable men to be called in as witnesses of his nuncupative last will and testament. These

Hindu ascetic with prayer beads (detail), illustration of an Indian *ragamala* verse, c. 1700.

individuals having been successively presented to the patient and taken their seats, he proceeded to inquire from his friend Tonisto the very lowest charge which he was in the habit of making for penning a will. "According to the strict rules of the profession," replied Tonisto, "it is only a florin, but in general the amount is decided by the feelings of the testator." "Well,

Japanese man sacrificing himself in honor of the Buddha Amitabha, French lithograph, 1811.

well, then," cried the patient, "take two florins, and set down what I tell you." The notary having invoked the divine name, drew out the preliminaries in the usual manner, bequeathing the body of the testator to the earth and his soul to the hands of God who gave it, with humble thanks for the many favors vouchsafed by Him to His unworthy creature. This exordium being read to Andrigetto, he flew into a violent

rage and commanded the notary to write down nothing but his own words, which he dictated as follows: "I, Andrigetto di Valsabbia, being of sound mind, though infirm of body, do hereby declare this to be my last will and testament: I give and bequeath my soul into the hands of the great Satan, the prince of devils." Hearing these words, the witnesses stood aghast; Raspante's quill started from the paper, and in evident horror and perturbation, he stopped. Looking the testator very earnestly in the face, he interposed: "Ah! Signor Andrigetto these are the words of a madman!" "How!" exclaimed Andrigetto, in a violent passion, "What do you mean? How dare you stop? Write word for word as I direct you, and nothing more, or you shall never be paid for a will of mine—proceed, I tell you!" Struck with the greatest horror and surprise, his friends attempted to remonstrate with him, lamenting that he should make use of language so opposite to his usual good sense, language which only madmen or blasphemers could be capable of using on such a subject and in so awful a situation as his.

He turned toward his attorney, requesting to know, in a voice of suppressed passion, whether he was prepared to go on, as he had already offered to pay double the usual charge for his labors. Apprehensive that Andrigetto might expire before he had made a disposition of his property, the notary promised to do as he was required—more especially when he heard the patient beginning to hiccup with the violence of his emotions—so that he was compelled to make a solemn vow to fulfil his client's instructions.

"Item," continued Andrigetto, "I hereby bequeath the wretched soul of my wicked agent, Tonisto Raspante, to the great Satan, in order that it may keep company with mine when it leaves this world, as it shortly must." "The Lord have mercy on me!" cried the poor attorney, shocked at the deep solemnity with which these last words were uttered, "The Lord have mercy on my soul!" and the pen dropped from his hand. "Recall," he continued, "my honored patron, recall those wicked words—do anything but destroy my eternal interests, my last, my dearest hopes." "Go on you rogue!" cried the testator, "and do not venture to interrupt me again; do not tell me about your soul. You have your pay and that is enough, so proceed quickly as I shall direct you. I leave my said attorney's soul to the devil, for this reason—that if he had not consented to draw up so many false and usurious contracts, but had driven me from his presence as soon as I proposed them, I should not now find myself reduced to the sad extremity of leaving both our souls to the king of hell, owing entirely to his shameful cupidity and want of common honesty." The attorney, though trembling at the name of the king of hell, yet fearful lest his patron might enter into further particulars far from creditable to him, wrote as he was commanded.

"Item," continued the patient, "I bequeath the soul of Father Neofito, my confessor, into the claws of Lucifer—aye, to thirty thousand pairs of devils." "Stop, Signor Andrigetto, pray stop," cried the priest, "and do not think of applying those dreadful words to me. You ought to put your trust in the Lord, in the Lord Jesus, whose mercies always abound, who came to save sinners, and is still inviting them night and day to repentance. He died for our sins, and for your sins, Signor Andrigetto; you have only to beseech pardon, and all will yet be well. The road is still open to restitution; hasten to make restitution then; for the Lord does not wish the death of a sinner. You have great wealth—remember the church; you will have masses said for your soul, and may yet sit in the seats of paradise." "Oh, you wicked and most wretched priest," retorted the patient, "by your vile avarice and simony, you have helped your own soul, as well as mine, into the pit of perdition. And do you now think of advising me to repent? Confusion on your villainy! Write, no-

tary, that I bequeath his soul to the very center of the place of torments; for had it not been for his bold and shameless conduct in absolving me from my numerous and repeated offenses, I should not now find myself in the strange predicament in which I am placed. What! Does the rogue think it would be now just to restore my evil-gotten gains and thus leave my poor family destitute? No, no—I am not quite such a fool as to do that, so please to go on. Item.

I am ready to meet my maker. Whether my maker is prepared for the ordeal of meeting me is another matter.
—Winston Churchill, 1949

To my dear lady Felicia I leave my pretty farm, situated in the district of Comacchio, in order to supply herself with the elegancies of life and occasionally treat her lovers as she has been hitherto in the habit of doing, thus preparing the way further to oblige me with her company in the other world, sharing with us the torments of eternity. The remainder of my property, personal as well as real, with all future interest and proceeds accruing thereon, I leave to my two legitimate and beloved sons, Commodo and Torquato, on condition that they give nothing for a single mass to be said for the soul of the deceased, but that they feast, swear, game, and fight to the best of their ability, in order that they may the sooner waste their substance so wickedly acquired, until, driven to despair, they may as speedily as possible hang themselves. And this I declare to be my last will and testament, as witness all present, not forgetting my attorney." Having signed this instrument and put his seal to it, Andrigetto turned away his face, and uttering a terrific howl, finally surrendered his impenitent soul to Pluto.

From The Nights of Straparola. *The Italian author's book of seventy-five stories served as inspiration for, among others, William Shakespeare and Molière, and introduced into European literature folktales such as "The Puss in Boots" and "Beauty and the Beast."*

1855: Brooklyn

BE NOT CURIOUS

I have said that the soul is not more than the body,
And I have said that the body is not more than the soul,
And nothing, not God, is greater to one than one's self is,
And whoever walks a furlong without sympathy walks to his own funeral dressed in his shroud,
And I or you pocketless of a dime may purchase the pick of the earth,
And to glance with an eye or show a bean in its pod confounds the learning of all times,
And there is no trade or employment but the young man following it may become a hero,
And there is no object so soft but it makes a hub for the wheel'd universe,
And I say to any man or woman, let your soul stand cool and composed before a million universes.
And I say to mankind, be not curious about God,
For I who am curious about each am not curious about God,
(No array of terms can say how much I am at peace about God and about death).

I hear and behold God in every object, yet understand God not in the least,
Nor do I understand who there can be more wonderful than myself.

Why should I wish to see God better than this day?
I see something of God each hour of the twenty-four, and each moment then,
In the faces of men and women I see God, and in my own face in the glass,
I find letters from God dropped in the street, and every one is sign'd by God's name,
And I leave them where they are, for I know that wheresoe'er I go,
Others will punctually come forever and ever.

> **Walt Whitman**, *from* Song of Myself. *Unable to find a publisher for the first edition of* Leaves of Grass *in 1855, Whitman sold a house to pay for its printing. The poet and essayist once wrote, "I respect Assyria, China, Teutonia, and the Hebrews / I adopt each theory, myth, god, and demigod." Elsewhere he stated, "Do I contradict myself? / Very well then I contradict myself, / (I am large, I contain multitudes.)"*

Annunciation, by Leonardo da Vinci, c. 1472–75.

1755: Edinburgh

AS IN A GREAT THEATER

We are placed in this world as in a great theater, where the true springs and causes of every event are entirely concealed from us; nor have we either sufficient wisdom to foresee, or power to prevent those ills with which we are continually threatened. We hang in perpetual suspense between life and death, health and sickness, plenty and want—which are distributed among the human species by secret and unknown causes, whose operation is oft unexpected, and always unaccountable. These *unknown causes*, then, become the constant object of our hope and fear, and while the passions are kept in perpetual alarm by an anxious expectation of the events, the imagination is equally employed in forming ideas of those powers on which we have so entire a dependence. Could men anatomize nature according to the most probable, at least the most intelligible philosophy, they would find that these causes are nothing but the particular fabric and structure of the minute parts of their own bodies and of external objects; and that by a regular and constant machinery all the events are produced, about which they are so much concerned. But this philosophy exceeds the comprehension of the ignorant multitude who can only conceive the *unknown causes* in a general and confused manner; though their imagination, perpetually employed on the same subject, must labor to form some particular and distinct idea of them. The more they consider these causes themselves and the uncertainty of their operation, the less satisfaction do they meet with in their researches; and, however unwilling, they must at last have abandoned so arduous an attempt, were it not for a propensity in human nature, which leads into a system that gives them some satisfaction.

There is a universal tendency among mankind to conceive all beings like themselves, and to transfer to every object those qualities with which they are familiarly acquainted. We find human faces in the moon, armies in the clouds, and by a natural propensity—if not corrected by experience and reflection—ascribe malice or goodwill to everything, that hurts or pleases us. Hence the frequency and beauty of the prosopopoeia in poetry, where trees, mountains, and streams are personified, and the inanimate parts of nature acquire sentiment and passion. And though these poetical figures and expressions gain not on the belief, they may serve at least to prove a certain tendency in the imagination, without which they could neither be beautiful nor natural. Nor is a river god or hamadryad always taken for a mere poetical or imaginary personage, but may sometimes enter into the real creed of the ignorant vulgar, while each grove or field is represented as possessed of a particular *genius* or invisible power, which inhabits and protects it. Nay, philosophers cannot entirely exempt themselves from this natural frailty, but have oft ascribed it to inanimate matter the horror of a *vacuum*, sympathies, antipathies, and other affections of human nature. The absurdity is not less, while we cast our eyes upward; and transferring, as is too usual, human passions and infirmities to the deity, represent him as jealous and revengeful, capricious and partial, and, in short, a wicked and foolish man, in every respect but his superior power and authority. No wonder, then, that mankind, being placed in such an absolute ignorance of causes, and being at the same time so anxious concerning their future fortune, should immediately acknowledge a dependence on invisible powers possessed of sentiment and intelligence. The *unknown causes* which continually employ their thought, appearing always in the same aspect, are all apprehended to be of the same kind or species. Nor is it long before we ascribe to them thought and reason and passion—and sometimes even the limbs and figures of men—in order to bring them nearer to a resemblance with ourselves.

David Hume, *from* The Natural History of Religion. *Hume's study of the humanities as a young man led to a nervous breakdown in 1729, requiring several years for recovery. Economist, historian, and philosopher of morality and epistemology, Hume called literature his "ruling passion," acknowledging his "insurmountable aversion to everything but the pursuits of philosophy and general learning."*

c. 1870: Brittany

ÉMILE ZOLA OBSERVES AN EXORCISM

Father Pintoux had been the parish priest of Saint-Marchal for the last forty years. He was now a little old man of seventy, dried up by his open-air life; with his brick-red, weather-beaten face and his shabby, threadbare old cassock, he looked like a peasant in his smock.

The story of his life was a simple one. He was a woodcutter's son from the neighboring village

Though the mills of God grind slowly, yet they
grind exceeding small;
Though with patience He stands waiting, with
exactness grinds He all.
— *Friedrich von Logau, 1654*

of Mériadec. A puny boy, bullied by his brothers, he had had the good fortune to be taken up by a patroness who arranged for him to be admitted to the little seminary of Guérande. Physical labor had always been anathema to him—the thought of wielding an axe to cut down trees scared him so much that he would have preferred to become a tramp. He had moreover always possessed a childlike faith which persisted at the seminary, together with an equally blind submission to authority. He believed everything his teachers told him, and never having been very bright, he avoided the need for thought by telling himself that God would do his thinking for him. He had taken holy orders with the same unquestioning submissiveness and with one single idea in mind: to exercise his ministry undisturbed. At first, the bishop of Nantes sent him round to a couple of smaller parishes, and finally realizing his simplemindedness, innocence, and complete lack of initiative, he had packed him off to Saint-Marchal and thought no more about him.

Saint-Marchal is a tiny hamlet in the wilds of lower Brittany. The Nantes-to-Brest railway did not pass within twenty-five miles of it; it was real wolf country, set on a high plateau battered by storms raging in from the Atlantic, which can be seen as a thin green line on the horizon. Saint-Marchal had almost four hundred inhabitants and poverty was widespread, for the soil is stony and there is a great shortage of water. The wretched villagers seemed to belong to quite a different world from that of the average Frenchman. And it was in this poor hamlet that Father Pintoux had grown old.

Little by little, the priest had settled into his narrow round of routine, like some old riding-school hack. Mass in the morning, catechism in the afternoon, and in the evening a game of cards with a neighbor. Since it was quite impossible to live on the few hundred francs he received from the parish, he had been forced to overcome his distaste for hard work and take to wielding a mattock in the vegetable garden at the back of his presbytery, where he grew beans and cabbages. He could be seen in his shirt-sleeves, bareheaded in the sun, grappling with a stony soil far too hard and heavy for his puny arms. Afterward he would put on his cassock and go off to hear confession from the girls of the village, still out of breath from his exertions and searching his memory for the Latin formulas which he trotted out automatically.

Father Pintoux had a whole collection of ready-made phrases and gestures which he had been using for the last half century and from which he never deviated. For him religion had become purely a matter of outward observance. His services went like clockwork. His devotion of earlier days had turned into mere empiricism and found satisfaction in the repetition, at every opportunity, of the same details culled from his missal. Had he returned to earth in the shape of one of those peaceful oxen lumbering stolidly through their pastures, he would have bowed down to the sun with the same conviction that he showed in kneeling before the figure of Christ.

Meanwhile, over the last forty years, he had officiated at the weddings of most of the villagers and baptized a whole generation of children. He was the patriarch of Saint-Marchal. At church festivals, they would bring him gifts of eggs and butter. It was he whom they consulted

Sioux Worshipping at the Red Boulders, by George Catlin, c. 1838.

on any matter of importance; he conducted lawsuits, reconciled families, and shared out inheritances. There was indeed nothing more natural than this regal status of the priest, for he alone was capable of reading the books, he alone was in communication with science and with God. He represented authority even more than the mayor, for he spoke in the name of the Lord, whereas the mayor spoke only in the name of the government—and heaven, which metes out hail and thunder, is the only power feared by peasants, the only one before which they would bend the knee.

In the whole village, there was not one single unbeliever. On Sundays, the church was packed, with the women on one side and the men on the other. When the priest came in carrying the chalice, he could see at a glance if everyone was present. As soon as one of his flock was an absentee, he would be required to offer an excuse, such as an illness preventing him from leaving the house; otherwise the priest would call down God's wrath upon the head of the lost sheep. From the pulpit, he would fulminate dire threats against the ungodly, conjuring up the horrors of hellfire, with cauldrons of boiling oil and souls in torment roasting on red-hot iron bars. Strong men and women would blanch, and after the service little children would be haunted by nightmares for the whole week. In fact, the priest would not have harmed a fly; but he was repeating sermons that he had heard from others, and he himself lived in awe of the divine wrath of a jealous God. He really believed these cruel and miraculous tales and legends. So Saint-Marchal lived in a state of humility and terror, like a primitive tribe prostrating itself beneath a cloud streaked with lightning and always on the point of loosing its thunderbolts.

One Sunday, having noticed that Marianne Roussel was not in her usual place beside the font, Father Pintoux set off after lunch to find out if she was ill. He had the stiff, halting gait of an old man; the only signs of life now left in his stolid, leathery old face were his tiny gray eyes, as sharp and innocent as a child's. On the way, a few peasants stopped him to ask him what the weather would be like tomorrow, and he looked up at the sky, wagged his head, and finally promised that it would be fine.

A few steps farther on, a woman's washing caught his eye; then he went into a backyard to look at a brood of chicks. For everybody in the village, he was one of the family. The only thing which differentiated him from the other villagers was his cassock; he shared their ideas and their speech, and he too looked as if he was walking in his sleep. Finally, he reached the Roussels' cottage. Marianne was outside, looking perfectly well and chatting to her tall neighbor Nanette.

"Well, Marianne, what's all this about? You missed mass this morning!"

And without giving her a chance to explain, he launched into his attack: it was wrong, the devil was always lying in wait and she would certainly end up in hell if she didn't go to church. In the end, Marianne managed to explain:

"It's my little girl, Father … She's very poorly. This morning I thought we'd lost her … So I had to stay at home."

"Little Catherine isn't well?"

"Yes Father, we've put her in our bed. Come and take a look."

In a large bed at the far end of the gloomy room, a little girl about ten years old was lying with a flushed face and closed eyes shivering with fever. The whole of her poor little body was trembling under the sheet. The priest went over and looked at her silently for a moment. Then he said slowly, "It's the good Lord punishing you, Marianne. You've offended Him by your bad example and He has laid His hand upon you."

He jerked his chin to emphasize each word, as if to indicate his approval of such divine vengeance. And Catherine had not been a very good girl, either. The previous Thursday during catechism, he had been obliged to send her out of church because she had been laughing and disturbing the other children. It happened to have rained very heavily that afternoon, and

"Watertown, South Dakota," 2008. Photograph by Alec Soth.

not daring to go home for fear of being scolded, the little girl had been drenched to the skin in a shower.

"She must have caught it last Thursday," her mother murmured. "She came home in a dreadful state."

"God is punishing her as He is punishing you," the priest went on. "Do you think He is happy when He sees a naughty little girl making fun of Him in His own house? Everything must be paid for, you know."

Nanette crossed herself and old Roussel, who was eating a bowl of soup at a table, nodded his head in approval. Yes, everything had to be paid for.

However, as the Roussels had no recollection of having given any cause for God's anger, they hoped that their young daughter would recover with the help of the angels. And if things were no better after a couple of days, they could even send for the doctor who lived at Pontenac, some fifteen miles away. Nanette gave a shrug; as far as she was concerned, doctors were of no use at all. Once heaven had passed judgment on someone, there was certainly no doctor who could save him.

"Rub her temples every hour with holy water," said the priest, "and say three Paternosters and two Ave Marias."

Then he knelt down and mumbled a quick prayer. The Roussels and Nanette said "Amen" with him and crossed themselves vigorously.

"It's not going to be anything much," said the priest as he left. "The child's body must cast out all its wickedness … I'll be back tomorrow."

But when Father Pintoux came to see the Roussels next day, he was greatly agitated, and in a voice trembling with emotion he recounted the appalling story that he had just been told by his bell-ringer: Catherine had committed an act of sacrilege. On Thursday, after being sent out of the catechism class, she had slipped off to play for a moment in the sacristy, where the bell-ringer had seen her take off the crown of the large plaster statue of the Virgin Mary and put it on her own head, making several curtsies all by

herself as she did so, doubtless in order to make fun of the Mother of God. The priest could not understand why heaven had not struck her down on the spot. But now she was surely doomed. Her illness had come from on high.

"But she did come home soaked to the skin on Thursday," Marianne said again. "Perhaps, after all, if we were to get her into a good sweat …"

"Oh, she's ill, very ill," old Roussel said in a low voice, sitting in a corner with his hands on his knees.

The important thing, I think, is not to be bitter. You know, if it turns out that there is a God, I don't think that he's evil. I think that the worst thing you could say about him is that basically he's an underachiever. After all, you know, there are worse things in life than death.
—*Woody Allen, 1975*

And the poor little girl seemed indeed on the point of death as she lay in the large bed with her short blond hair all dishevelled, gasping feverishly for breath through her burning lips. Behind her half-closed lids, her eyes were glazed and staring, and in her fever she kept moaning, "Oh, it's hurting me, it's hurting dreadfully!" It was pitiful to see this tender young girl in such pain, clenching her tiny fists in her lonely struggle against death.

Meanwhile the story of the sacrilege had spread through the village, and all the neighbors had come flocking to the house. It was rumored that Father Pintoux was going to attempt to chase out the devil who had got into the body of the Roussel girl. Soon there were a dozen people gathered in the front room. They were all whispering together and recalling other well-known incidents of the same sort.

"She was such a quiet, well-behaved little girl," said her father. "Something must have got into her, that's for sure."

The priest had started praying. He walked round the room, reciting his Latin prayers, and dipping a twig into a plateful of holy water, each time he reached the child he sprinkled some over her, making a sign of the cross in the air. Catherine was still moaning, writhing and arching her back while she babbled incoherently in her delirium, laughing and sobbing simultaneously. Suddenly she started up with staring eyes, calling out to the people she saw around her; then she fell back, singing a children's song until her voice died away into silence.

The men and women in the room shrank back trembling, afraid of seeing a monster spring out of the poor feverish girl's open

The wrath of the lion is the wisdom of God.
—*William Blake, 1793*

mouth. She must certainly be possessed by the devil if she started like that as soon as a drop of holy water touched her. Surely the devil was going to throttle her and put an end to it all.

At the foot of the bed, Marianne was in tears: Catherine was all she had, and now she was going to lose her without even knowing what had caused her death. Once more, she mentioned a doctor and begged her husband to drive quickly over to Pontenac, but old Roussel was still slumped stupidly in his corner and merely shook his head apathetically in reply. He was resigned to the death of his daughter, like all old peasants who submit to higher powers which they cannot understand. Why bother to send for a doctor when Father Pintoux had announced that God wished to take away their child? Father Pintoux certainly knew better than anyone. All you can do is submit; your turn will come too, and the best thing was to be always on your best behavior.

When he saw that the holy water was making the little girl suffer and not bringing her any relief, Father Pintoux clapped his hands lightly, as he did in church when he wanted the congregation to kneel. They all fell on their knees. He remained standing for a moment, saying, "Let us pray together and ask our Lord to perform a miracle."

His brown leathery face lit up with the radiance of his faith, and despite his stoop and his weather-beaten peasantlike appearance, he had a majestic look as he fell on his knees and, with all the fervor of his seminary days, prayed God to show mercy on the poor sinner. The murmur of prayer grew louder and the anxious atmosphere in the room was filled by the icy chill of superstition, the helpless ignorance of people crushed by life's adversity. The little girl gave one final convulsive shudder and then lay flat in the bed, gasping as if in relief. Then all at once she gave a deep sigh and lay still. She was dead.

"*Requiescat in pace,*" said the priest, raising his voice.

"Amen!" came the response from the villagers.

And they all rose to their feet and left, greatly affected by the scene, while Marianne stifled her sobs in her apron and old Roussel, utterly bewildered and unable to realize what he was doing, opened his clasp knife and cut himself a slice of bread.

When Father Pintoux left he was greeted by the whole village as the representative of the dread Master who can exercise his power of life and death at any time. It so happened that municipal elections were being held on the following Sunday and the villagers clustered round him to ask him how they should vote. He repeated the instructions which he had received from the bishop's palace the previous day. Next Sunday, not one of the villagers failed to attend Mass and the bishop's candidate was elected without a single dissenting voice. Father Pintoux ruled in Saint-Marchal like God himself, like some old rough-hewn wooden idol with power to dispense thunderbolts and horrible diseases.

From "Priests and Sinners." The novelist and political activist was an early advocate for the Impressionists in the 1860s and 1870s. In 1871 Zola published his first novel in The Rougon Family Fortune series, writing nineteen more installments over the next twenty-two years. As a leader of literary naturalism, he copublished in 1880 a collection of short stories with Guy de Maupassant and J.-K. Huysmans.

Jonah and the Whale, by Fred Aris, c. 1975.

1520: Wittenberg

AMONG SCORPIONS

To Leo X, pope at Rome, Martin Luther wishes salvation in Christ Jesus our Lord. Amen.

Living among the monsters of this age with whom I am now for the third year waging war, I am compelled occasionally to look up to you, Leo, most blessed father, and to think of you. Indeed, since you are occasionally regarded as the sole cause of my warfare, I cannot help thinking of you. It is true that I have been so bold as to despise and look down upon those who have tried to frighten me with the majesty of your name and authority. There is one thing, however, which I cannot ignore and which is the cause of my writing once more to Your Blessedness. It has come to my attention that I am accused of great indiscretion—said to be my great fault, in which, it is said, I have not spared even your person.

I freely vow that I have, to my knowledge, spoken only good and honorable words concerning you whenever I have thought of you. If I had ever done otherwise, I myself could by no means condone it but should agree entirely with the judgment which others have formed of me, and I should do nothing more gladly than recant such indiscretion and impiety. Indeed, your reputation and the fame of your blameless life, celebrated as they are throughout the world by the writings of many great men, are too well known and too honorable to be assailed by anyone, no matter how great he is. I am not so foolish as to attack one whom all people praise.

I have, to be sure, sharply attacked ungodly doctrines in general, and I have snapped at my opponents, not because of their bad morals but because of their ungodliness. Rather than repent this in the least, I have determined to persist in that fervent zeal and to despise the judgment of men, following the example of Christ who in his zeal called his opponents "a brood of vipers," "blind fools," "hypocrites," and "children of the devil."

I have truly despised your see, the Roman Curia, which, however, neither you nor anyone else can deny is more corrupt than any Babylon or Sodom ever was, and which, as far as I can

Now is a great time for new religions to pop up. There are people who get religious about jogging, they get religious about sex, and you talk to some of these people who are avowed swingers—they'll bore your head off. God, it's just painful to listen to them. Fifteen minutes in a roomful of these people is like turning your head into a husk. Health foods have become the basis of a religion. Let's see, ESP, of course, flying saucers, anything is fertile ground now. There's a new messiah born every day.
—Tom Wolfe, 1980

see, is characterized by a completely depraved, hopeless, and notorious godlessness. I have been thoroughly incensed over the fact that good Christians are mocked in your name and under the cloak of the Roman church. I have resisted and will continue to resist your see as long as the spirit of faith lives in me. Not that I shall strive for the impossible or hope that by my efforts alone anything will be accomplished in that most disordered Babylon where the fury of so many flatterers is turned against me; but I acknowledge my indebtedness to my Christian brethren, whom I am duty-bound to warn so that fewer of them may be destroyed by the plagues of Rome, at least so that their destruction may be less cruel.

As you well know, there has been flowing from Rome these many years—like a flood covering the world—nothing but a devastation of men's bodies and souls and possessions, the

worst examples of the worst of all things. All this is clearer than day to all, and the Roman church, once the holiest of all, has become the most licentious den of thieves, the most shameless of all brothels, the kingdom of sin, death, and hell. It is so bad that even the Antichrist himself, if he should come, could think of nothing to add to its wickedness.

Meanwhile you, Leo, sit as a lamb in the midst of wolves—like Daniel in the midst of lions. With Ezekiel you live among scorpions. How can you alone oppose these monsters? Even if you would call to your aid three or four well-learned and thoroughly reliable cardinals, what are these among so many?

It was your duty and that of your cardinals to remedy these evils, but the gout of these evils makes a mockery of the healing hand, and neither chariot nor horse responds to the rein. Moved by this affection for you, I have always been sorry, most excellent Leo, that you were made pope in these times, for you are worthy of being pope in better days. The Roman Curia does not deserve to have you or men like you, but it should have Satan himself as pope, for he now actually rules in that Babylon more than you do.

Would that you might discard that which your most profligate enemies boastfully claim to be your glory and might live on a small priestly income of your own or on your family inheritance! What do you accomplish in the Roman Curia, my Leo? The more criminal and detestable a man is, the more gladly will he use your name to destroy men's possessions and souls, to increase crime, to suppress faith and truth and God's whole church. O most unhappy Leo, you are sitting on a most dangerous throne. I am telling you the truth, because I wish you well.

Martin Luther, *from a letter to Pope Leo X. Luther was struck by lightning during a violent thunderstorm in 1505; he vowed to serve God as a monk if he lived. By 1517 he was disseminating his "Ninety-five Theses," number eighty-six of which asked, "Why does not the pope, whose wealth today is greater than the wealth of the richest Crassus, build this one basilica of St. Peter with his own money rather than with the money of poor believers?"*

1928: Argentina

THE GOSPEL ACCORDING TO JORGE LUIS BORGES

The incident took place on the Los Alamos ranch, south of the small town of Junín, in late March of 1928. Its protagonist was a medical student named Baltasar Espinosa. We might define him for the moment as a Buenos Aires youth much like many others, with no traits worthier of note than the gift for public speaking that had won him more than one prize at the English school in Ramos Mejía and an almost unlimited goodness. He didn't like to argue; he preferred that his interlocutor, rather than he himself, be right. And though he found the chance twists and turns of gambling interesting, he was a poor gambler, because he didn't like to win. He was intelligent and open to learning, but he was lazy; at thirty-three he had not yet completed the last requirements for his degree. (The work he still owed, incidentally, was for his favorite class.) His father, like all the gentlemen of his day, a freethinker, had instructed Espinosa in the doctrines of Herbert Spencer, but once, before he set off on a trip to Montevideo, his mother had asked him to say the Lord's Prayer every night and make the sign of the cross, and never in all the years that followed did he break that promise. He did not lack courage; one morning, with more indifference than wrath, he had traded two or three blows with some of his classmates that were trying to force him to join a strike at the university. He abounded in debatable habits and opinions, out of a spirit of acquiescence: his country mattered less to him than the danger that people in other countries might think the Argentines still wore feathers; he venerated France but had contempt for the French; he had little respect for Americans but took pride in the fact that there were skyscrapers in Buenos Aires; he thought that the gauchos of the plains were better horsemen than the gauchos of the mountains. When his cousin Daniel invited him to spend the summer at Los Alamos, he immediately accepted—not because he liked the country but out of a natural desire to please, and because he could find no good reason for saying no.

The main house at the ranch was large and a bit run down; the quarters for the foreman, a man named Gutre, stood nearby. There were three members of the Gutre family: the father, the son—who was singularly rough and

Muhammad and the archangel Gabriel, sixteenth century.

unpolished—and a girl of uncertain paternity. They were tall, strong, and bony, with reddish hair and Indian features. They rarely spoke. The foreman's wife had died years before.

In the country, Espinosa came to learn things he hadn't known, had never even suspected; for example, that when you're approaching a house there's no reason to gallop and that nobody goes out on a horse unless there's a job to be done. As the summer wore on, he learned to distinguish birds by their call.

God is a complex of ideas formed by the tribe, the nation, and humanity, which awake and organize social feelings and aim to link the individual to society and to bridle the zoological individualism. —Maxim Gorky, 1913

Within a few days, Daniel had to go to Buenos Aires to close a deal on some livestock. At the most, he said, the trip would take a week. Espinosa, who was already a little tired of his cousin's *bonnes fortunes* and his indefatigable interest in the vagaries of men's tailoring, stayed behind on the ranch with his textbooks. The heat was oppressive, and not even nightfall brought relief. Then one morning toward dawn, he was awakened by thunder. Wind lashed the casuarina trees. Espinosa heard the first drops of rain and gave thanks to God. Suddenly the wind blew cold. That afternoon, the Salado overflowed.

The next morning, as he stood on the porch looking out over the flooded plains, Baltasar Espinosa realized that the metaphor equating the pampas with the sea was not—at least that morning—an altogether false one, though Hudson had noted that the sea seems the grander of the two because we view it not from horseback or our own height, but from the deck of a ship. The rain did not let up; the Gutres, helped (or hindered) by the city dweller, saved a good part of the livestock, though many animals were drowned. There were four roads leading to the ranch; all were underwater. On the third day, when a leaking roof threatened the foreman's house, Espinosa gave the Gutres a room at the back of the main house, alongside the toolshed. The move brought Espinosa and the Gutres closer, and they began to eat together in the large dining room. Conversation was not easy; the Gutres, who knew so much about things in the country, did not know how to explain them. One night Espinosa asked them if people still remembered anything about the Indian raids, back when the military command for the frontier had been in Junín. They told him they did, but they would have given the same answer if he had asked them about the day Charles I had been beheaded. Espinosa recalled that his father used to say that all the cases of longevity that occur in the country are the result of either poor memory or a vague notion of dates—gauchos quite often know neither the year they were born in nor the name of the man that fathered them.

In the entire house the only reading material to be found were several copies of a farming magazine, a manual of veterinary medicine, a deluxe edition of the romantic verse drama *Tabaré*, a copy of *The History of the Shorthorn in Argentina*, several erotic and detective stories, and a recent novel that Espinosa had not read—*Don Segundo Sombra*, by Ricardo Güiraldes. In order to put some life into the inevitable after-dinner attempt at conversation, Espinosa read a couple of chapters of the novel to the Gutres, who did not know how to read or write. Unfortunately, the foreman had been a cattle drover himself, and he could not be interested in the adventures of another such a one. It was easy work, he said; they always carried along a pack mule with everything they might need. If he had not been a cattle drover, he announced, he'd never have seen Lake Gómez, or the Bragado River, or even the Nuñez ranch in Chacabuco …

In the kitchen there was a guitar; before the incident I am narrating, the laborers would sit in a circle and someone would pick up the guitar and strum it, though never managing actually to play it. That was called "giving it a strum."

Espinosa, who was letting his beard grow out, would stop before the mirror to look at his changed face; he smiled to think that he'd soon be boring the fellows in Buenos Aires with his stories about the Salado overrunning its banks. Curiously, he missed places in the city he never went and would never go—a street corner on Cabrera where a mailbox stood, two cement lions on a porch on Calle Jujuy a few blocks from the Plaza del Once, a tile-floored corner grocery store and bar (whose location he couldn't quite remember). As for his father and his brothers, by now Daniel would have told them that he had been isolated—the word was etymologically precise—by the floodwaters.

Exploring the house still cut off by the high water, he came upon a Bible printed in English. On its last pages the Guthries (that was their real name) had kept their family history. They had come originally from Inverness and had arrived in the New World—doubtlessly as peasant laborers—in the early nineteenth century; they had intermarried with Indians. The chronicle came to an end in the 1870s; they no longer knew how to write. Within a few generations they had forgotten their English; by the time Espinosa met them, even Spanish gave them some difficulty. They had no faith, though in their veins, alongside the superstitions of the pampas, there still ran a dim current of the Calvinist's harsh fanaticism. Espinosa mentioned his find to them, but they hardly seemed to hear him.

He leafed through the book, and his fingers opened it to the first verses of the Gospel according to Mark. To try his hand at translating, and perhaps to see if they might understand a little of it, he decided that that would be the text he read the Gutres after dinner. He was surprised that they listened first attentively and then with mute fascination. The presence of gold letters on the binding may have given it increased authority. "It's in their blood," he thought. It also occurred to him that throughout history, humankind has told two stories: the story of a lost ship sailing the Mediterranean seas in quest of a beloved isle, and the story of a god who allows himself to be crucified on Golgotha. He recalled his elocution classes in Ramos Mejía, and he rose to his feet to preach the parables.

c. 1260: Japan

WHEEL OF TRUTH

This spot among the mountains is secluded from the worldly life, and there is no human habitation in the neighborhood—east, west, north, or south. I am now living in such a lonely hermitage, but in my bosom, in Nichiren's fleshly body, is secretly deposited the great mystery which the Lord Shākyamuni revealed on Vulture Peak, and has entrusted to me. Therefore I know that my breast is the place where all Buddhas are immersed in contemplation, that they turn the Wheel of Truth upon my tongue, that my throat is giving birth to them, and that they are attaining the Supreme Enlightenment in my mouth. This place is the abode of such a man, who is mysteriously realizing the Lotus of Truth in his life—surely such a place is no less dignified than the Paradise of Vulture Peak. As the Truth is noble, so is the man who embodies it; as the man is noble, so is the place where he resides.

Nichiren, *from a letter. The monk conducted a study of the various sects of Buddhism, declaring in 1253 that* The Lotus Sutra *was the only true path. For predicting impending disasters in Japan if the country did not accept the* Sutra's *teaching, he was exiled to the island of Sado, where he wrote an account of his enlightenment. The government pardoned Nichiren in 1274, fearing that his prophecies were coming true.*

In the following days, the Gutres would wolf down the spitted beef and canned sardines in order to arrive sooner at the Gospel.

The girl had a little lamb; it was her pet, and she prettied it with a sky blue ribbon. One day it cut itself on a piece of barbed wire; to stanch the blood, the Gutres were about to put spiderwebs on the wound, but Espinosa treated it with pills. The gratitude awakened by that cure amazed him. At first, he had not trusted the Gutres and had hidden away in one of his books the two hundred forty pesos he'd brought; now with Daniel gone, he had taken the master's place and begun to give timid orders, which were immediately followed. The Gutres would trail him through the rooms and along the hallway, as though they were lost. As he read, he noticed that they would sweep away the crumbs he had left on the table. One afternoon he surprised them as they were discussing him in brief, respectful words. When he came to the end of the Gospel According to St. Mark, he started to read another of the three remaining gospels, but the father asked him to reread the one he'd just finished, so they could understand it better. Espinosa felt they were like children, who prefer repetition to variety or novelty. One night he dreamed of the Flood (which is not surprising) and was awakened by the hammering of the building of the Ark, but he told himself it was thunder. And in

Those who by God's commands have waged war, or who, wielding the public power, and in conformity with the divine laws, have put criminals to death—these have by no means violated the commandment "Thou shalt not kill."
—St. Augustine, 426

fact the rain, which had let up for a while, had begun again; it was very cold. The Gutres told him the rain had broken through the roof of the toolshed; when they got the beams repaired, they said, they'd show him where. He was no longer a stranger, a foreigner, and they all treated him with respect—he was almost spoiled. None of them liked coffee, but there was always a little cup for him, with spoonfuls of sugar stirred in.

That second storm took place on a Tuesday. Thursday night there was a soft knock on his door; because of his doubts about the Gutres he always locked it. He got up and opened the door; it was the girl. In the darkness he couldn't see her, but he could tell by her footsteps that she was barefoot, and afterward, in the bed, that she was naked—that in fact she had come from the back of the house that way. She did not embrace him, or speak a word; she lay down beside him and she was shivering. It was the first time she had lain with a man. When she left, she did not kiss him; Espinosa realized that he didn't even know her name. Impelled by some sentiment he did not attempt to understand, he swore that when he returned to Buenos Aires, he'd tell no one of the incident.

The next day began like all the others, except that the father spoke to Espinosa to ask whether Christ had allowed himself to be killed in order to save all mankind. Espinosa, who was a freethinker like his father but felt obliged to defend what he had read them, paused.

"Yes," he finally replied. "To save all mankind from hell."

"What *is* hell?" Gutre then asked him.

"A place underground where souls will burn in fire forever."

"And those that drove the nails will also be saved?"

"Yes," replied Espinosa, whose theology was a bit shaky. (He had worried that the foreman wanted to have a word with him about what had happened last night with his daughter.)

After lunch they asked him to read the last chapters again.

Espinosa had a long siesta that afternoon, although it was a light sleep, interrupted by persistent hammering and vague premonitions. Toward evening he got up and went out into the hall.

"The water's going down," he said, as though thinking out loud. "It won't be long now."

"Not long now," repeated Gutre, like an echo.

The three of them had followed him. Kneeling on the floor, they asked his blessing. Then they cursed him, spat on him, and drove him to the back of the house. The girl was weeping. Espinosa realized what awaited him on the other side of the door. When they opened it, he saw the sky. A bird screamed. *It's a goldfinch*, Espinosa thought. There was no roof on the shed; they had torn down the roof beams to build the Cross.

From "The Gospel According to Mark." Borges was born in Buenos Aires in 1899 and read his first books in English, among them The Adventures of Huckleberry Finn *and* Don Quixote. *Living abroad during World War I, he returned to his native city in 1921, soon publishing his first book of poems,* Fervor of Buenos Aires. *Borges later worked at a library named for an ancestor, until Juan Perón's government dismissed him for supporting the Allies in World War II.*

1922: Moscow

THE GREAT ESCAPE

No, you never will bind him
To your signs and your burdens!
The least chink—he's inside it,
Like the supplest of gymnasts.

By the drawbridges
And flocks in migration,
By the telegraph poles,
God's escaping us.

No, you never will train him
To abide and to share!
He, in feelings' resident slush,
Is a gray floe of ice.

No, you never will catch him!
On a thrifty dish, God
Never thrives in the window
Like domestic begonias!

All, beneath the roof's vault,
Were awaiting the builder,
The call. Poets and pilots
—All gave up despair.

He's the sprint—and he's moving.
The whole volume of stars
Is, from alpha to omega,
Just a trace of his cloak.

Marina Tsvetaeva, *from "God (3)." During the Russian Civil War, Tsvetaeva composed* The Swans' Camp, *a cycle of poems relating her experiences as the wife of a White Army officer. In 1922 she left the Soviet Union, eventually settling in Paris. She published* Homesick for the Motherland *in 1935 and returned to Moscow in 1939, joining her husband, who was soon arrested. Tsvetaeva committed suicide in 1941.*

1843: Kreuznach

OPIUM DEN

The critique of religion is the prerequisite of every critique. Man, who has found only his own reflection in the fantastic reality of heaven, where he sought a supernatural being, will no longer be disposed to find only the semblance of himself, only a nonhuman being, here where he seeks and must seek his true reality.

The foundation of irreligious criticism is this: man makes religion; religion does not make man. Religion is, in fact, the self-consciousness and self-esteem of man who has either not yet gained himself or has lost himself again. But man is no abstract being squatting outside the world. Man is the world of man, the state, society. This state, this society, produce religion, which is an inverted world consciousness, because they are an inverted world. Religion is the general theory of this world, its encyclopedic compendium, its logic in popular form, its spiritualistic *point d'honneur*, its enthusiasm, its moral sanction, its solemn complement, its universal basis of consolation and justification. It is the fantastic realization of the human being because the human being has attained no true reality. Thus, the struggle against religion is indirectly the struggle against that world of which religion is the spiritual aroma.

The wretchedness of religion is at once an expression of and a protest against real wretchedness. Religion is the sigh of the oppressed creature, the heart of a heartless world, and the soul of soulless conditions. It is the opium of the people.

The abolition of religion as the illusory happiness of the people is a demand for their true happiness. The call to abandon illusions about their condition is the call to abandon a condition which requires illusions. Thus, the critique of religion is the critique in embryo of the vale of tears of which religion is the halo.

Criticism has plucked the imaginary flowers from the chain, not so that man shall bear the chain without fantasy or consolation, but so

Ritual figurine used for cursing enemies, Egypt, c. 300.

that he shall cast off the chain and gather the living flower. The critique of religion disillusions man so that he will think, act, and fashion his reality as a man who has lost his illusions and regained his reason, so that he will revolve about himself as his own true sun. Religion is only the illusory sun about which man revolves so long as he does not revolve about himself.

It is the task of history, therefore—once the other-world of truth has vanished—to establish the truth of this world. It is above all the task of philosophy, which is in the service of history, to unmask human self-alienation in its secular forms, once its sacred form has been unmasked. Thus, the critique of heaven is transformed into the critique of the earth, the critique of religion into the critique of law, the critique of theology into the critique of politics.

Karl Marx, *from* A Contribution to the Critique of Hegel's Philosophy of Right. *Fearing the effects of anti-Semitism on his family, Marx's father had the boy christened in the Evangelical Established Church at the age of six. Playing the parlor game "Confessions" in the mid-1860s, the father of modern communism said his "idea of happiness" was "to fight" and his "favorite virtue" was "simplicity"; his friend Engels answered, respectively, "Chateau Margaux 1848" and "jollity."*

1949: Tennessee

Nothing was working the way Haze had expected it to. He had spent every evening preaching, but the membership of the Church Without Christ was still only one person: himself. There had been a sort of follower but that had been a mistake. That had been a boy about sixteen years old who had wanted someone to go to a whorehouse with him because he had never been to one before. He knew where the place was but he didn't want to go without a person of experience, and when he heard Haze, he hung around until he stopped preaching and then asked him to go. But it was all a mistake because after they had gone and got out again and Haze had asked him to be a member of the Church Without Christ, or more than that, a disciple, an apostle, the boy said he was sorry but he couldn't be a member of that church because he was a lapsed Catholic. He said that what they had just done was a mortal sin, and that should they die unrepentant of it they would suffer eternal punishment and never see God. Haze had not enjoyed the whorehouse anywhere near as much as the boy had, and he had wasted half his evening. He shouted that there was no such thing as sin or judgment, but the boy only shook his head and asked him if he would like to go again the next night.

If Haze had believed in praying, he would have prayed for a disciple, but as it was all he could do was worry about it a lot. Then two nights after the boy, the disciple appeared.

That night he preached outside of four different picture shows and every time he looked up, he saw the same big face smiling at him. The man was plumpish, and he had curly blond hair that was cut with showy sideburns. He wore a black suit with a silver stripe in it and a wide-brimmed white hat pushed onto the back of his head, and he had on tight-fitting black pointed shoes and no socks. He looked like an ex-preacher turned cowboy, or an ex-cowboy turned mortician. He was not handsome but under his smile, there was an honest look that fitted into his face like a set of false teeth.

Every time Haze looked at him, the man winked.

At the last picture show he preached in front of, there were three people listening to him besides the man. "Do you people care anything about the truth?" he asked. "The only way to the truth is through blasphemy, but do you care? Are you going to pay any attention to what I've been saying, or are you just going to walk off like everybody else?"

Zeus alone has cures for everything.
—Greek fragment

There were two men and a woman with a cat-faced baby sprawled over her shoulder. She had been looking at Haze as if he were in a booth at the fair. "Well, come on," she said, "he's finished. We got to be going." She turned away and the two men fell in behind her.

"Go ahead and go," Haze said, "but remember that the truth don't lurk around every street corner."

The man who had been following reached up quickly and pulled Haze's pants leg and gave him a wink. "Come on back heah you folks," he said. "I want to tell you all about *me*."

The woman turned around again, and he smiled at her as if he had been struck all along with her good looks. She had a square red face and her hair was freshly set. "I wisht I had my gittarr here," the man said, "cause I just somehow can say sweet things to music bettern plain. And when you talk about Jesus you need a little music, don't you, friends?" He looked at the two men as if he were appealing to the good judgment that was impressed on their faces. They had on brown felt hats and black town suits, and they looked like older and younger brother. "Listen, friends," the disciple said confidentially, "two months ago before I met the Prophet here, you wouldn't know me for the same man. I didn't have a friend in the world. Do you know what it's like not to have a friend in the world?"

"It ain't no worsen havinum that would put a knife in your back when you wasn't looking," the older man said, barely parting his lips.

"Friend, you said a mouthful when you said that," the man said. "If we had time, I would have you repeat that just so ever'body could hear it like I did." The picture show was over and more people were coming up. "Friends," the man said, "I know you're all interested in the Prophet

here," pointing to Haze on the nose of the car, "and if you'll just give me time I'm going to tell you what him and his idears've done for me. Don't crowd because I'm willing to stay here all night and tell you if it takes that long."

Haze stood where he was, as if he weren't sure what he was hearing.

"Friends," the man said, "lemme innerduce myself. My name is Onnie Jay Holy and I'm telling it to you so you can check up and see I don't tell you any lie. I'm a preacher and I don't mind who knows it, but I wouldn't have you believe nothing you can't feel in your own hearts. You people coming up on the edge push right on up in here where you can hear good," he said. "I'm not selling a thing, I'm giving something away!" A considerable number of people had stopped.

"Friends," he said, "two months ago you wouldn't know me for the same man. I didn't have a friend in the world. Do you know what it's like not to have a friend in the world?"

A loud voice said, "It ain't no worsen havinum that would put ..."

"Why, friends," Onnie Jay Holy said, "not to have a friend in the world is just about the most miserable and lonesome thing that can happen to a man or woman! And that's the way it was with me. I was ready to hang myself or to despair completely. Not even my own dear old mother loved me—and it wasn't because I wasn't sweet inside, it was because I never known how to make the natural sweetness inside me show. Every person that comes onto this earth," he said, stretching out his arms, "is born sweet and full of love. A little child loves ever'body, friends, and its nature is sweetness—until something happens. Something happens, friends, I don't need to tell people like you that can think for theirselves. As that little child gets bigger, its sweetness don't show so much, cares and troubles come to perplext it, and all its sweetness is driven inside it. Then it gets miserable and lonesome and sick, friends. It says, 'Where is all my sweetness gone? Where are all the friends that loved me?' and all the time, that little beat-up rose of its sweetness is inside, not a petal dropped, and on the outside is just a mean lonesomeness. It may want to take its own life or yours or mine, or to despair completely, friends." He said it in a sad nasal voice, but he was smiling all the time so that they could tell he had been through what he was talking about and come out on top. "That was the way it was with me, friends. I know what of I speak," he said, and folded his hands in front of him. "But all the time that I was ready to hang myself or to despair completely, I was sweet inside, like ever'body else, and I only needed something to bring it out. I only needed a little help, friends.

"Then I met this Prophet here," he said, pointing at Haze on the nose of the car. "That was two months ago, folks, that I heard how he was out to help me, how he was preaching the Church of Christ Without Christ, the church that was going to get a new jesus to help me bring my sweet nature into the open where ever'body could enjoy it. That was two months ago, friends, and now you wouldn't know me for the same man. I love ever'one of you people and I want you to listen to him and me and join our church, the Holy Church of Christ Without Christ, the new church with the new jesus, and then you'll all be helped like me!"

From Wise Blood. *O'Connor sought to explore "religious consciousness without a religion" in her first novel, part of which she had written as an MFA student at the University of Iowa. Diagnosed with lupus in 1951, she wrote most of her short stories and novels, among them "A Good Man Is Hard to Find" and* The Violent Bear It Away, *at her home in Milledgeville, Georgia, where she died in 1964.*

1431: **Rouen**

VOICES OF GOD

Saturday, February 24, in the Chapel Royal of the Castle of Rouen. The bishop and sixty-two assessors present.

In their presence we required the aforenamed Joan of Arc to swear to speak the truth simply and absolutely on the questions to be addressed to her, without adding any restriction to her oath. We three times thus admonished her. She answered, "Give me leave to speak. By my faith! You may well ask me such things as I will not tell you. Perhaps on many of the things you may ask me I shall not tell you truly—especially on those that touch on my revelations—for you may constrain me to say things that I have sworn not to say; then I should be perjured, which you ought not to wish." [*Addressing the bishop*] "I tell you, take good heed of what you say, you who are my judge—you take a great responsibility in thus charging me."

"Will you swear, simply and absolutely?"

"I will say willingly what I know, and yet not all. I am come in God's name; I have nothing to do here—let me be sent back to God, whence I came."

"A last time we require you to swear, and urgently admonish you to speak the truth on all that concerns your trial; you expose yourself to a great peril by such a refusal."

"I am ready to speak truth on what I know touching the trial."

And in this manner was she sworn.

Then, by our order, she was questioned by Master Jean Beaupère, a well-known doctor, as follows: "How long is it since you have had food and drink?"

"Since yesterday afternoon."

"How long is it since you heard your voices?"

"I heard them yesterday and today."

"At what hour yesterday did you hear them?"

Brazilian soccer star Kaká celebrates a goal at the FIFA Club World Cup, Japan, 2007.

"Yesterday I heard them three times— once in the morning, once at vespers, and again when the Ave Maria rang in the evening. I have even heard them oftener than that."

"What were you doing yesterday morning when the voice came to you?"

"I was asleep; the voice awoke me."

"Was it by touching you on the arm?"

"It awoke me without touching me."

"Was it in your room?"

"Not so far as I know, but in the castle."

"Did you thank it? And did you go on your knees?"

"I did thank it. I was sitting on the bed; I joined my hands; I implored its help. The voice said to me, 'Answer boldly.' I asked advice as to how I should answer, begging it to entreat for this the counsel of the Lord. The Voice said to me, 'Answer boldly; God will help you.' Before I had prayed it to give me counsel, it said to me several words I could not readily understand. After I was awake, it said to me, 'Answer boldly.'" [*Addressing herself to the said bishop*] "You say you are my judge. Take care what you are doing; for in truth I am sent by God, and you place yourself in great danger."

Master Beaupère, continuing, said, "The voice that you say appears to you, does it come directly from an angel, or directly from God; or does it come from one of the saints?"

"The voice comes to me from God, and I do not tell you all I know about it—I have far greater fear of doing wrong in saying to you things that would displease it, than I have of answering you. As to this question, I beg you to grant me delay."

"Is it displeasing to God to speak the truth?"

"My voices have entrusted to me certain things to tell to King Charles VII, not to you. This very night they told me many things for the welfare of my king, which I would he might know at once, even if I should drink no wine until Easter … The king would be the more joyful at his dinner!"

"Can you not so deal with your voices that they will convey this news to your king?"

"I know not if the voice would obey, and if it be God's will. If it please God, He will know how to reveal it to the king, and I shall be well content."

"Why does this voice not speak anymore to your king, as it did when you were in his presence?"

"I do not know if it be the will of God. Without the grace of God I should not know how to do anything."

"Has your counsel revealed to you that you will escape from prison?"

"I have nothing to tell you about that."

"The last two occasions on which you have heard this voice, did a brightness come?"

"The brightness comes at the same time as the voice."

"The voice from whom you ask counsel, has it a face and eyes?"

"You shall not know yet. There is a saying among children, that 'Sometimes one is hanged for speaking the truth.'"

"Do you know if you are in the grace of God?"

"If I am not, may God place me there; if I am, may God so keep me. I should be the saddest in all the world if I knew that I were not in the grace of God. But if I were in a state of sin, do you think the voice would come to me? I would that everyone could hear the voice as I hear it."

From the trial of Joan of Arc. Having led the French to victory over the English at the battles of Orléans and Patay, Joan of Arc was captured and put on trial for witchcraft in 1431. Found guilty of heresy by Peter Cauchon, Bishop of Beauvais, the nineteen-year-old peasant girl was burned at the stake in the marketplace of Rouen. She never recanted her belief that the voices she heard were sent by God.

384: Rome

LET NOT DEMONS DANCE

I will say it boldly: though God can do all things, he cannot raise a virgin up after she has fallen. He is able to free one who has been corrupted from the penalty of her sin, but he refuses her the crown. Let us be fearful lest in our case also the prophecy "Good virgins shall faint" be fulfilled. Note that it is of good virgins he speaks, for there are bad ones as well. The scripture says, "Everyone who looks at a woman with lust has already committed adultery with her in his heart." Virginity therefore can be lost even by a thought. Those are the evil virgins, virgins in the flesh but not in the spirit—foolish virgins, who, having no oil in their lamps, are shut out by the Bridegroom.

But if even those virgins are virgins, and yet are not saved by their bodily virginity when they have other faults, what shall be done to those who have prostituted the members of Christ and changed the temple of the Holy Spirit into a brothel? Straightaway they shall hear the words, "Come down and sit in the dust, O virgin daughter of Babylon; sit in the dust, for there is no throne for the daughter of the Chaldeans; no more shall you be called tender and delicate. Take the millstone and grind meal; uncover your locks, make bare your legs, pass over the rivers; your nakedness shall be uncovered, and your shame shall be seen." Now she shall be made naked and her skirts shall be placed upon her face. She shall sit by the waters of loneliness and lay down her pitcher and shall open her feet to everyone that passes by and shall be polluted to the crown of her head. Better had it been for her to have submitted to marriage with a man and to have walked on the plain, rather than to strain for the heights and fall into the depths of hell.

Let not the faithful city of Zion become a harlot, I pray you; let not demons dance and sirens and satyrs nest in the place that once sheltered the Trinity. Loose not the belt that confines the bosom. As soon as lust begins to tickle the senses and the soft fires of pleasure envelop us with their delightful warmth, let us

Buddha head, stucco, third century.

break forth and cry, "The lord is on my side: I will not fear what the flesh can do to me." When for a moment the inner man shows signs of wavering between vice and virtue, say, "Why are you cast down, O my soul, and why are you disquieted within me? Hope in God, for I shall yet praise Him who is the health of my countenance and my God." I would not have you allow any such thoughts to rise. Let nothing disorderly, nothing that is of Babylon find shelter in your breast. Slay the enemy while he is small—nip evil in the bud. Hearken to the words of the psalmist: "Hapless daughter of Babylon, happy shall he be who rewards you as you have served us. Happy shall he be who takes and dashes your little ones against the stones." It is impossible that the body's natural heat should not sometimes assail a man and kindle sensual desire, but he is praised and accounted blessed, who, when thoughts begin to rise, gives them no quarter, but dashes them straightway against the rock. "And the rock is Christ."

St. Jerome, *from a letter to Eustochium. In 375 Jerome dreamed he was brought before a tribunal of the Lord and judged to be a Ciceronian, not a Christian; he vowed never again to read pagan literature. After living for a time in the Syrian desert as a hermit, he served as a secretary to Pope Damasus, who commissioned him to produce a Latin version of the Bible. St. Jerome completed the Vulgate around 405.*

1808: Weimar

HEAVEN'S FLAME

Gretchen: Promise me, Heinrich!

Faust: Anything I can.

Gretchen: Then tell me how you feel about religion.
You're such a good man, so good hearted,
And yet I can't think you have much use for it.

Faust: Child, let's not talk about it! You know I love you;
I'd sacrifice my life for those I love,
There's no one whom I'd rob of his church and faith.

Gretchen: That isn't right, one must believe!

Faust: Must one?

Gretchen: Oh, if only I could make you feel it!
And you don't revere the sacraments.

Faust: I do revere them.

Gretchen: But you don't want them, though.
It's such a long time since you've been to mass,
To confession. Do you believe in God?

Faust: Dearest, who is there that can say,
"I believe in God"?
You may ask the priests that, the philosophers—
But what they say will only seem to mock you.

Gretchen: So then you don't believe?

Faust: You lovely vision, don't mistake me!
Who is there that can name him?
Who is there that can testify,
"I believe in him"?
Who is there that can feel
And still can dare to say,
"I don't believe in him"?
The All-Embracing,
The All-Sustaining,
Does not he embrace, sustain,

You, me, himself?
Does not the sky arch over us?
Does not the earth stand fast beneath us?
Do not the everlasting stars
Rise over us with friendly glances?
We look into each other's eyes:
Didn't all things press in on your heart,
Weaving in everlasting mystery
Invisibly—and visibly—beside you?
Fill your heart with it, fill it to the brim,
And when your bliss has reached its height,
Then call it what you will—
Call it Love! Happiness! Soul! God!
I have no name for it.
Feeling is everything:
The name is sound and smoke,
Overclouding heaven's flame.

Gretchen: That's all very fine and good;
Our priest says almost the same thing
But in a little different words.

Faust: Each soul beneath the light
Of heaven says it, each in his own tongue;
Then why not I in mine?

Gretchen: It sounds all right when you say it that way,
But just the same there's something wrong with it;
Because you're not a Christian.

Johann Wolfgang von Goethe, *from* Faust. *Having returned to Frankfurt from Leipzig University in 1768, Goethe began studying the alchemical writings of Paracelsus and Basil Valentine and performing experiments in his own laboratory. The poet, statesman, playwright, novelist, and scientist began his masterwork around 1771; he published* Faust: A Fragment *in 1790 and* Faust: Part One *eighteen years after that.*

1823: England

PAINTED WOOD

Would it not be hard upon a little girl, who is busy in dressing up a favorite doll, to pull it to pieces before her face in order to show her the bits of wood, the wool, and rags it is composed of? So it would be hard upon that great baby, the world, to take any of its idols to pieces and show that they are nothing but painted wood. Neither of them would thank you, but consider the offer as an insult. The little girl knows as well as you do that her doll is a cheat—but she shuts her eyes to it, for she finds her account in keeping up the deception. Her doll is her pretty little self. In its glazed eyes, its cherry cheeks, its flaxen locks, its finery, and its baby house, she has a fairy vision of her own future charms, her future triumphs, a thousand hearts led captive, and an establishment for life. Harmless illusion, that can create something out of nothing, can make that which is good for nothing in itself so fine in appearance, and clothe a shapeless piece of deal board with the attributes of a divinity! But the great world has been doing little else but playing at *make-believe* all its lifetime. For several thousand years its chief rage was to paint larger pieces of wood and smear them with gore and call them gods and offer victims to them—slaughtered hecatombs, the fat of goats and oxen, or human sacrifices—showing in this its love of show, of cruelty, and imposture. The more stupid, brutish, helpless, and contemptible they were, the more furious, bigoted, and implacable were their votaries in their behalf. The more absurd the fiction, the louder was the noise made to hide it—the more mischievous its tendency, the more did it excite all the frenzy of the passions. Superstition nursed with peculiar zeal her rickety, deformed, and preposterous offspring. She passed by the nobler races of animals even, to pay divine honors to the odious and unclean—she took toads and serpents, cats, rats, dogs, crocodiles, goats, and monkeys, and hugged them to her bosom and dandled them into deities, and set up altars to them, and drenched the earth with tears and blood in their defense—and those who did not believe in them were cursed and forbidden the use of bread, fire, and water. And to worship them was piety, and their images were held sacred, and their race became gods in perpetuity and by divine right. To touch them was sacrilege; to kill them, death, even in your defense. If they stung you, you must die; if they infested the land with their numbers and their pollutions, there was no remedy. The nuisance was intolerable, impassive, immortal. Fear, religious horror, disgust, hatred, heightened the flame of bigotry and intolerance. There was nothing so odious or contemptible but it found a sanctuary in the more odious and contemptible perversity of human nature. The barbarous gods of antiquity reigned *in contempt of their worshippers!*

This game was carried on through all the first ages of the world and is still kept up in many parts of it, and it is impossible to describe the wars, massacres, horrors, miseries, and crimes to which it gave color, sanctity, and sway. The idea of a God, beneficent and just, the invisible maker of all things, was abhorrent to their gross material notions. No, they must have gods of their own making that they could see and handle, that they knew to be nothing in themselves but senseless images—and these they daubed over with the gaudy emblems of their own pride and passions, and these they lauded to the skies, and grew fierce, obscene, frantic before them, as the representatives of their sordid ignorance and barbaric vices. Truth, good, were idle names to them, without a meaning. They must have a lie, a palpable, pernicious lie, to pamper their crude, unhallowed conceptions with and to exercise the untameable fierceness of their wills.

William Hazlitt, *from "On the Spirit of Monarchy." The son of a Unitarian preacher who supported the American Revolution, Hazlitt grew up in Ireland and the United States. Charles Lamb and William Wordsworth encouraged him to become a painter, but in 1805 he published his first book,* On the Principles of Human Action. *Over the next decade, Hazlitt established himself as a prominent essayist, writing on art, politics, and drama.*

c. 1368: Shiraz

A GREAT SECRET

If this world
Was not held in God's bucket

How could an ocean stand upside down
On its head and never lose a drop?

If your life was not contained in God's cup

How could you be so brave and laugh,
Dance in the face of death?

Hafiz,
There is a private chamber in the soul
That knows a great secret

Of which no tongue can speak.

Your existence my dear, O love my dear,
Has been sealed and marked

"Too sacred," "too sacred," by the Beloved—
To ever end!

Indeed God
Has written a thousand promises
All over your heart

That say,
Life, life, life,
Is far too sacred to
Ever end.

> **Hafiz**, *"God's Bucket." Hafiz sang the praises of multiple rulers at the court of Shiraz while also lecturing on theology. It is said that after Tamerlane took over Persia, he made a visit to Shiraz to spend time with the great poet; the conqueror remained there for two months.*

1997: Iowa City

MARILYNNE ROBINSON RAISES AN OBJECTION

Whether Darwin himself intended to debunk religion is not a matter of importance, since he was perceived to have done so by those who embraced his views. His theory, as science, is irrelevant to the question of the truth of religion. It is only as an inversion of Christian ethicalism that it truly engages religion. And in those terms it is appropriately the subject of challenge from any humane perspective, religious or other. Insofar as ethical implications are claimed for it, it is not science, yet historically it has sheltered under the immunities granted to science. The churches generally have accepted the idea of evolution with great and understandable calm. The God of Abraham, Isaac, and Jacob, or of Luther, Calvin, and Ignatius of Loyola, or of Dietrich Bonhoeffer, Simone Weil, and Martin Luther King, is no Watchmaker. To find him at the end of even the longest chain of being or causality would be to discover that he was a thing (however majestic) among things. Not God, in other words.

If one looks at the creation narrative in Genesis one finds no Watchmaker, as the Darwinists would have us believe, but a God who stands outside his creation and calls it into being by, in effect, willing its existence. This terse account does as little to invoke the model of a human artisan as it could do. The creation and blessing of everything, from light to the great sea creatures to whatever creeps on the earth, is done in the same formulaic terms. It all has the same origin, and it is all good. There is no suggestion of hierarchy in the order in which things come into being any more than in the language that names them, with the exception of man/woman, who are made in God's image and given dominion over the rest of creation.

The narrative stabilizes essential theological assertions—first of all, that God is not embodied in any part of creation. He is not light, nor is he the sun, as the gods of other ancient peoples were thought to be. He is in no sense limited or local. He is not the force of good or order struggling against forces of evil or chaos, but the sole creator of a creation that is in whole and in part "very good." There are no loci of special holiness, humanity aside, and nothing evil or alarming or unclean. The sun and moon are simply "lights" and the markers of days and seasons. The alternation of day and night are not the endless recurrence of a terrifying primal struggle but the frame of a great order, identified by the repeated reference to evening and morning with the ordering of creation itself. All these things articulate a vision of being which is sharply distinct from those expressed in competing ancient cosmogonies. The narrative, with its refrain, tells of the days in a week, and culminates in the Sabbath, which is therefore as fundamental a reality as creation itself. It is as if God's rest were the crown of his work. This is a very powerful statement of the value of the Sabbath, so essential to the life of the Jews, and it seems to me it probably accounts for the fact of the narrative's describing creation as the business of a week.

Certainly this cosmogony describes a natural order which is freestanding and complete, with rainfall and seasons established, as well as the fecundity of all living things. In *Human, All Too Human*, Nietzsche [*Sils Maria*, page 142] says:

> In the imagination of religious people all nature is a summary of the actions of conscious and voluntary creatures, an enormous complex or *arbitrariness*. No conclusion may be drawn with regard to everything that is outside of us, that anything will *be* so and so, *must* be so and so; the approximately sure, reliable are *we*—man is the *rule*, nature is *irregularity*.

This statement is wrong, point for point, as a characterization of the world of the Genesis cosmogony, which is not in the least degree animistic or demon haunted or dependent for its functioning on divine intervention. If ancient people had consciously set out to articulate a worldview congenial to science, it is hard to imagine how, in the terms available to them, they could have done

Gained in Translation
The evolving Bible

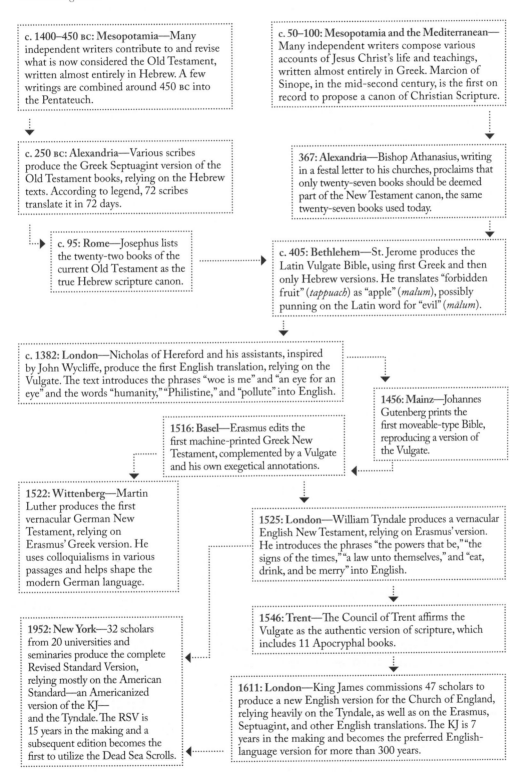

c. 1400–450 BC: Mesopotamia—Many independent writers contribute to and revise what is now considered the Old Testament, written almost entirely in Hebrew. A few writings are combined around 450 BC into the Pentateuch.

c. 50–100: Mesopotamia and the Mediterranean—Many independent writers compose various accounts of Jesus Christ's life and teachings, written almost entirely in Greek. Marcion of Sinope, in the mid-second century, is the first on record to propose a canon of Christian Scripture.

c. 250 BC: Alexandria—Various scribes produce the Greek Septuagint version of the Old Testament books, relying on the Hebrew texts. According to legend, 72 scribes translate it in 72 days.

367: Alexandria—Bishop Athanasius, writing in a festal letter to his churches, proclaims that only twenty-seven books should be deemed part of the New Testament canon, the same twenty-seven books used today.

c. 95: Rome—Josephus lists the twenty-two books of the current Old Testament as the true Hebrew scripture canon.

c. 405: Bethlehem—St. Jerome produces the Latin Vulgate Bible, using first Greek and then only Hebrew versions. He translates "forbidden fruit" (*tappuach*) as "apple" (*malum*), possibly punning on the Latin word for "evil" (*mālum*).

c. 1382: London—Nicholas of Hereford and his assistants, inspired by John Wycliffe, produce the first English translation, relying on the Vulgate. The text introduces the phrases "woe is me" and "an eye for an eye" and the words "humanity," "Philistine," and "pollute" into English.

1456: Mainz—Johannes Gutenberg prints the first moveable-type Bible, reproducing a version of the Vulgate.

1516: Basel—Erasmus edits the first machine-printed Greek New Testament, complemented by a Vulgate and his own exegetical annotations.

1522: Wittenberg—Martin Luther produces the first vernacular German New Testament, relying on Erasmus' Greek version. He uses colloquialisms in various passages and helps shape the modern German language.

1525: London—William Tyndale produces a vernacular English New Testament, relying on Erasmus' version. He introduces the phrases "the powers that be," "the signs of the times," "a law unto themselves," and "eat, drink, and be merry" into English.

1952: New York—32 scholars from 20 universities and seminaries produce the complete Revised Standard Version, relying mostly on the American Standard—an Americanized version of the KJ—and the Tyndale. The RSV is 15 years in the making and a subsequent edition becomes the first to utilize the Dead Sea Scrolls.

1546: Trent—The Council of Trent affirms the Vulgate as the authentic version of scripture, which includes 11 Apocryphal books.

1611: London—King James commissions 47 scholars to produce a new English version for the Church of England, relying heavily on the Tyndale, as well as on the Erasmus, Septuagint, and other English translations. The KJ is 7 years in the making and becomes the preferred English-language version for more than 300 years.

better. And in fact, Judeo-Christian culture has been uniquely hospitable to science.

But the point to be stressed is that religious people—by definition, I would say—do not look for proof of the existence of God, or understand God in a way that makes his existence liable to proof or disproof. It is naive to talk about proof in that way, which is why Darwinists need not apologize for their failure to prove the existence of the process of natural selection, which they freely concede they have not done. That attempts at proofs of God's existence have been made from time to time—under the influence of the prestige of Aristotle or of early science—does not mean that religious belief has sought or depended on that kind of affirmation, as any reader of theology is well aware. Faith is called faith for a reason. Darwinism is another faith—a loyalty to a vision of the nature of things despite its inaccessibility to demonstration.

The creationist position has long been owned by the religious right, and the Darwinist position by the irreligious right. The differences between these camps are intractable because they are meaningless. People who insist that the sacredness of scripture depends on belief in creation in a literal six days seem never to insist on a literal reading of "to him who asks, give," or "sell what you have and give the money to the poor." In fact, their politics and economics align themselves quite precisely with those of their adversaries, who yearn to disburden themselves of the weak and to unshackle the great creative forces of competition. The defenders of "religion" have made religion seem foolish, while rendering it mute in the face of a prolonged and highly effective assault on the poor. The defenders of "science" have imputed objectivity and rigor to an account of reality whose origins and consequences are indisputably economic, social, and political.

Creationism is the best thing that could have happened to Darwinism, the caricature of religion that has seemed to justify Darwinist contempt for the whole of religion. Creationism has tended to obscure the fact that religion—precisely as the hope of the powerless and the mitigator of the abuse of the weak—has indeed come under determined attack by people who have claimed the authority of science, and that Darwin's work was quite rightly seized upon by antireligionists who had other fish to fry than the mere demystification of cosmogony. I am speaking, as I know it is rude to do, of the social Darwinists, the eugenicists, the imperialists, the scientific socialists who showed such firmness in reshaping civilization in Eastern Europe, China, Cambodia, and elsewhere, and, yes, of the Nazis. Darwin influenced the nationalist writer Heinrich von Treitschke and the biologist Ernst Haeckel, who influenced Hitler and also the milieu in which he flourished.

If there is felt to be a missing link between Darwinism and these distinctive phenomena of modern history, it is because we pretend that only Darwin's most presentable book would have had circulation and impact. Reading *The Descent of Man*, one finds Darwin the obsessive taxonomist marveling that Hindus, who are apparently so unlike Europeans, are in fact also Aryans, while Jews, who look just like Europeans, are in fact Asiatics. This sort of language is a reminder of the kind of thinking that was going on in Europe at that time, which Darwin's cheerful interest in the extermination of races, and his insistence on ranking races in terms of their nearness to the apes, could only have abetted.

It does bear mentioning that the full title of his first book is *On the Origin of Species by Means of Natural Selection, or the Preservation of Favoured Races in the Struggle for Life*. However generously this title is interpreted, clearly it does not assume that biological systems evolve by chance and not design, as Darwin is always said to have done. It clearly implies that whatever is is right, and—even less tenably— that whatever is is the product of raw struggle, and—still less tenably—that there is a teleology behind it all, one which favors and preserves. Darwinists seem unable to refrain from theology, as the supplanters of it. The old God may have let the rain fall on the just and the unjust alike, but this new god is more implacable in his judgments, and very straightforward, killing off those who die, to state the matter baldly. What need of this theology except to imply that there is wisdom and blessing and meaning in "selection," which the phenomenon itself does not by any means imply? If the temperature on earth rose or fell by five degrees, this same god would curse where he had cherished and love what he had despised, which is only to say that natural selection must indeed be thought of as blind, from the preserving and favoring point of view, if consistency is to be respected at all.

Surely we must assume that a biosphere generated out of any circumstances able to sustain life is as good as any other, that if we make a desert of this planet, for example, and the god of survival turns his countenance upon the lurkers and scuttlers who emerge as fittest, under the new regime, we can have no grounds for saying that things have changed for the worse or for the better, in Darwinist terms. In other words, absent teleology, there are no grounds for saying that survival means any-

thing more or other than survival. Darwinists praise complexity and variety as consequences of evolution, though the success of single-celled animals would seem to raise questions. I am sure we all admire ostriches, but to call a Darwinist creation good because it is credited with providing them is simply another version of the old argument from design, proving in this use of it not the existence of God but the appropriateness of making a judgment of value: that natural selection, whose existence is to be assumed, is splendid and beneficent and therefore to be embraced.

From "Darwinism." Robinson in 1981 published her first novel, Housekeeping, *and in 2004 her second novel,* Gilead, *which was awarded a Pulitzer Prize. In an interview with* The Paris Review, *she said, "Religion has been profoundly effective in enlarging human imagination and expression. It's only very recently that you couldn't see how the high arts are intimately connected to religion." Her third novel,* Home, *was published in 2008.*

Charlton Heston, film portrait for *The Ten Commandments*, directed by Cecil B. DeMille, 1956.

ACTS OF FAITH

1991: Rio de Janeiro

ALMA GUILLERMOPRIETO IN THE PRESENCE OF THE SPIRITS

The gods are on display at the Spiritist Tent of Granny Maria Antonia of the Congo, one of the more successful of many thousands of Umbanda temples in Rio. The temple is not a tent at all but a spacious, comfortable two-story house with a long open-air corridor and a shining tile-walled meeting hall on the ground floor. It is called a tent, or tepee, in honor of the spirits of various Indians—among them the Indian of the Seven Crossroads, the Indian of the Coral Cobra, and the Indian Who Tears Up Tree Stumps—who are believed to have lived long ago in the Brazilian jungle. The Granny who is honored in the temple's name is a well-known Old Black Woman, the spirit of a slave who was born in Africa and died in Brazil. At this temple, Granny Maria Antonia is the principal spirit incorporated by Stella Virginia dos Santos Soares, who runs it. She is a tall, imposing black woman of such extraordinary efficiency in every gesture that one cannot help having faith in her—and hundreds of people do. She has dozens of regular initiates, mostly white and quite well off, and

she is also extremely popular among the black slum dwellers on a hill behind the middle-class neighborhood, where her temple stands.

When worshippers arrive for ceremonies that take place every Friday night, they stop in the corridor to pray briefly before half a dozen shrines, where the gods live. During the years of slavery in Brazil, which lasted until 1888, blacks managed to worship their own African gods—Orishas, in Yoruba—only by disguising them as Catholic saints. Candomblé, a religion that sprang up in the northern city of Salvador da Bahia, standardized a canon of camouflaged gods, and Umbanda followers in Rio borrowed it. St. George, for example, is actually Ogum, the god of wars and metals, who, like his dragon-slaying Christian counterpart, carries a sword. According to legend, St. Barbara's pagan father, who sought to have her executed for becoming a Christian, was felled by lightning, and so Iansâ, the warrior goddess of the forests and of lightning, is worshipped under her name. Yemanjá, the gentle mother goddess of the oceans, who dresses in blue and white,

Jain pilgrim praying to a statue of Lord Bahubali, 1993. Photograph by Raghu Rai.

is the Virgin Mary—in her incarnation as the Virgin of the Immaculate Conception, who wears the same colors. Most of the plaster-cast figurines in the shrines at Granny Maria Antonia's were made specifically for Umbanda worship, and they would look a little strange inside a Catholic church: the colors are too bright, St. George looks too angry, and the Virgin Mary looks strangely buxom and hippy. On a separate altar the statues of an Indian and an Old Black Man are more recognizable: the Indian is holding an arrow and wears a long headdress of feathers, like Sitting Bull's, and the Old Black Man is portrayed sitting pensively on a tree stump, smoking a corncob pipe.

God is only a great imaginative experience.
—D. H. Lawrence, 1930

Although the Indians and Old Black Folks are not Orishas but mere spirits, their cult is what defines Umbanda. Indeed, the religion is said to have started one evening in 1908 after the participants in a middle-class Spiritist seance refused to allow an Indian spirit to speak. The seance regulars, who were white, were used to communing with the likes of Voltaire [*Ferney,* page 109] and Plato, and when the Indian of the Seven Crossroads tried to butt in, he was told that Indians were "forces of darkness," and was asked to go away. The Indian got angry, and speaking through a sickly adolescent whose vocal cords he had borrowed before, he swore that he would found a religion in which Indians and Old Black Folks would finally have a voice. In Umbanda's religious hierarchy, they are ranked as inferior to the Orishas, but have a central advantage over them: in Candomblé, when the Orishas take possession of their initiates they make their presence known by executing characteristic dance movements, but they remain silent. When the Umbanda spirits appear, they talk. Indians, on their allotted night, suggest potions and incantations for the medical problems of their devotees. Old Black Folks, who appear on separate evenings, impart wisdom and spiritual counsel.

On a night when an Indian session was to take place, I found Stella Virginia dos Santos Soares selling soft drinks and chicken empanadas to her followers at a refreshment stand she runs at the entrance to the temple. After the snack, the faithful headed for dressing rooms in the back to change from their work clothes into all-white costumes that looked like hospital uniforms. The resemblance is no coincidence. Stella is a former nurse who loved her work, and she tries to bring as much of its character as possible into her ritual center. "Standard white uniforms are more egalitarian," she told me. "There are very rich and very poor people here, but once they've changed there's no way of knowing the difference." Briskly, she instructed an assistant to show me and a photographer friend to our assigned places for the ceremony, which, with the aid of a clock on one of the shiny, hospital-like walls, was to begin at eight sharp.

Stella summoned everyone into the meeting hall and directed the rest of the seating arrangements. Those who were wearing street clothes—noninitiate suppliants—sat in pews at the back. In the middle, ranged in rows according to rank, stood the white-clad initiates, and they were flanked by white-clad apprentices, who sat on tile-covered benches against the walls with a gleaming metal spittoon on the floor between every two people. Stella stood at the front, facing the congregation. Behind her, chairs for special guests were on one side, and on the other stood a drummer and half a dozen singers. In the center of the front wall was the altar, topped by an image of Jesus Christ, who appeared to be blessing ranks of Umbanda saints below. With startling speed, the ceremony got under way: the drummer beat out a complicated rhythm, the singers chanted an invocation to each of the saints and then to an Indian named Seu Tupinambá. At that point, Stella's body jerked up, down, and sideways, and she sank into a crouch. She remained in that position for a few seconds, sighed, and then straightened up and lit a big cigar.

Soon all the initiates had incorporated Indians and lit up. Indian spirits like to smoke and spit, and Stella doesn't like messes—that's why she provides the spittoons. They were in use throughout the ceremony, which proceeded at a breakneck pace and developed a sweaty, dreamy intensity. While the chanting continued, Seu Tupinambá, whom Stella had now incorporated, gave orders. The suppliants at the back were told to come forward seven at a time, barefoot and without their jewelry, and when they were lined up in front of the altar Seu Tupinambá strode past them, waving his arms energetically above their heads. At the end of each pass, he disposed of the evil energies he had absorbed by shaking his hands in the direction of the apprentices on the benches; they received this discharge and howled, metabolizing it into harmless force. When all the suppliants had received this initial cleansing, they were told to line up again, in rows facing the altar, this time one per cigar-smoking initiate. Each initiate blew smoke around the aura of a suppliant and with loving care performed healing gestures with his arms. At last, the initiates and the apprentices, their medical mission accomplished, were allowed to attend to themselves. They danced, sang, and went into little spinning frenzies. The apprentices fell into long, suffering trances that shook their bodies and sometimes made them weep, and the initiates took care of them, watching to see that they did not bump into anything or otherwise hurt themselves. Every once in a while, for no apparent reason, Seu Tupinambá or another of the temple elders went up to someone and offered a warm, healing embrace. Then, at a signal from Seu Tupinambá, everyone lined up again, sang farewell to the spirit guests, and shuddered briefly as the otherworldly visitors departed. By ten thirty, it was all over. The former Indians clustered once again around the refreshment stand to sip beer, laugh, and chatter loudly.

"Why do I do this?" a woman named Gloria said later. "I've asked myself that question a hundred times, and I can't come up with a logical answer." Gloria is part of Stella's high command, a middle-aged woman with bleached hair and a friendly, intense manner. She lives in one of many airy, terraced high-rises that dot the temple neighborhood, a bastion of the middle, middle class that has gradually settled here since 1900, far away from the frivolity of the oceanfront neighborhoods to the south. There are bakeries, and family restaurants serving heavy Portuguese food, and all-girl schools housed in birthday-cake, fin-de-siécle manors. Everything bespeaks respectability, and so did Gloria's attire and that of her husband, who had also turned into an Indian at the earlier session and now sat silent while Gloria speculated about the origins of her faith.

Typically, the couple had first come to Stella's some fifteen years ago because Gloria's husband had a health problem that doctors

'Twas only fear first in the world made gods.
—Ben Jonson, 1603

couldn't cure. The sessions helped almost immediately, even though for the first year or so the couple did nothing but sit quietly in the back pews. Then a day came when the spirits arrived and took possession of their bodies, and there was no turning back. "Now, I ask you, how could a couple like us, well-educated, well-off, professionally successful, fall into this?" Gloria said. "You know, there are some sessions when I turn into a child, and when I think of the things this child makes me do I think I must have a screw loose! I jump around, turn somersaults, talk nonsense. But the thing is, even on evenings when we think how much nicer it would be to rent a videocassette and stay home, we know that there are people waiting who need our help. For us to stay away, it would be like a surgeon leaving the hospital waiting. So we don't stay away."

From The Heart That Bleeds. *Guillermoprieto was one of two journalists in 1982 to break the story of a massacre of nine hundred villagers at El Mozote by the U.S.-backed El Salvadoran army. Before becoming a noted reporter on Latin America, she was a professional dancer, at one time teaching high school students in Cuba in 1970—the subject for her memoir* Dancing with Cuba, *published in 2004.*

1648: Poland

ISAAC BASHEVIS SINGER SAVES A SOUL

Wanda, not Jacob, had thought of playing the mute, realizing Yiddish would take her too long to learn; the few words she knew she spoke like a gentile. Her idea of passing herself off as a "Cossack bride" who could now only speak the language of the steppes was discarded because she didn't know that tongue either. She was not an adroit liar and would have been unmasked immediately. Jacob and she underwent many hardships and dangers before she decided on the role of a mute. They went to distant Pilitz

I can't see (or feel) the conflict between love and religion. To me they're the same thing.
—Elizabeth Bowen, c. 1970

because Jacob was too famous in Lublin and the surrounding areas as the slave who had returned. At night when Sarah—as all Jewish converts were called—closed the shutters, Jacob spoke with her and instructed her in their religion. He had already taught her the prayers and how to write Yiddish and now they studied the Pentateuch, the Books of Samuel and Kings, the Code of the Jewish Law; he told her stories from the Gemara and Midrash. Her diligence was amazing, her memory good; many of the questions she asked were the same the commentators had raised. Teaching her, he dared not lift his voice. Not only did he dread the gentiles and their laws, but also the Jews who would expel him from the village if they learned his wife was a convert. Sarah's presence in Pilitz imperiled the town. If the Polish authorities learned that a Christian girl had been seduced into Judaism, there would be reprisals. God knows what accusations would be made. The priests only wanted a pretext. And if the Jews got wind of it, the elders would immediately investigate the circumstances of the conversion and would guess correctly that Sarah had left her own religion because of Jacob—women being little

interested in speculative matters—and Jacob would be excommunicated.

There was so much concern with the lineage and matrimonial connections of scholars that Jacob had not divulged that he was learned. The few scholarly books he had brought he kept hidden. He built his house with thick walls and constructed an alcove, windowless and hidden from the world by a clump of trees, where he and his beloved wife could study in secret. True, they had lived together illicitly, but since then they had fulfilled the law of Moses and Israel by standing under the canopy. Sarah now fervently believed in God and the Torah and obeyed all the laws. Now and then she erred, doing things upside down according to her peasant understanding or speaking in a manner that was inappropriate. But Jacob corrected her kindly and made her understand the reason for each law and custom. Teaching others, Jacob realized, one also instructed oneself; correcting Sarah's behavior, answering her questions, eradicating her errors, many problems about which he would not have otherwise thought were clarified for him. Often her questions demanded answers which were not to be found in this world. She asked, "If murder is a crime, why did God permit the Israelites to wage war and even kill old people and small children?" If the nations distant from the Jews, such as her own people, were ignorant of the Torah, how could they be blamed for being idol worshippers? If Father Abraham was a saint, why did he drive Hagar and her son Ishmael into the desert with a gourd of water? The question that recurred more often than any other was why did the good suffer and the evil prosper. Jacob told her repeatedly he couldn't solve all the world's riddles, but Sarah kept on insisting, "You know everything."

He had warned her many times about the unclean days, reminding her that when she was menstruating she could not sit on the same bench with him, take any object from his hand, nor even eat at the same table unless there was a screen between her plate and his. He was not allowed to sit on her bed, nor she on his; not even the headboards of their beds ought to touch at this time. But these were some of the things that Sarah either forgot or ignored, for she kept on insisting she must be near him. She was capable of running over and kissing him in the middle of her period. Jacob rebuked her and told her such acts were forbidden by the Torah, but she took these restrictions lightly, and this caused Jacob sorrow. She was very scrupulous about less important things. She immersed all the dishes in the ritual bath and kept on inquiring about milk and meat. At times she forgot she was a mute and broke into song. Jacob trembled. Not only was there the danger of her being heard, but a pious daughter of Israel should not provoke lust with the lascivious sound of her voice. Nor had she let the bath attendant shave her head like the other women's, though Jacob had asked her to. Sarah cut her own hair with shears; occasionally ringlets pushed out from under her kerchief.

Though Jacob had built them a house, Sarah complained nightly that she wished to leave Pilitz. She could not remain silent forever, and she feared what would happen to her child. The young must be taught to speak, and given love. She kept asking whether her Yiddish had improved; Jacob assured her she was doing well, but it wasn't so. She mispronounced the words, twisted the constructions, and whatever she uttered came out upside down. Often her mistakes made Jacob laugh. Even a few words dropping from her tongue and there was no mistaking she had been born a gentile. Now that she was pregnant Jacob was more frightened than ever. A wom-an in labor cannot control her screams. Unless she could endure the birth pangs in silence, Sarah would give herself away.

At night when Sarah and he lay in their beds which were arranged so as to form a right angle (the room wasn't long enough to have one at the foot of the other), the couple whispered to each other for hours without tiring. Jacob informed Sarah about the moral life, spicing his text with little parables. She spoke of how much she loved him. They often recalled the summers he had lived in the barn when she had brought food to him. Now those days were far off and as shadowy

Michael Alphonsus Shen Fuzong, a Chinese convert, by Godfrey Kneller, 1685.

Parvati, consort of Shiva,
Indian bronze, thirteenth century.

"What can a daughter of Israel do?"

"Bear children and serve God."

"I intend to bear you a dozen."

He would not lie with her immediately, but first told her stories of upright men and women. She asked what went on in paradise and what would occur when the Messiah came. Would Jacob still be her husband? Would they speak Hebrew? Would he take her with him to the rebuilt temple? When the Messiah came, Jacob said, each day would be as long as a year, the sun would be seven times as bright, and the saints would feed on leviathan and the wild ox and drink the wine prepared for the days of redemption.

"How many wives will each man have?" Sarah asked.

"I'll have only you."

"I'll be old by then."

"We'll be young forever."

"What kind of a dress will I wear?"

Lying with Jacob was for her a foretaste of paradise. She often wished that the night would last forever and she could continue to listen to his words and receive his caresses. That hour in the darkness was her reward for what she had endured during the day. When she fell asleep, her dreams took her to her native village; she entered the hut where she had lived; she stood on the mountain. Strange events involving Antek, Basha, and her mother occurred. Her father, once more alive, spoke wisely to her, and though she forgot his words as soon as she awoke, their resonance rang in her ears. Sometimes she dreamed Jacob had left her, and she cried in her sleep. Jacob always awakened her.

"Oh Jacob, you're still here. Thank God." His face would become hot and wet from her tears.

as a dream. Sarah found it difficult to believe that the village still existed and that Basha and Antek and possibly her mother still lived there. According to the law, Jacob said, she no longer was a member of her family. A convert was like a newborn child and had a fresh soul. Sarah was like Mother Eve who had been formed from Adam's rib—her husband was her only relative. "But," Sarah argued, "my father is still my father," and she began to cry about Jan Bzik who had had so hard a life and now lay buried among idolaters. "You will have to bring him into paradise," she told Jacob. "I won't go without him."

The moment the candle was extinguished she would call him to her bed. "You gentile," Jacob said jokingly. "Don't you know that a daughter of Israel mustn't be immodest, or she'll be divorced without a settlement?"

From The Slave. *Completing his rabbinical studies at a Warsaw seminary, Singer worked as a proofreader and translator in his native Poland before immigrating in 1935 to the United States, where he was hired at the country's leading Yiddish newspaper. He composed almost all of his works in Yiddish, among them* The Family Moskat *and* Gimpel the Fool, and Other Stories, *and often worked personally with translators to render the texts into English.*

c. 750: China

Creeks and summits are brilliant at sunset.
I laze in a boat, my way in the wind's hands.

Watching wild landscapes I forget distance
and come to the water's edge.

Gazing at lovely far woods and clouds
I guess I've lost my way.

How could I know this lucid stream
would turn, leading me into mountains?

I abandon my boat, pick up a light staff
and come upon something wonderful,

four or five old monks in contemplation,
enjoying the shade of pines and cypresses.

Before the forest dawns they read Sanskrit.
Their nightly meditation quiets the peaks.

Here even shepherd boys know the Dao.
Woodcutters bring in worldly news.

They sleep at night in the woods
with incense, on mats clean as jade.

Their robes are steeped in valley fragrances;
the stone cliffs shine under a mountain moon.

I fear I will lose this refuge forever
so at daybreak I fix it in my mind.

People of Peach Tree Spring, goodbye.
I'll be back when flowers turn red.

> **Wang Wei**, *an untitled poem. A critic writing more than three hundred years after Wang Wei's death remarked, "Taste Wang Wei's poetry—there are paintings in it; look at his paintings—they are full of poetry." Wang Wei began his long government career working for the Imperial Directorate of Music. Later in life, he spent increasing stretches of time in the hills around his country estate, studying Buddhism and conversing with monks.*

c. 1100: Constantinople

FIRE AND SMOKE

Since Basil was the protagonist behind the Bogomil heresy and showed no sign whatever of remorse, the members of the Holy Synod, the chief Naziarioi, as well as Nicholas, the patriarch of that time, unanimously decided that he must be burned. The emperor Alexius, who had interviewed the man at length on many occasions, cast his vote for the same verdict. He had recognized Basil's perversity and knew that his attachment to the heresy was irrevocable. A huge fire was set, therefore, in the

Religion! How it dominates man's mind, how it humiliates and degrades his soul. God is everything, man is nothing, says religion. But out of that nothing God has created a kingdom so despotic, so tyrannical, so cruel, so terribly exacting that naught but gloom and tears and blood have ruled the world since gods began.
—Emma Goldman, 1910

Hippodrome. An enormous trench had been dug and a mass of logs, every one a tall tree, had been piled up to the height of a mountain. Then the pyre was lit, and a great multitude of people slowly gathered in the arena and on its steps; everybody waited impatiently to see what would happen. On the other side a cross had been set up, and the godless fellow was given an opportunity to recant—if by some chance through dread of the fire he changed his mind and walked over to the cross, he could still escape the burning.

The Bogomils were there in force too, watching their leader Basil. Far from giving way, it was obvious that he despised all punishment and threats, and while he was still some distance from the flames, he laughed at them and boasted that angels would rescue him from the midst of the fire. He quoted David's psalm, softly chanting, "It shall not come nigh thee; only with thine eyes shalt thou behold." But

when the crowd stood aside and let him see clearly that awe-inspiring sight (for even far off he could feel the fire and saw the flames rising and shooting out fiery sparks with a noise like thunder, sparks which leaped high in the air to the top of the stone obelisk which stands in the center of the Hippodrome), then for all his boldness he seemed to flinch before the pyre, and appeared troubled. He darted his eyes now here, now there, struck his hands together and beat his thighs, like a man at his wits' end.

And yet, affected though he was at the mere sight of it, he was still hard as steel; his iron will was not softened by the fire. Maybe in this hour of supreme need and misfortune a great madness possessed him, so that he lost his mind and was utterly unable to decide what was best for himself; or perhaps—and this was more likely—the devil that possessed his soul had shed about him a profound darkness. So there stood this Basil, despicable, helpless before every threat, every terror, gaping now at the pyre, now at the spectators. Everyone thought he was quite mad, for he neither rushed to the flames, nor did he altogether turn back, but stayed rooted to the spot where he had first entered the arena, motionless. Now there was much talk going on, as everyone repeated the marvelous prophecies he had made, and the public executioners were afraid lest somehow the demons that protected Basil might perform some extraordinary miracle through the grace of God—that the scoundrel might be snatched from the scene of this tremendous fire and then be seen in some public place where many people met, and thus the last error might be worse than the first. So they decided to put him to the test.

While he was talking marvels and boasting that he would be seen unharmed in the midst of the flames, they took his cloak and said, "Let's see if the fire will catch your clothes!" And straightway they hurled it into the center of the pyre. So confident was Basil in the demon that was deluding him that he cried, "Behold my cloak flying up to the sky!" Recognizing the robe from its hem, they seized him and threw him—clothes, shoes, and all—into the fire. The flames, as if in rage against him, so thoroughly devoured the wretch that there was no odor and not the slightest change to the smoke, with just one thin, wispy plume rising from the center of the flames. For although the elements are stirred against the wicked, they do spare those who are dear to God—just as they once did those young men in Babylon and died down because they were beloved by God, with the fire forming a golden chamber around them. But on this occasion the executioners who lifted the wretched Basil up in their arms had barely placed him on the fire when the flames seemed to leap forward and snatch the charlatan. The crowd standing by roared in excitement, desperate to throw on the fire all the rest of Basil's pernicious sect, but the emperor would not allow this to happen. On his orders they were instead kept in custody in the porticoes and colonnades of the Great Palace. The spectators then dispersed. Later these atheists were transferred to a prison of maximum security, and after languishing there for a long time died in their wickedness.

Anna Comnena, *from* The Alexiad. *In 1118 the Byzantine princess attempted to depose her brother from the throne; her failure to do so obliged her to forfeit her property, and she retreated to a nunnery, where she wrote her work of history. Enhanced with allusions to Plato, Homer, Aristotle, and Euripides,* The Alexiad *describes the rule of her father, Alexius I, and the beginning of the First Crusade.*

The Angelus, by Jean-François Millet, c. 1857–59.

1901: Edinburgh

CHANNEL OF BLOOD

There can be no doubt that as a matter of fact a religious life, exclusively pursued, does tend to make the person exceptional and eccentric. I speak not now of your ordinary religious believer who follows the conventional observances of his country, whether it be Buddhist, Christian, or Mohammedan. His religion has been made for him by others, communicated to him by tradition, determined to fixed forms by imitation, and retained by habit. It would profit us little to study this secondhand religious life. We must make search rather for the original experiences which were the pattern setters to all this mass of suggested feeling and imitated conduct. These experiences we can only find in individuals for whom religion exists not as a dull habit, but as an acute fever rather. But such individuals are "geniuses" in the religious line, and like many other geniuses who have brought forth fruits effective enough for commemoration in the pages of biography, such religious geniuses have often shown symptoms of nervous instability. Even more perhaps than other kinds of genius, religious leaders have been subject to abnormal psychical visitations. Invariably, they have been creatures of exalted emotional sensibility.

Often they have led a discordant inner life and had melancholy during a part of their career. They have known no measure, been liable to obsessions and fixed ideas—and frequently they have fallen into trances, heard voices, seen visions, and presented all sorts of peculiarities which are ordinarily classed as pathological. Often, moreover, these pathological features in their career have helped to give them their religious authority and influence.

If you ask for a concrete example, there can be no better one than is furnished by the person of George Fox. The Quaker religion which he founded is something which it is impossible to overpraise. In a day of shams, it was a religion of veracity rooted in spiritual inwardness, and a return to something more like the original gospel truth than men had ever known in England. So far as our Christian sects today are evolving into liberality, they are simply reverting in essence to the position which Fox and the early Quakers so long ago assumed. No one can pretend for a moment that in point of spiritual sagacity and capacity, Fox's mind was unsound. Everyone who confronted him personally, from Oliver Cromwell down to county magistrates and jailers, seems to have acknowledged his superior power. Yet from the point of view of his nervous constitution, Fox was a psychopath of the deepest dye. His journal abounds in entries of this sort:

> As I was walking with several friends, I lifted up my head and saw three steeple-house spires, and they struck at my life. I asked them what place that was? They said, Lichfield. Immediately the word of the Lord came to me, that I must go thither. I came within a mile of Lichfield, where, in a great field, shepherds were keeping their sheep. Then was I commanded by the Lord to pull off my shoes. I stood still, for it was winter, but the word of the Lord was like a fire in me. So I put off my shoes and left them with the shepherds, and the poor shepherds trembled and were astonished. Then I walked on about a mile, and as soon as I was got within the city, the word of the Lord came to me again, saying: "Cry, 'Woe to the bloody city of Lichfield!'" So I went up and down the streets, crying with a loud voice, "Woe to the bloody city of Lichfield!" And no one laid hands on me. As I went thus crying through the streets, there seemed to me to be a channel of blood running down the streets. When I had declared what was upon me and felt myself clear, I went out of the town in peace; and returning to the shepherds gave them some money, and took my shoes from them again. But the fire of the Lord was so on my feet, and all over me, that I did not bother to put on my shoes again—and was at a stand whether I should or no, till I felt freedom from the Lord so to do. Then, after I had washed my feet, I

put on my shoes again. After this a deep consideration came upon me, for what reason I should be sent to cry against that city, and call it the bloody city! For though the parliament had the minister one while, and the king another, and much blood had been shed in the town during the wars between them, yet there was no more than had befallen many other places. But afterward I came to understand, that in the Emperor Diocletian's time a thousand Christians were martyred in Lichfield. So I was to go without my shoes through the channel of their blood, and into the pool of their blood in the marketplace, that I might raise up the memorial of the blood of those martyrs which had been shed above a thousand years before and lay cold in their streets. So the sense of this blood was upon me, and I obeyed the word of the Lord.

Bent as we are on studying religion's existential conditions, we cannot possibly ignore these pathological aspects of the subject. We must describe and name them just as if they occurred in nonreligious men. It is true that we instinctively recoil from seeing an object to which our emotions and affections are committed handled by the intellect as any other object is handled. The first thing the intellect does with an object is to class it along with something else. But any object that is infinitely important to us and awakens our devotion feels to us also as if it must be sui generis and unique. Probably a crab would be filled with a sense of personal outrage if it could hear us class it without ado or apology as a crustacean, and thus dispose of it. "I am no such thing," it would say, "I am myself, myself alone."

William James, *from* The Varieties of Religious Experience. *At different times in James' thirty-five-year academic career he served as a professor of physiology, psychology, and philosophy, educating, among others, Theodore Roosevelt, W. E. B. Du Bois, and Gertrude Stein. Fascinated by the "altered states of consciousness" that all religions inspired cross culturally, he experimented with hypnosis and nitrous-oxide intoxication.*

Articles of Faith
Price list

HEAD:	
Jewish yarmulke	$9.95
Isalmic hijab	$2.95

FOREHEAD:	
Hindu bindi (7-pack)	$3.99
Leather-strapped Jewish tefillin	$385.00

NECK:	
Wiccan pentagram	$13.99
4k white-gold diamond Christian cross necklace	$237.99

WRISTS:	
WWJD (What Would Jesus Do) adjustable wristband	$4.99
Red satin-string Kabbalah bracelet with 9k golden Hamsa charm for good luck	$39.99

FINGERS:	
14k white-gold Christian chastity ring	$145.00
Tibetan Buddhist "Om Mani Padme Hum" sterling silver and gold prayer-wheel ring	$59.00

BODY:	
Hemp-hooded Maharishi robe	$581.70
Custom-made American Indian Buckskin Dress	$385.00

LEGS:	
Polynesian Etua tattoo of tortoise offering protection from the gods	$300.00
Plaid pleated Catholic schoolgirls' skirt	$12.99

FEET:	
Our Lady of Guadalupe canvas shoes	$60.00
Bare feet for Buddhist meditation	$0.00

1565: Ávila

COMMUNION

Very often raptures seemed to leave my body as light as if it had lost all its weight, and sometimes so light that I hardly knew whether my feet were touching the ground. But during the rapture itself, the body is very often like a corpse, unable to do anything of itself. It remains all the time in whatever attitude it was in when the rapture came on it—seated, for example, and with the hands open or closed. The subject rarely loses consciousness; I have occasionally lost it entirely, but not very often and only for a short time. Generally the senses

c. 363: Antioch

HELPING HAND

I have behaved to all the Galileans with such kindness and benevolence that none of them has suffered violence anywhere or been dragged into a temple or threatened into anything else of the sort against his own will. But the followers of the Arian church, in the insolence bred by their wealth, have attacked the followers of the Gnostic Valentine and have committed in Edessa such rash acts as could never occur in a well-ordered city. Therefore, since by their most admirable law they are bidden to sell all they have and give to the poor that so they may attain more easily to the kingdom of the skies, in order to aid those persons in that effort, I have ordered that all their funds—namely those belonging to the church of the people of Edessa—are to be taken over that they may be given to the soldiers, and that its property be confiscated to my private purse. This is in order that poverty may teach them to behave properly and that they may not be deprived of that heavenly kingdom for which they still hope.

Julian the Apostate, *from a letter to Hecebolius. The nephew of the first Christian Roman emperor Constantine, Julian announced his conversion to paganism in 361. He imagined himself the head of the pagan hierarchy, banishing bishops, burning churches, and proclaiming that Christianity was riddled with fables and falsehoods.*

are disturbed, and though absolutely powerless to perform any outward action, the subject still sees and hears things, though only dimly, as if from far away. I do not say that he can see and hear when the rapture is at its height—and by its height I mean those times when the faculties are lost because they are closely united with God. While it lasts none of the senses perceives or knows what is taking place. We can have no way of understanding this—while we are on earth at least—or rather God cannot wish us to, since we have not the capacity for such understanding. This I have learned for myself.

What I am describing lasts only a moment. But as the surge and impulse of the spirit have been violent, the will remains absorbed, even when the other faculties begin to stir again, and remains mistress over all these workings in the body. The eyes are generally closed, although we may not wish to close them, and if occasionally they remain open, the soul, as I have just said, does not perceive anything or pay attention to what it sees.

A person can do very little in this condition, and so will not be capable of doing much when the faculties come to themselves again. But let him to whom the Lord grants this favor not be discouraged when he finds himself in this state, with his body unable to move for many hours, and with his understanding and memory wandering at times. True, generally they are absorbed in the praise of God, or in an attempt to comprehend or understand what has happened to them. Yet even for this they are not sufficiently awake, but are like people who have slept and dreamed for a long time, and have not yet properly woken up.

Now comes the distress of having to return to life. Now the soul has grown wings that can bear it, and has shed its weak feathers. Now the standard is lifted high for Christ, and it really seems as if the captain of the fort is climbing, or being lifted, to the highest tower, there to raise it aloft in God's name. The soul looks down on those below, like one in a safe place who fears no dangers now, but courts them instead, since they seem to give it the certain

Mawlawiyah, a Sufi order, known to the West as "whirling dervishes," Turkey, c. 1875.

assurance of victory. This is clearly shown by the soul's contempt in this state for the things of this world, which it values at nothing. One who is high up attains many things. The soul has no desire to seek or possess free will; all it wants is to perform the Lord's will, and it prays Him that it may, giving Him at the same time the keys of its own will.

If the raptures are true raptures, the fruits and advantages mentioned remain with the soul; if they do not, I should very much doubt if they came from God. I have myself seen, and I know by experience that the soul in rapture is mistress of everything, and gains such freedom in one hour or even less that it cannot recognize itself.

What power the soul has when the Lord raises it to a height from which it looks down on everything and is not enmeshed in it! How ashamed it is of the time when it was so enmeshed! It is indeed amazed at its own blindness and feels pity for those who are still blind, especially if they are men of prayer to whom God is granting consolations. It longs to cry

aloud and call their attention to their delusions; and sometimes it actually does so, only to bring down a storm of persecutions on its head. Particularly if the person in question is a woman, it is accused of lacking humility, and of wishing to teach those from whom it should learn. So they condemn it, and not without reason, for they know nothing of the force that impels it. At times it cannot help itself, or refrain from enlightening those whom it loves and wishes to see freed from the prison of this life. For the state in which it has once been living is neither more nor less than a prison, and this it realizes.

St. Teresa, *from her* Life. *At the age of twenty-one in 1536, St. Teresa entered a Carmelite convent that allowed its sisters to wear jewelry and perfume. She later referred to it as "an inn just off the road of hell." Her numerous visions included one in which an angel repeatedly plunged an arrow into her heart, leaving her "all on fire with a great love of God." Gian Lorenzo Bernini famously sculpted the episode in marble nearly one hundred years later.*

1779: Monticello

CHURCH AND STATE

Well aware that Almighty God hath created the mind free; that all attempts to influence it by temporal punishments or burdens or by civil incapacitations tend only to beget habits of hypocrisy and meanness—and are a departure from the plan of the Holy Author of our religion, who being Lord both of body and mind, yet chose not to propagate it by coercions on either, as was in his Almighty power to do; that the impious presumption of legislators and rulers, civil as well as ecclesiastical, who, being themselves but fallible and uninspired men have assumed dominion over the faith of others, setting up their own opinions and modes of thinking as the only true and infallible, and as such endeavoring to impose them on others, hath established and maintained false religions over the greatest part of the world and through all time; that to compel a man to furnish contributions of money for the propagation of opinions which he disbelieves is sinful and tyrannical; that even forcing him to support this or that teacher of his own religious persuasion is depriving him of the comfortable liberty of giving his contributions to the particular pastor whose morals he would make his pattern and whose powers he feels most persuasive to righteousness—and is withdrawing from the ministry those temporal rewards which, proceeding from an approbation of their personal conduct, are an additional incitement to earnest and unremitting labors for the instruction of mankind; that our civil rights have no dependence on our religious opinions, more than our opinions in physics or geometry; that, therefore, the proscribing any citizen as unworthy of the public confidence by laying upon him an incapacity of being called to the offices of trust and emolument unless he profess or renounce this or that religious opinion, is depriving him injuriously of those privileges and advantages to which in common with his fellow citizens he has a natural right; that it tends also to corrupt the principles of that very religion it is meant to encourage, by bribing with a monopoly of worldly honors and emoluments, those who will externally profess and conform to it; that though indeed these are criminals who do not withstand such temptation, yet neither are those innocent who lay the bait in their way; that to suffer the civil magistrate to intrude his powers into the field of opinion and to restrain the profession or propagation of principles on the supposition of their ill tendency is a dangerous fallacy, which at once destroys all religious liberty—because he, being of course judge of that tendency, will make his opinions the rule of judgment and approve or condemn the sentiments of others only as they shall square with or differ from his own; that it is time enough for the rightful purposes of civil government, for its offices to interfere when principles break out into overt acts against peace and good order; and finally, that truth is great and will prevail if left to herself, that she is the proper and sufficient antagonist to error and has nothing to fear from the conflict unless by human interposition disarmed of her natural weapons, free argument and debate, errors ceasing to be dangerous when it is permitted freely to contradict them.

Be it therefore enacted by the General Assembly: That no man shall be compelled to frequent or support any religious worship, place, or ministry whatsoever, nor shall be enforced, restrained, molested, or burdened in his body or goods, nor shall otherwise suffer on account of his religious opinions or belief; but that all men shall be free to profess—and by argument to maintain—their opinions in matters of religion, and that the same shall in nowise diminish, enlarge, or affect their civil capacities.

> **Thomas Jefferson**, *from "The Virginia Statute for Religious Freedom." The inscription on Jefferson's headstone reads, "Here was buried Thomas Jefferson, author of the Declaration of American Independence, of the Statute of Virginia for Religious Freedom, and father of the University of Virginia." He was also the nation's first secretary of state, second vice president, and third president.*

332 BC: Egypt

DEIFICATION

Alexander went to Pharos, which at that time was an island lying a little above the Canobic mouth of the river Nile, though it has now been joined to the mainland by a mole. As soon as he saw the commodious situation of the place—it being a long neck of land stretching like an isthmus between large lagoons and shallow waters on one side and the sea on the other, the latter at the end of it making a spacious harbor—he ordered the plan of a city to be drawn out answerable to the place. To do which, for want of chalk, and the soil being black, they laid out their lines with flour, taking in a pretty large compass of ground in a semicircular figure, and drawing into the inside of the circumference equal straight lines from each end, thus giving it something of the form of a cloak or cape. While he was pleasing himself with his design, all of a sudden an infinite number of great birds of several kinds rising like a black cloud out of the river and the lake devoured every morsel of the flour that had been used in setting out the lines; at which omen even Alexander himself was troubled, till the augurs restored his confidence again by telling him it was a sign the city he was about to build would not only abound in all things within itself but also be the nurse and feeder of many nations. He commanded the workmen to proceed, while he went to visit the temple of Amun.

This was a long and painful and dangerous journey, but Alexander was not easily to be diverted from anything he was bent upon. For fortune, having hitherto seconded him in

Buddha descending from heaven, Thai wall painting, eighteenth century.

his designs, made him resolute and firm in his opinions, and the boldness of his temper raised a sort of passion in him for surmounting difficulties—as if it were not enough to be always victorious in the field unless places and seasons and nature herself submitted to him. In this journey, the relief and assistance the gods afforded him in his distresses were more remarkable and obtained greater belief than the oracles he received afterward, which, however, were valued and credited the more on account of those occurrences. For first, plentiful rains that fell preserved them from any fear of perishing by drought and—allaying the extreme dryness of the sand, which now became

The most dangerous madmen are those created by religion, and people whose aim is to disrupt society always know how to make good use of them.
—*Denis Diderot, 1777*

moist and firm to travel on—cleared and purified the air. Besides this, when they were out of their way and were wandering up and down because the marks which were wont to direct the guides were disordered and lost, they were set right again by some ravens, which flew before them when on their march and waited for them when they lingered and fell behind. And the greatest miracle, as Callisthenes tells us, was that if any of the company went astray in the night, they never ceased croaking and making a noise till by that means they had brought them into the right way again. Having passed through the wilderness, they came to the place where the high priest, at the first salutation, bade Alexander welcome from his father Amun. And being asked by him whether any of his father's murderers had escaped punishment, he charged him to speak with more respect, since his was not a mortal father. Then Alexander, changing his expression, desired to know of him whether the empire of the world was reserved for him. This, the god answered, he should obtain, which gave him so much satisfaction that he made splendid offerings to Jupiter, and gave the priests very rich presents.

Among the sayings of one Psammon, a philosopher whom he heard in Egypt, he most approved of this: that all men are governed by God, because in everything, that which is chief and commands is divine. But what he pronounced himself upon this subject was even more like a philosopher, for he said God was the common father of us all, but more particularly of the best of us. To the barbarians he carried himself very haughtily, as if he were fully persuaded of his divine birth and parentage, but to the Grecians more moderately and with less affectation of divinity, except once in writing to the Athenians about Samos, he told them that he should not himself have bestowed upon them that free and glorious city. "You received it," he says, "from the bounty of him who at that time was called my lord and father," meaning Philip. However, afterward being wounded with an arrow, and feeling much pain, he turned to those about him, and told them, "This, my friends, is real flowing blood, not ichor, 'such as immortal gods are wont to shed.'"

And another time, when it thundered so much that everybody was afraid, and Anaxarchus the sophist asked him if he who was Jupiter's son could do anything like this, Alexander said, laughing, "No, I have no desire to be formidable to my friends." From what I have said upon this subject, it is apparent that Alexander in himself was not foolishly affected, or had the vanity to think himself really a god, but merely used his claims to divinity as a means of maintaining among other people the sense of his superiority.

Plutarch, *from* Parallel Lives. *Son of Philip II of Macedon and pupil of Aristotle, Alexander the Great as a child read* The Iliad, *which inspired him to model himself on the half-god, half-man Achilles. The Panhellenic leader was known to dress up like various deities and have incense burned in his honor. Plutarch's* Parallel Lives, *consisting of paired biographies of Greek and Roman statesmen, was a source for a few of William Shakespeare's plays.*

1943: Warsaw

GOD HIDES HIS FACE

I cannot say, after all I have lived through, that my relation to God is unchanged. But with absolute certainty I can say that my faith in Him has not altered by a hair's breadth. In earlier times, when my life was good, my relation to Him was as if to one who gave me gifts without end, and to whom I was therefore always somewhat in debt. Now my relation to Him is as to one who is also in my debt—greatly in my debt. And because I feel that He, too, is in my debt, I consider that I have the right to *admonish* Him. I do not say, like Job, that God should lay His finger on my sins so that I may know how I have earned this. For greater and better men than I are convinced that it is no longer a question of punishment for sins and transgressions. On the contrary, something unique is happening in the world: *hastoras ponim*—God has hidden His face.

God has hidden His face from the world and delivered mankind over to its own savage urges and instincts. This is why I believe that when the forces of evil dominate the world, it is, alas, completely natural that the first victims will be those who represent the holy and the pure. To each of us as individuals, perhaps this brings no comfort. Yet as the destiny of our people is determined not by worldly but by otherworldly laws, not material and physical but spiritual and godly, so must the true believer see in these events a part of God's great leveling of the scales, in which even human tragedies weigh little. But this does not mean that the devout among my people must simply approve what is ordained and say, "The Lord is just and His decrees are just." To say that we have earned the blows we have received is to slander ourselves. It is a defamation of the *Shem Hameforash*, a profanation of His Holy Name—a desecration of the name Jew, a desecration of the name God. It is one and the same. God is blasphemed when we blaspheme ourselves.

In such a circumstance I have, naturally, no expectation of a miracle and do not beg of Him, my Lord, that He should take pity on me. Let Him veil His face in indifference to me as He has veiled it to millions of others of His

Mary Magdalene, from the Isenheim Altarpiece (detail), by Matthias Grünewald, c. 1512–15.

people. I am no exception to the rule. I expect no preference. I will no longer try to save myself, and I will not flee again from here. I will lighten the work of the fire and pour gasoline over my clothes. I still have three bottles of gasoline in reserve, after pouring several dozen over the heads of the murderers.

That was a great moment in my life, and I was convulsed with laughter. I could never have imagined that the death of people, even enemies—even enemies such as these—could fill me with such joy. Foolish humanists may say what they will, revenge and the longing for

The gods are on the side of the stronger.
—Tacitus, c. 109

retribution have always fueled the resistance of the oppressed to the very last, and will always do so. Nothing else brings such solace to their souls. Until now I had never really understood the passage in the Talmud that says, "Vengeance is holy, for it is mentioned between two names of God, as it is written: *A God of vengeance is the Lord!*" Now I understand it. Now I feel it, and now I know why my heart rejoices when I remember how for thousands of years we have called upon our God: "God of Vengeance!" *El Nekamot Adonoi*.

And now, when I am in a position to view life and the world from this clearest of perspectives, such as is rarely granted a man before death, I realize that there is this exclusive and characteristic difference between our God and the God in whom the peoples of Europe believe: while our God is the God of vengeance and our Torah threatens death for the smallest of transgressions, it is also told in the Talmud how in ancient times, when the Sanhedrin was our people's highest court—when we were still a free people in our own land—a single death sentence from the High Council in seventy years was enough to make people call "you murderers" after the judges. The God of the other peoples, however, whom they call "the God of Love," has offered to love every creature created

in His image, and yet they have been murdering us without pity in His name day in, day out, for almost two thousand years.

Yes, I speak of vengeance. Only rarely have we seen true vengeance, but when we have experienced it, it was so comforting, and so sweet—such deep solace and intense happiness—that to me it was as if a new life had opened up. A tank suddenly broke through into our alley and was bombarded from every fortified house around it with bottles of burning gasoline. But not one of them found its mark the way it was supposed to. The tank continued to advance undamaged. I waited with my friends until the tank was rumbling past, literally right under our noses, then we all attacked it at the same moment through the half-walled-up windows. The tank immediately burst into flames and six burning Nazis leaped out of it. Yes, they burned! They burned like the Jews whom they burned, but they screamed more than the Jews. The Jews do not scream. They embrace death as their deliverer. The Warsaw Ghetto is dying in battle, it is going down in gunfire, in fighting, and in flames—but there is no screaming.

I still have three bottles of gasoline left, and they are as precious to me as wine to a drinker. When not long from now I empty one of them over me, I will put the sheets of paper on which I am writing these lines into the empty bottle and hide it here between the bricks in the wall beneath the window. If anyone should ever find them and read them, he will perhaps understand the feeling of a Jew—one of millions—who died abandoned by God, in Whom he so deeply believes. I will explode the two other bottles over the heads of the thugs when my last moment is come.

Zvi Kolitz, *from "Yosl Rakover Talks to God." While visiting Brazil as an emissary for the World Zionist Congress in 1946, Kolitz was asked to write an article for a local paper's Yom Kippur edition; his contribution was this fictional memoir. The Lithuanian-born author had no direct experience with life in the Warsaw Ghetto, but since the work was later reprinted without his name it was for many years considered an authentic document.*

c. 547 BC: Lydia

FOOL'S GOLD

Croesus attempted to win the favor of the Delphian Apollo by a magnificent sacrifice. Of every kind of appropriate animal he slaughtered three thousand; he burned in a huge pile a number of precious objects—couches overlaid with gold or silver, golden cups, tunics, and other richly colored garments—in the hope of binding the god more closely to his interest. And he issued a command that every Lydian was also to offer a sacrifice according to his means. After this ceremony he melted down an enormous quantity of gold into 117 ingots about eighteen inches long, nine inches wide, and three inches thick—four of the ingots were of refined gold weighing approximately 142 pounds each; the rest were alloyed and weighed about 114 pounds. He also caused the image of a lion to be made of refined gold, in weight some 570 pounds. This statue, when the temple at Delphi was burned down, fell from the gold bricks which formed its base and lies today in the Corinthian treasury. It lost about two hundred pounds weight in the fire and now weighs only 370 pounds.

This was by no means all that Croesus sent to Delphi; there were also two huge mixing bowls, one of gold which was placed on the right-hand side of the entrance to the temple, the other of silver, on the left. These also were moved at the time of the fire, and the golden one, which weighs nearly a quarter of a ton, now stands in the treasury of the Clazomenians, and the silver one, which holds over five thousand gallons, is in the corner of the antechapel. Its capacity is known because the Delphians use it for mixing wine at the festival called Theophania. It is a most remarkable piece of work. In addition Croesus sent four silver casks, which are in the Corinthian treasury, and two sprinklers for lustral water, one of gold, the other of silver; the former has the name of the Lacedaemonians engraved upon it, and they claim to have presented it. But this is not true. Croesus presented it along with all the rest, and some Delphian (I know his name but will not mention it) cut the inscription to please the Lacedaemonians. I admit that the boy through whose hand the water runs is a Lacedaemonian gift, but not either of the two sprinklers. There were many other gifts of no great importance, including round silver basins; but I must not forget to mention a figure of a woman, in gold, four and a half feet high, said by the Delphians

1887: Indiana

IT'S THAT SIMPLE

We feel bound explicitly to avow our unshaken persuasion that all war is utterly incompatible with the plain precepts of our divine Lord and Lawgiver, and the whole spirit of His gospel, and that no plea of necessity or policy, however urgent or peculiar, can avail to release either individuals or nations from the paramount allegiance which they owe to Him who hath said, "Love your enemies." In enjoining this love, and the forgiveness of injuries, He who has brought us to Himself has not prescribed for man precepts which are incapable of being carried into practice, or of which the practice is to be postponed until all shall be persuaded to act upon them.

We cannot doubt that they are incumbent now, and that we have in the prophetic scriptures the distinct intimation of their direct application, not only to individuals, but to nations also. When nations conform their laws to this divine teaching, wars must necessarily cease.

We would, in humility, but in faithfulness to our Lord, express our firm persuasion that all the exigencies of civil government and social order may be met under the banner of the Prince of Peace, in strict conformity with His commands.

The Society of Friends, *from "The Richmond Declaration." In 1682 the persecuted lawyer William Penn founded the Pennsylvania colony as a "holy experiment," based on Quaker ideals and religious liberty. In 1887 ninety-five Quaker delegates signed "The Richmond Declaration" to create a lasting statement of faith. It remains in use today, providing, among other things, the basis for the Friends' claim for conscientious-objector status.*

Priest with an offering table, limestone, c. 1340 BC.

these are the only true oracles in the world, has given you gifts such as your power of divination deserves, and now asks you if he should march against Persia and if it would be wise to seek an alliance." To this question both oracles returned a similar answer: they foretold that if Croesus attacked the Persians, he would destroy a great empire, and they advised him to find out which of the Greek states was the most powerful and to come to an understanding with it.

Croesus was overjoyed when he learned the answer which the oracles had given, and was fully confident of destroying the power of Cyrus. To express his satisfaction he sent a further present to Delphi of two gold staters for every man, having first inquired how many men there were. The Delphians in return granted in perpetuity to Croesus and the people of Lydia the right of citizenship for any who wished, together with exemption from dues, front seats at state functions, and priority in consulting the oracle.

When Croesus had given the Delphians their presents, he consulted the oracle a third time, for one true answer had made him greedy for more. On this occasion he asked if his reign would be a long one. The priestess answered:

When comes the day that a mule shall sit
    on the Median throne,
Then, tender-footed Lydian, by pebbly
    Hermus
Run and abide not, nor think it shame to
    be a coward.

This reply gave Croesus more pleasure than anything he had yet heard; for he did not suppose that a mule was likely to become king of the Medes, and that meant that he and his line would remain in power forever.

to represent the woman who baked Croesus' bread. Lastly, he sent his own wife's necklaces and girdles. These, then, were the offerings which Croesus sent to Delphi. To the shrine of Amphiaraus—the story of whose valor and misfortune he knew—he sent a shield of solid gold and a spear, also of solid gold throughout, both shaft and head; the shield and spear were still at Thebes in my own day, in the temple of Ismenian Apollo.

The Lydians who were to bring the presents to the temples were instructed by Croesus to ask the oracles if he should undertake the campaign against Persia, and if he should strengthen his army by some alliance. On their arrival, therefore, they offered the gifts with proper ceremony and put their question in the following words: "Croesus, King of Lydia and other nations, in the belief that

Herodotus, *from* The Histories. *According to Herodotus, Croesus went to war, having faith in the divine prediction that if he attacked Persia he would "destroy a great empire." The Delphic Oracle proved accurate, but the great empire Croesus destroyed was his own. Cyrus the Great ordered the captive king to be burned, but Apollo saved him at the last moment.*

778: Saragossa

SPLITTING HAIRS

The day passes, the evening comes, and Franks and pagans fight on with their swords. Those who have led these two hosts into battle are brave men. They have not forgotten their war cries—the emir, Baligant, shouts, "*Precieuse!*" and Charles raises his famous battle cry of "Mountjoy!" And by their clear ringing voices the two men recognize each other, and they meet in the middle of the field and ride to attack each other, and exchange heavy blows, each one's spear smashing into the other's ringed shield. And each shield is pierced above the broad boss, and the folds of both of their hauberks are rent, but on neither side do the spears enter the flesh. Their cinches break and their saddles tip over and both kings fall to the ground, but they leap to their feet at once and bravely draw their swords. Now nothing can separate them, and the fight cannot end except with the death of one or the other.

Charles of sweet France is gifted with great courage, and the Emir shows neither dread nor hesitation. They draw their swords, showing the naked blades, and they deal each other heavy blows on their shields, cutting through the leather coverings and the two outer layers of wood, so that the nails fall and the buckles are broken in pieces. Then, bare of shields, they hack at each other's coats of mail, and the sparks leap from their bright helmets. This combat cannot be brought to an end without one or the other confessing that he is in the wrong.

The emir says, "Charles, consider the matter carefully and make up your mind to repent for what you have done to me. You have killed my son, if I am not mistaken, and you are wrongfully disputing with me the possession of my own country. If you will become my vassal and swear fealty to me, you may come with me and serve me from here to the East."

Charles answers, "To my way of thinking that would be vile and base. It is not for me to render either peace or love to a pagan. Submit to the creed which God has revealed to us, become a Christian, and my love for you will never end as long as you put your faith in the omnipotent King and serve Him."

Baligant says, "You have begun a bad sermon!" Then they raise their swords and resume the fight.

The emir is a strong and skillful fighter. He strikes Charlemagne upon his helmet of burnished steel and splits and smashes it above his head, bringing the sword down into the fine hair, sheering off a palm's breadth and more of flesh,

Without doubt God is the universal moving force, but each being is moved according to the nature that God has given it. He directs angels, man, animals, brute matter, in sum all created things—but each according to its nature—and man having been created free, he is freely led. This rule is truly the eternal law and in it we must believe.   —Joseph de Maistre, 1821

and laying bare the bone. Charles staggers and almost falls, but it is not God's will that he should be killed or beaten. St. Gabriel comes to his side, asking, "Great king, what are you doing?"

When he hears the holy voice of the angel, Charles loses all fear of death, and his vigor and clearness of mind return. He strikes the Emir a blow with the sword of France, cleaves the helmet flashing with jewels, cuts open the head and spills the brains, and splits the whole face down through the white beard. It is a corpse, past all hope of recovery, which that stroke hurls to the ground. Charles calls "Mountjoy!" to rally his vassals, and at his shout Duke Naimes comes to him bringing with him the Emperor's horse Tencendur, and the king mounts.

The pagans flee. It is not the will of God that they should remain. Now the French have achieved the triumph which they had hoped for.

> *From* The Song of Roland. *Considered one of the exemplary "chansons de gestes" or "songs of deeds," the French epic poem dating from around 1100 glorifies the Battle of Roncesvalles, a historically negligable skirmish between Charlemagne and Basque forces.*

c. 2300 BC: Sumer

MUSIC OF MOURNING

Lady of all powers,
In whom light appears,
Radiant one
Beloved of heaven and earth,
Tiara-crowned
Priestess of the Highest God,
My lady, you are the guardian
Of all greatness.
Your hand holds the seven powers:
You lift the powers of being,
You have hung them over your fingers,
You have gathered the many powers,
You have clasped them now
Like necklaces onto your breast.

Like a dragon,
You poisoned the land—
When you roared at the earth
In your thunder,
Nothing green could live.
A flood fell from the mountain:
You, Inanna,
Foremost in heaven and earth.
Lady riding a beast,
You rained fire on the heads of men.
Taking your power from the Highest,
Following the commands of the Highest,
Lady of all the great rites,
Who can understand all that is yours?

In the forefront
Of the battle,
All is struck down by you—
O winged Lady,
Like a bird
You scavenge the land.
Like a charging storm
You charge,
Like a roaring storm
You roar,
You thunder in thunder,
Snort in rampaging winds.
Your feet are continually restless.
Carrying your harp of sighs,
You breathe out the music of mourning.

It was in your service
That I first entered
The holy temple,
I, Enheduanna,
The highest priestess.
I carried the ritual basket,
I chanted your praise.
Now I have been cast out
To the place of lepers.
Day comes,
And the brightness
Is hidden around me.
Shadows cover the light,
Drape it in sandstorms.
My beautiful mouth knows only confusion.
Even my sex is dust.

Enheduanna, *from "The Hymn to Inanna."*
Enheduanna is the earliest author in the world
known by name. As the daughter of King Sargon,
she was appointed the high priestess to the moon
goddess whose praises she sung in her verse.

1960: Mt. Judge

JOHN UPDIKE HEARS
A POINT OF CONTENTION

Reverend Eccles drives across the town, tacking on the diagonal streets along a course parallel to the distant ridge of the mountain. Fritz Kruppenbach, Mt. Judge's Lutheran minister for twenty-seven years, lives in a high brick house not far from the cemetery. The motorcycle belonging to his college-age son is on its side in the driveway, partly dismantled. The sloping lawn, graded in fussy terraces, has the unnatural chartreuse

> *Even a god cannot change the past.*
> —*Agathon, c. 445 BC*

evenness that comes with much fertilizing, much weed killing, and much mowing. Mrs. Kruppenbach comes to the door in a gray dress that makes no compromise with the season. Her gray hair girdles her head with braids of great compactness. When she lets all that hair down, she must be a witch. "He's mowing out back," she says.

"I'd like to talk to him for just a few minutes. It's a problem that involves our two congregations."

"Go up to his room, why do-an tcha? I'll fetch him."

The house is flooded with the smell of beef roasting. Eccles sits by the window of Kruppenbach's den on an oak-backed choir pew left over from some renovation. Seated on the bench he feels an adolescent compulsion to pray but instead peers across the valley at the green fragments of the golf course where he would like to be.

The house shudders to the master's step. Kruppenbach comes up the stairs into his den, angry at being taken from his lawn mowing. He wears old black pants and an undershirt soaked with sweat. His shoulders are coated with wiry gray wool.

"Hello Chack," he says at pulpit volume, with no intonation of greeting. His German accent makes his words seem like stones, set angrily one on top of another. "What is it?"

Eccles, not daring "Fritz" with the older man, laughs and blurts, "Hello!"

Kruppenbach grimaces. He has a massive square head, crew-cut. He is a man of brick: as if he had been born as a baby literally of clay and decades of exposure have baked him to the color and hardness of brick. He repeats, "What?"

"You have a family called Angstrom."

"Yes."

"The father's a printer."

"Yes."

"Their son, Harry, deserted his wife over two months ago; her people, the Springers, are in my church."

"Yes, well. The boy. The boy's a *Schussel.*"

Eccles isn't certain what that means. He supposes that Kruppenbach doesn't sit down because he doesn't want to stain his furniture with his own sweat. His continuing to stand puts Eccles in a petitionary position, sitting on the bench like a choirboy. The odor of meat cooking grows more insistent as he explains what he thinks happened: how Harry has been in a sense spoiled by his athletic successes; how the wife, to be fair, had perhaps showed little imagination in their marriage; how he himself, as minister, had tried to keep the boy's conscience in touch with his wife without pressing him into a premature reunion—for the boy's problem wasn't so much a lack of feeling as an uncontrolled excess of it; how the four parents, for various reasons, were of little help; how he had witnessed, just minutes ago, a quarrel between the Angstroms that perhaps offered a clue as to why their son—

"Do you think," Kruppenbach at last interrupts, "do you think this is your job, to meddle in these people's lives? I know what they teach you at seminary now: this psychology and that. But I don't agree with it. You think now your job is to be an unpaid doctor, to run around and plug up the holes and make everything smooth. I don't think that. I don't think that's your job."

"I only—"

"No, now let me finish. I've been in Mt. Judge twenty-seven years and you've been here

The Talmudists, by Jacob Kramer, c. 1919.

two. I've listened to your story but I wasn't listening to what it said about the people, I was listening to what it said about you. What I heard was this: the story of a minister of God selling his message for a few scraps of gossip and a few games of golf. What do you think now it looks like to God, one childish husband leaving one childish wife? Do you ever think anymore what God sees? Or have you grown beyond that?"

"No, of course not. But it seems to me our role in a situation like this—"

"It seems to you our role is to be cops, cops without handcuffs, without guns, without anything but our human good nature. Isn't it right? Don't answer, just think if I'm not right. Well, I say that's a devil's idea. I say, let the cops be cops and look after their laws that have nothing to do with us."

"I agree, up to a point—"

"There *is* no up to a point! There is no reason or measure in what we must do." His thick forefinger, woolly between the knuckles, has begun to tap emphasis on the back of a leather chair. "If God wants to end misery He'll declare

the Kingdom now." Jack feels a blush begin to burn his face. "How big do you think your little friends look among the billions that God sees? In Bombay now they die in the streets every minute. You say role. I say you don't know what your role is, or you'd be home locked in prayer. *There* is your role: to make yourself an exemplar of faith. *There* is where comfort comes from: faith, not what little finagling a body can do here and there, stirring the bucket. In running back and forth you run from the duty given you by God, to make your faith powerful, so when the call comes you can go out and tell them, 'Yes, he is dead, but you will see him again in heaven. Yes, you suffer, but you must *love* your pain, because it is *Christ's* pain.' When on Sunday morning then, when we go before their faces, we must walk up not worn out with misery but full of Christ, *hot*"—he clenches his hairy fists—"with Christ, on *fire*: *burn* them with the force of our belief. That is why they come; why else would they pay us? Anything else we can do or say anyone can do and say. They have doctors and lawyers for that. It's all in the Book—a thief with faith is

A Diablerie, by Cornelis Saftleven, c. 1650.

worth all the Pharisees. Make no mistake. Now I'm serious. Make no mistake. There is nothing but Christ for us. All the rest, all this decency and busyness, is nothing. It is devil's work."

"Fritz," Mrs. Kruppenbach's voice calls carefully up the stairs. "Supper."

The red man in his undershirt looks down at Eccles and asks, "Will you kneel a moment with me and pray for Christ to come into this room?"

"No. No I won't. I'm too angry. It would be hypocritical."

The refusal, unthinkable from a layman, makes Kruppenbach, not softer, but stiller. "Hypocrisy," he says mildly. "You have no seriousness. Don't you believe in damnation? Didn't you know when you put that collar on what you risked?" In the brick skin of his face his eyes seem small imperfections, pink and glazed with water as if smarting in intense heat.

He turns without waiting for Jack to answer and goes downstairs for supper. Jack descends behind him and continues out the door. His heart is beating like a scolded child's and his knees are weak with fury. He had come for an exchange of information and been flagellated with an insane spiel. Unctuous old thundering Hun, no conception of the ministry as a legacy of light, probably himself scrambled into it out of a butcher's shop. Jack realizes that these are spiteful and unworthy thoughts but he can't stop them. His depression is so deep that he tries to gouge it deeper by telling himself, *He's right, he's right*, and thus springing tears and purging himself, however absurdly, above the perfect green circle of the Buick steering wheel. But he can't cry; he's parched. His shame and failure hang downward in him, heavy but fruitless.

From Rabbit, Run. *"My subject," Updike once said, "is the American Protestant small-town middle class." As a child he wanted to be a cartoonist for either Walt Disney or* The New Yorker, *the magazine with which he began his prolific affiliation as a writer in 1955. Over the course of the next fifty-four years, Updike won two Pulitzer Prizes and published twenty-three novels He died at the age of seventy-six on January 27, 2009.*

C. 410 BC: Thebes

EURIPIDES BEHOLDS DIONYSUS

[*Enter Pentheus. He addresses the audience, without at first noticing Cadmus and Teiresias, who stand at the opposite side of the stage.*]

Pentheus: I happen to have been away from Thebes; reports
Of this astounding scandal have just been brought to me.
Our women, it seems, have left their homes on some pretense
Of Bacchic worship and are now gadding about
On the wooded mountain slopes, dancing in honor of
This upstart god Dionysus, whoever he may be.
Amidst these groups of worshippers, they tell me, stand
Bowls full of wine; and our women go creeping off
This way and that to lonely places and give themselves
To lecherous men. They are maenad priestesses, if you please!
Aphrodite supplants Bacchus in their ritual.
Well, those I've caught, my guards are keeping safe; we've tied
Their hands, and lodged them at state expense. Those still at large
On the mountain I am going to hunt out—and that
Includes my own mother Agave and her sisters
Ino and Autonoe. Once they're fast in iron fetters,
I'll put a stop to this outrageous Bacchism.
They tell me, too, some oriental conjurer
Has come from Lydia, a magician with golden hair
Flowing in scented ringlets, his face flushed with wine,
His eyes lit with the charm of Aphrodite; and he
Entices young girls with his Bacchic mysteries,
Spends days and nights consorting with them. Once let me
Get that fellow inside my walls—I'll cut his head
From his shoulders; that will stop him drumming with his thyrsus,
Tossing his long hair. *He's* the one—this foreigner—
Who says Dionysus is a god; who says he was
Sewn up in Zeus' thigh. The truth about Dionysus
Is that he's dead, burnt to a cinder by lightning
Along with his mother, because she said Zeus lay with her.
Whoever the man may be, is not his arrogance
An outrage? Has he not earned a rope around his neck?
[*Pentheus turns to go, and sees Cadmus and Teiresias*]
Why, look! Another miracle! Here's Teiresias
The prophet—in a fawn skin; and my mother's father—
A Bacchant with a fennel wand! Well, there's a sight
For laughter! [*but he is raging, not laughing*]
Sir, I am ashamed to see two men
Of your age with so little sense of decency.
Come, you're my grandfather: throw down that ivy wreath,

Get rid of that thyrsus!—*You* persuaded him to this,
Teiresias. By introducing a new god, you hope
To advance your augurer's business, to collect more fees
For inspecting sacrifices. Listen: your gray hairs
Are your protection; otherwise you'd be sitting now
In prison with all these crazy females, for promoting
Pernicious practices. As for women, I tell you this:
Wherever the sparkle of sweet wine adorns their feasts,
No good will follow from such Bacchic ceremonies.

Teiresias: When a good speaker has a sound case to present,
Then eloquence is no great feat. Your fluent tongue
Promises wisdom, but the content of your speech
Is ignorant. Power and eloquence in a headstrong man
Spell folly; such a man is a peril to the state.
This new god, whom you ridicule—no words of mine
Could well express the ascendancy he will achieve
In Hellas. There are two powers, young man, which are supreme
In human affairs: first, Demeter—the same goddess
Is also Earth; give her which name you please—and she
Supplies mankind with solid food. After her came
Dionysus, Semele's son; the blessing he procured
And gave to men is counterpart to that of bread:
The clear juice of the grape. When mortals drink their fill
Of wine, the sufferings of our unhappy race
Are banished; each day's troubles are forgotten in sleep.
There is no other cure for sorrow. Dionysus,
Himself a god, is thus poured out in offering
To the gods, so that through him come blessings on mankind.
And this god is a prophet; the Bacchic ecstasy
And frenzy hold a strong prophetic element.
When he fills irresistibly a human body
He gives those so possessed power to foretell the future.
In Ares' province too Dionysus has his share;
Sometimes an army, weaponed and drawn up for battle,
Has fled in wild panic before a spear was raised.
This too is an insanity sent by Dionysus.
Ay, and the day will come when, on the very crags
Of Delphi, you shall see him leaping, amidst the blaze
Of torches, over the twin-peaked ridge, waving aloft
And brandishing his Bacchic staff, while all Hellas
Exalts him. Pentheus, pay heed to my words. You rely
On force; but it is not force that governs human affairs.
Do not mistake for wisdom that opinion which
May rise from a sick mind. Welcome this god to Thebes,
Offer libations to him, celebrate his rites,
Put on his garland. Dionysus will not compel

Women to be chaste, since in all matters self-control
Resides in our own natures. You should consider this;
For in the Bacchic ritual, as elsewhere, a woman
Will be safe from corruption if her mind is chaste.
Think of this too: when crowds stand at the city gates
And Thebes extols the name of Pentheus, you rejoice;
So too, I think, the god is glad to receive honor.
Well, I at least, and Cadmus, whom you mock, will wear
The ivy wreath and join the dancing—we are a pair
Of gray heads, but this is our duty; and no words
Of yours shall lure me into fighting against gods.
For a most cruel insanity has warped your mind;
While drugs may well have caused it, they can bring no cure.

Cadmus: My dear son, Teiresias has given you good advice.
Don't stray beyond pious tradition; live with us.
Your wits have flown to the winds, your sense is foolishness.
Even if, as you say, Dionysus is no god,
Let him have *your* acknowledgement; lie royally,
That Semele may get honor as having borne a god,
And credit come to us and to all our family.
Remember, too, Actaeon's miserable fate—
Torn and devoured by hounds which he himself had bred,
Because he filled the mountains with the boast that he
Was a more skillful hunter than Artemis herself.
Don't share his fate, my son! Come, let me crown your head
With a wreath of ivy; join us in worshipping this god.

Pentheus: Keep your hands off! Go to your Bacchic rites, and don't
Wipe off your crazy folly on me. But I will punish
This man who has been your instructor in lunacy.
Go, someone, quickly to his seat of augury,
Smash it with crowbars, topple the walls, throw all his things
In wild confusion, turn the whole place upside down,
Fling out his holy fripperies to the hurricane winds!
This sacrilege will sting him more than anything else.
The rest of you—go, comb the country and track down
That effeminate foreigner, who plagues our women with
This new disease, fouls the whole land with lechery;
And once you catch him, tie him up and bring him here
To me; I'll deal with him. He shall be stoned to death.
He'll wish he'd never brought his Bacchic rites to Thebes.

From The Bacchae. *The last of the three great tragedians after Aeschylus and Sophocles, Euripides was known in the ancient world as "the philosopher of the stage" for his meditative monologues—a device that Aristophanes blamed for the "death of tragedy." Of his ninety-two known plays, only nineteen are extant, among them* Hippolytus, Medea, *and* Trojan Women.

c. 1905: United States

CLAD IN ROBES OF SPOTLESS WHITE

"Big meeting" is an institution something like a camp meeting, the difference being that it is held in a permanent church, and not in a temporary structure. All the churches of some one denomination—of course, either Methodist or Baptist—in a county, or perhaps in several adjoining counties, are closed, and the congregations unite at some centrally located church for a series of meetings lasting a week. It is really a social as well as a religious function. The people

> *The psychoanalysis of individual human beings teaches us with quite special insistence that the god of each of them is formed in the likeness of his father, that his personal relation to God depends on his relation to his father in the flesh and oscillates and changes along with that relation—and that at bottom God is nothing other than an exalted father.*
> —Sigmund Freud, 1913

come in great numbers, making the trip, according to their financial status, in buggies drawn by sleek, fleet-footed mules, in ox carts, or on foot. It was amusing to see some of the latter class trudging down the hot and dusty road, with their shoes—which were brand new—strung across their shoulders. When they got near the church, they sat on the side of the road and, with many grimaces, tenderly packed their feet into those instruments of torture. This furnished, indeed, a trying test of their religion. The famous preachers come from near and far and take turns in warning sinners of the day of wrath. Food, in the form of those two Southern luxuries, fried chicken and roast pork, is plentiful, and no one need go hungry. On the opening Sunday the women are immaculate in starched, stiff, white dresses adorned with ribbons, either red or blue. Even a great many of the men wear streamers of varicolored ribbons in the buttonholes of their coats. A few of them carefully

cultivate a forelock of hair by wrapping it in twine, and on such festive occasions decorate it with a narrow ribbon streamer. Big meetings afford a fine opportunity for the younger people to meet each other dressed in their Sunday clothes, and much rustic courting—which is as enjoyable as any other kind—is indulged in.

This big meeting which I was lucky enough to catch was particularly well attended; the extra-large attendance was due principally to two attractions: a man by the name of John Brown, who was renowned as the most powerful preacher for miles around, and a wonderful leader of singing, who was known as Singing Johnson. These two men were a study and a revelation to me. They caused me to reflect upon how great an influence their types have been in the development of the Negro in America. Both these types are now looked upon generally with condescension or contempt by the progressive element among the colored people, but it should never be forgotten that it was they who led the race from paganism and kept it steadfast to Christianity through all the long, dark years of slavery.

John Brown was a jet-black man of medium size, with a strikingly intelligent head and face, and a voice like an organ peal. He preached each night after several lesser lights had successively held the pulpit during an hour or so. As far as subject matter is concerned, all of the sermons were alike: each began with the fall of man, ran through various trials and tribulations of the Hebrew children, on to the redemption by Christ, and ended with a fervid picture of the judgment day and the fate of the damned. But John Brown possessed magnetism and an imagination so free and daring that he was able to carry through what the other preachers would not attempt. He knew all the arts and tricks of oratory, the modulation of the voice to almost a whisper, the pause for effect, the rise through light, rapid-fire sentences to the terrific, thundering outburst of an electrifying climax. In addition, he had the intuition of a born theatrical manager. Night after night this man held me fascinated. He convinced me that, after all, eloquence consists more in the manner of saying than in what is said. It is largely a matter of tone pictures.

The most striking example of John Brown's magnetism and imagination was his "heavenly march"; I shall never forget how it impressed me when I heard it. He opened his sermon in the usual way; then, proclaiming to his listeners that he was going to take them on the heavenly march, he seized the Bible under his arm and began to pace up and down the pulpit platform. The congregation immediately began with their feet a tramp, tramp, tramp, in time with the preacher's march in the pulpit, all the while singing in an undertone a hymn about marching to Zion. Suddenly he cried, "Halt!" Every foot stopped with the precision of a company of well-drilled soldiers, and the singing ceased. The morning star had been reached. Here the preacher described the beauties of that celestial body. Then the march, the tramp, tramp, tramp, and the singing were again taken up. Another "Halt!" They had reached the evening star. And so on, past the sun and moon—the intensity of religious emotion all the time increasing—along the milky way, on up to the gates of heaven. Here the halt was longer, and the preacher described at length the gates and walls of the New Jerusalem. Then he took his hearers through the

Evening at the Golden Temple, Amritsar, by Derek Hare, c. 2000.

pearly gates, along the golden streets, pointing out the glories of the city, pausing occasionally to greet some patriarchal members of the church, well-known to most of his listeners in life, who had had "the tears wiped from their eyes, were clad in robes of spotless white, with crowns of gold upon their heads and harps within their hands," and ended his march before the great white throne. To the reader this may sound ridiculous, but listened to under the circumstances, it was highly and effectively dramatic. I was a more or less sophisticated and nonreligious man of the world, but the torrent of the preacher's words, moving with the rhythm and glowing with the eloquence of primitive poetry, swept me along, and I, too, felt like joining in the shouts of "Amen! Hallelujah!"

John Brown's powers in describing the delights of heaven were no greater than those in depicting the horrors of hell. I saw great, strapping fellows trembling and weeping like children at the "mourners' bench." His warnings to sinners were truly terrible. I shall never forget one expression that he used, which for originality and aptness could not be excelled. In my opinion, it is more graphic and for us far more expressive than St. Paul's: "It is hard to kick against the pricks." He struck the attitude of a pugilist and thundered out, "Young man, your arm's too short to box with God!"

> **James Weldon Johnson,** *from* The Autobiography of an Ex-Colored Man. *The lawyer, Broadway songwriter, and civil-rights activist worked on Theodore Roosevelt's 1904 presidential campaign, later serving as a U.S. consul to Venezuela and Nicaragua. He anonymously published his only novel,* The Autobiography, *in 1912, joined the staff of the NAACP in 1916, and was a leading member of the Harlem Renaissance in the 1920s.*

c. 260 bc: China

PROPER ORDER

Through rites, heaven and earth join in harmony, the sun and moon shine, the four seasons proceed in order, the stars and constellations march, the rivers flow, and all things flourish, men's likes and dislikes are regulated, and their joys and hates made appropriate. Those below are obedient, those above are enlightened; all things change but do not become disordered—only he who turns his back upon rites will be destroyed. Are they not wonderful indeed? When they are properly established and brought to the peak of perfection, no one in the world can add to or detract from them. Through them the root and the branch are put in proper order; beginning and end are justified; the most elegant forms embody all distinctions; the most penetrating insight explains all things. In the world those who obey the dictates of ritual will achieve order; those who turn against them will suffer disorder. Those who obey them will win safety; those who turn against them will court danger. Those who obey them will be preserved; those who turn against them will be lost. This is something that the petty man cannot comprehend.

The meaning of ritual is deep indeed. He who tries to enter it with the kind of perception that distinguishes hard and white, same and different, will drown there. The meaning of ritual is great indeed. He who tries to enter it with the uncouth and inane theories of the system makers will perish there. The meaning of ritual is lofty indeed. He who tries to enter with the violent and arrogant ways of those who despise common customs and consider themselves to be above other men will meet his downfall there.

He who dwells in ritual and can ponder it well may be said to know how to think; he who dwells in ritual and does not change his ways may be said to be steadfast. He who knows how to think and to be steadfast, and in addition has a true love for ritual—he is a sage. Heaven is the acme of loftiness, earth the acme of depth, the boundless the acme of breadth, and the sage the acme of the Way. Therefore the scholar studies how to become a sage; he does not study merely to become one of the people without direction.

> **Xunzi,** *from "A Discussion of Ritual." Xunzi was the first great Confucian philosopher to write in the essay form, instead of relying on pithy epigrams or dialogues. Living during the Warring States period, he concluded that "the nature of man is evil; his goodness is only acquired training."*

819: Chang'an

REMONSTRANCE

I humbly submit that Buddhism is but one of the religious systems obtaining among the barbarian tribes, that only during the later Han dynasty did it filter into the Middle Kingdom, and that it never existed in the golden age of the past.

It was not until the reign of Mingdi of the Han that Buddhism first appeared. His reign lasted no longer than eighteen years, and after him disturbance followed upon disturbance, and reigns were all short. From the time of the five dynasties, Song, Qi, Liang, Chen, and Yuan Wei onward, as the worship of Buddha slowly increased, dynasties became more short-lived. Wudi of Liang alone reigned as long as forty-eight years. During his reign he three times consecrated his life to Buddha, made no animal sacrifices in his ancestral temple, and ate but one meal a day of vegetables and fruit. Yet in the end he was driven out by the rebel Hou Jing and died of starvation in Tai-cheng, and his state was immediately destroyed. By worshipping Buddha he looked for prosperity but found only disaster—a sufficient proof that Buddha is not worthy of worship.

When Gaozu succeeded the fallen house of Sui, he determined to eradicate Buddhism. But the ministers of the time were lacking in foresight and ability, they had no real understanding of the way of the ancient kings, nor of the things that are right both for then and now. Thus they were unable to assist the wise resolution of their ruler and save their country from this plague. To my constant regret the attempt stopped short. But you, your majesty, are possessed of a skill in the arts of peace and war, of wisdom and courage the like of which has not been seen for several thousand years. When you first ascended the throne you prohibited recruitment of Buddhist monks and Daoist priests and the foundation of new temples and monasteries and I firmly believed that the intentions of Gaozu would be carried out by your hand, or if this were still impossible, that

at least their religions would not be allowed to spread and flourish.

And now, your majesty, I hear that you have ordered all Buddhist monks to escort a bone of the Buddha from Fengxiang and that a pavilion be erected from which you will in person watch its entrance into the Imperial Palace. You have further ordered every Buddhist temple to receive this object with due homage. Stupid as I am, I feel convinced that it

Reason and experience both forbid us to expect that national morality can prevail in exclusion of religious principle.
—*George Washington, 1796*

is not out of regard for Buddha that you, your majesty, are praying for blessings by doing him this honor, but that you are organizing this absurd pantomime for the benefit of the people of the capital and for their gratification in this year of plenty and happiness. For a mind so enlightened as your majesty's could never believe such nonsense. The minds of the common people however are as easy to becloud as they are difficult to enlighten. If they see your majesty acting in this way, they will think that you are wholeheartedly worshipping the Buddha, and will say, "His majesty is a great sage, and even he worships the Buddha with all his heart. Who are we that we should any of us grudge our lives in his service?" They will cauterize the crowns of their heads, burn off their fingers, and in bands of tens or hundreds cast off their clothing and scatter their money and from daylight to darkness follow one another in the cold fear of being too late. Young and old in one mad rush will forsake their trades and callings and, unless you issue some prohibition, will flock round the temples, hacking their arms and mutilating their bodies to do him homage. And the laughter that such unseemly and degenerate behavior will everywhere provoke will be no light matter.

The Buddha was born a barbarian; he was unacquainted with the language of the Middle

Vishnu rescuing the elephant king Gajendra from a water monster, c. 1825.

Kingdom, and his dress was of a different cut. His tongue did not speak nor was his body clothed in the manner prescribed by the kings of old; he knew nothing of the duty of minister to prince, or the relationship of son to father. Were he still alive today, were he to come to court at the bidding of his country, your majesty would give him no greater reception than an interview in the Strangers' Hall, a ceremonial banquet, and the gift of a suit of clothes, after which you would have him sent under guard to the frontier to prevent him from misleading your people. There is then all the less reason now that he has been dead so long for allowing this decayed and rotten bone, this filthy and disgusting relic to enter the Forbidden Palace. "I stand in awe of supernatural beings," said Confucius, "but keep them at a distance." And the feudal lords of olden times when making a visit of condolence even within their own state would still not approach without sending a shaman to precede them and drive away all evil influences with a branch of peach wood. But now and for no given reason your majesty proposes to view in person the reception of this decayed and disgusting object without even

sending ahead the shaman with his peach-wood wand—and to my shame and indignation none of your ministers says that this is wrong, none of your censors has exposed the error.

I beg that this bone be handed over to the authorities to throw into water or fire, that Buddhism be destroyed root and branch forever, that the doubts of your people be settled once and for all and their descendants saved from heresy. For if you make it known to your people that the actions of the true sage surpass ten thousand times ten thousand those of ordinary men, with what wondering joy will you be acclaimed! And if the Buddha should indeed possess the power to bring down evil, let all the bane and punishment fall upon my head, and as heaven is my witness I shall not complain.

In the fullness of my emotion, I humbly present this memorial for your attention.

Han Yu, *from* Memorial on the Bone of Buddha. *For his spirited attack on Buddhism, Han Yu nearly lost his life; the emperor's request for capital punishment was commuted to a one-year banishment to South China. A poet, essayist, and early proponent of neo-Confucianism, Han Yu received the official honorary epithet "Master of Letters" upon his death.*

1764: Ferney

DIVISION OF THE SPOILS

Last night I was meditating. I was absorbed in the contemplation of nature, admiring the immensity, the courses, the relations of those infinite globes, which are above the admiration of the vulgar.

I admired still more the intelligence that presides over this vast machinery. I said to myself: A man must be blind not to be impressed by this spectacle; he must be stupid not to recognize its author; he must be mad not to adore him. What tribute of adoration ought I to render him? Should not this tribute be the same throughout the extent of space, since the same Supreme Power reigns equally in all that extent?

Does not a thinking being, inhabiting a star of the Milky Way, owe him the same homage as the thinking being on this little globe where we are? Light is the same to the Dog Star as to us—morality, too, must be the same.

If a feeling and thinking being in the Dog Star is born of a tender father and mother, who have labored for his welfare, he owes them as much love and duty as we here owe to our parents. If anyone in the Milky Way sees one who is lame and indigent and does not relieve him, though able to do it, he is guilty in the sight of every globe.

The heart has everywhere the same duties; on the steps of the throne of God—if he has a throne—and at the bottom of the great abyss, if there be an abyss.

I was wrapped in these reflections, when one of those genii who fill the spaces between worlds came down to me to inform me that the judgments of God are different from ours, and how much a good action is preferable to controversy.

He transported me into a desert covered all over with bones piled one upon another, and between these heaps of dead there were avenues of evergreen trees, and at the end of each avenue, a tall man of august aspect gazing with compassion on these sad remains.

"Alas, my archangel," I said, "where have you brought me?"

"To desolation," he answered.

"And who are those fine old patriarchs whom I see motionless and melancholy at the end of those green avenues, and who seem to weep over this immense multitude of dead?"

"Poor human creature! You will know," replied the genius, "but first you must weep."

He began with the first heap. "These," he said, "are the 23,000 Jews who danced before a calf, together with the 24,000 who were slain

The state dictates and coerces; religion teaches and persuades. The state enacts laws; religion gives commandments. The state is armed with physical force and makes use of it if need be; the force of religion is love and benevolence. The former renounces the undutiful and thrusts him out; the latter receives him in its bosom and yet in the last moments of his present life, tries, not quite unavailingly, to instruct, or at least, to console him.

—Moses Mendelssohn, 1783

while ravishing Midianitish women: the number of the slaughtered for similar offenses or mistakes amounts to nearly 300,000.

"At the following avenues are the bones of Christians, butchered by one another on account of metaphysical disputes. They are divided into several piles of four centuries each—it was necessary to separate them, for had they been all together, they would have reached the sky."

"What!" I exclaimed, "Have brethren thus treated their brethren, and have I the misfortune to be one of this brotherhood?"

"Here," said the spirit, "are the twelve million Americans, slain in their own country for not having been baptized."

"Ah! My god! Why were these frightening skeletons not left to whiten in the hemisphere where the bodies were born, and where they were murdered in so many various ways? Why are all these abominable monuments of barbarity and fanaticism assembled here?"

"For thy instruction."

"Since you are willing to instruct me," I said to the genius, "tell me if there are any other people than the Christians and Jews whom zeal and religion, unhappily turned into fanaticism, have prompted to so many horrible cruelties?"

"Yes," he said, "the Muslims have been stained by the same inhuman acts, but rarely—and when their victims have cried out '*amman!*' (mercy!) and have offered them tribute, they have pardoned them. As for other nations, not one of them since the beginning of the world has ever made a purely religious war. Now, follow me!" I followed.

A little beyond these heaps of dead, we found other heaps—these were the bags of gold and silver, and each pile had its label: SUB-STANCE OF THE HERETICS MASSACRED IN THE EIGHTEENTH CENTURY, IN THE SEVENTEENTH, IN THE SIXTEENTH, and so on. GOLD AND SIL-VER OF THE SLAUGHTERED AMERICANS, etc., etc. And all these piles were surmounted by crosses, mitres, croziers, and tiaras, enriched with jewels.

"What, my genius—was it then to possess these riches that these carcasses were accumulated?"

"Yes, my son."

I shed tears, and when I had earned by my grief to be taken to the end of the green avenues, he conducted me there.

"Contemplate," he said, "the heroes of humanity who have been the benefactors of the earth, and who united to banish from the world, as far as they were able, violence and rapine. Question them."

Voltaire, *from* The Philosophical Dictionary. *After the death of Louis XIV, Voltaire became popular in Paris for his witty "society verse," until he insulted the Duc d'Orléans and was imprisoned at the Bastille for almost a year in 1717. Poet, philosopher, and author of* Candide, *Voltaire drew inspiration from Diderot and d'Alembert's* Encyclopedia *for his* Dictionary.

c. 1185: Syria

THE POWER OF PRAYER

I myself have witnessed a case of God's benevolence (may He be exalted) and His good protection. The Franks (may God curse them) encamped against us with their cavalry and infantry, with the Orontes between us. The river was at full spate to such a degree that they could neither cross over to us, nor we to them. So they encamped on the mountain in their tents. A band of them then came down toward the orchards on their side, and letting their horses graze freely on the green fodder, they went to sleep. Now, a group of youths from the infantry of Shayzar stripped down, flinging off their clothes, picked up their swords and swam over to those men sleeping there. They killed a few of them, but the Franks outnumbered our comrades, so our men threw themselves into the water and crossed back over. Meanwhile, the Frankish army had streamed down from the mountain like a flash flood. On their side stood a mosque known as the Mosque of Abu al-Majd ibn Sumayya, in which lived a man known as Hasan the Ascetic. He was standing on the roof of some rooms in the mosque praying, wearing a black woollen garment. We stood watching him without any way to get over to him.

The Franks had come and were now stopped at the door to the mosque. They climbed up toward him while we thought to ourselves, "There is no power or strength save in God! They're going to kill him now!"

But he, by God, never interrupted his prayers and remained in his place. The Franks turned around and went down, mounted their horses, and rode away, while Hasan remained standing where he was, praying. There is no doubt in my mind that God (glory be to Him) blinded them to him and concealed him from their gaze. Glory be to the Almighty, the Merciful!

Usama ibn Munqidh, *from* The Book of Contemplation. *Born the same year that Pope Urban II inaugurated the First Crusade at the Council of Clermont, Usama became one of the primary Muslim chroniclers of the clash of civilizations. In old age the historian, diplomat, and warrior gave council to Sultan Saladin and wrote this largely autobiographical narrative, as well as his guide to proper conduct,* Kernel of Refinement.

c. 1850 bc: Moriah

BURNT OFFERING

God tested Abraham. He said to him, "Abraham!" And he said, "Here I am." He said, "Take your son, your only son Isaac, whom you love, and go to the land of Moriah and offer him there as a burnt offering on one of the mountains that I shall show you."

So Abraham rose early in the morning, saddled his donkey, and took two of his young men with him and his son Isaac. He cut the wood for the burnt offering and set out and went to the place in the distance that God had shown him. On the third day, Abraham looked up and saw the place far away. Then Abraham said to his young men, "Stay here with the donkey; the boy and I will go over there; we will worship, and then we will come back to you." Abraham took the wood of the burnt offering and laid it on his son Isaac, and he himself carried the fire and the knife. So the two of them walked on together. Isaac said to his father Abraham, "Father!" And he said, "Here I am, my son." He said, "The fire and the wood are here, but where is the lamb for a burnt offering?" Abraham said, "God himself will provide the lamb for a burnt offering, my son." So the two of them walked on together.

When they came to the place that God had shown him, Abraham built an altar there and laid the wood in order. He bound his son Isaac and laid him on the altar on top of the wood. Then Abraham reached out his hand and took the knife to kill his son. But the angel of the Lord called to him from heaven, and said, "Abraham, Abraham!" And he said, "Here I am." He said, "Do not lay your hand on the boy or do anything to him, for now I know that you fear God, since you have not withheld your son, your only son from me." And Abraham looked up and saw a ram caught in a thicket by its horns. Abraham went and took the ram and offered it up as a burnt offering instead of his son. So Abraham called that place "The Lord will provide," as it is said to this day, "On the mount of the Lord it shall be provided."

The angel of the Lord called to Abraham a second time from heaven and said, "By myself I have sworn, says the Lord: because you have done this, and have not withheld your son, your only son, I will indeed bless you, and I will make your offspring as numerous as the stars of heaven and as the sand that is on the seashore. And your offspring shall possess the gate of their enemies, and by your offspring shall all the nations of the earth gain blessing for themselves, because you have obeyed my voice."

> *From the Book of Genesis. Josephus believed that Isaac was twenty-five years old at the time of his binding, the Talmudic sages believed he was thirty-seven, and Muslims believe that it was not Isaac but his older brother Ishmael. Søren Kierkegaard in* Fear and Trembling *wrote that Abraham was an example of a "knight of faith," who demonstrated absolute faith in the absolute.*

Thumbs Up, Thumbs Down

Films Condemned by the
U.S. Conference of Catholic Bishops

Some Like It Hot, 1959
From Russia with Love, 1963
The Good, the Bad, and the Ugly, 1966
A Clockwork Orange, 1971
Rocky Horror Picture Show, 1975
Grease, 1978
Thelma and Louise, 1991
The *Harold and Kumar* movies, 2004 / 2008
Year One, 2009

Films from the
Vatican's Top 45

Nosferatu, 1922
Wizard of Oz, 1939
It's a Wonderful Life, 1946
The Bicycle Thief, 1948
On the Waterfront, 1954
8 ½, 1963
2001: A Space Odyssey, 1968
Chariots of Fire, 1981
Gandhi, 1982
Schindler's List, 1993

c. 1922: Nunavut

INTO THE WILD

When I was to be a shaman, I chose suffering through the two things that are most dangerous to us humans: suffering through hunger and suffering through cold. First I hungered five days and was then allowed to drink a mouthful of warm water; the old ones say that only if the water is warm will the gods Pinga and Hila notice the novice and help him. Thereafter I went hungry another fifteen days and again was given a mouthful of warm water. After that I hungered for ten days and then could begin to eat, though it only had to be the sort of food on which there is never any taboo, preferably fleshy meat—and never intestines, head, heart, or other entrails, nor meat that had been touched by wolf or wolverine while it lay in a cache. I was to keep to this diet for five moons and then the next five moons might eat everything, but after that I was again forced to eat the meat diet that is prescribed for all those who must do penance in order to become clean.

My instructor was my wife's father, Perqánâq. When I was to be exhibited to Pinga and Hila, he dragged me on a little sledge that was no bigger than I could just sit on it; he dragged me far over on the other side of Hikoligjuaq. It was a very long day's journey inland to a place we call Kingârjuit. It was in winter time and took place at night with the new moon; one could just see the very first streak of the moon; it had just appeared in the sky. I was not fetched again until the next moon was of the same size. Perqánâq built a small snow hut at the place where I was to be, this snow hut being no bigger than that I could just get under cover and sit down. I was given no sleeping skin to protect me against the cold, only a little piece of caribou skin to sit upon. There I was shut in … The entrance was closed with a block, but no soft snow was thrown over the hut to make it warm. When I had sat there five days, Perqánâq came with tepid water, wrapped in a watertight caribou-skin bag.

Not until fifteen days afterward did he come again and hand me the same, just giving himself time to hand it to me, and then he was gone again, for even the old shaman must not interrupt my solitude. The snow hut in which I sat was built far from the trails of men, and when Perqánâq had found the spot where he thought it ought to be built, he stopped the little sledge at a distance, and there I had to remain seated until the snow hut was ready. Not even I, who was after all the one to have to stay there, might set my footprints in the vicinity of the hut, and old Perqánâq had to carry me from the sledge over to the hut so that I could crawl in. As soon as I had become alone, Perqánâq enjoined me to think of one single thing all the time I was to be there, to want only one single thing, and that was to draw Pinga's attention to the fact that there I sat and wished to be a shaman … Pinga should own me. My novitiate took place in the middle of the coldest winter, and I—who never got anything to warm me—was very cold, and it was so tiring having to sit without daring to lie down, that sometimes it was as if I died a little. Only toward the end of the thirty days did a helping spirit come to me, a lovely and beautiful helping spirit, whom I had never thought of—it was a white woman. She came to me while I had collapsed, exhausted, and was sleeping. But still I saw her lifelike, hovering over me, and from that day I could not close my eyes or dream without seeing her. There is this remarkable thing about my helping spirit—that I have never seen her while awake, but only in dreams. She came to me from Pinga and was a sign that Pinga had now noticed me and would give me powers that would make me a shaman.

> Igjugârjuk, *from a narritive recorded by Knud Rasmussen in* Intellectual Culture of the Caribou Eskimos. *After his month-long initiation rite ended, Igjugârjuk reported, "I was now so completely emaciated that the veins on my hands and body and feet had quite disappeared." Back in his village, he was required to be celibate for a year. The Danish anthropologist Rasmussen published the shaman's oral history, and other fellow Inuits', in 1930.*

1916: Dublin

CONTRITION

—A holy saint was once vouchsafed a vision of hell. It seemed to him that he stood in the midst of a great hall, dark and silent save for the ticking of a great clock. The ticking went on unceasingly; and it seemed to this saint that the sound of the ticking was the ceaseless repetition of the words: ever, never; ever, never. Ever to be in hell, never to be in heaven; ever to be shut off from the presence of God, never to enjoy the beatific vision; ever to be eaten with flames, gnawed by vermin, goaded with burning spikes, never to be free from those pains; ever to have the conscience upbraid one, the memory enrage, the mind filled with darkness and despair, never to escape; ever to curse and revile the foul demons who gloat fiendishly over the misery of their dupes, never to behold the shining raiment of the blessed spirits; ever to cry out of the abyss of fire to God for an instant, a single instant, of respite from such awful agony, never to receive, even for an instant, God's pardon; ever to suffer, never to enjoy; ever to be damned, never to be saved; ever, never; ever, never. Oh, what a dreadful punishment! An eternity of endless agony, of endless bodily and spiritual torment, without one ray of hope, without one moment of cessation, of agony limitless in intensity, of torment infinitely varied, of torture that sustains eternally that which it eternally devours, of anguish that everlastingly preys upon the spirit while it racks the flesh, an eternity, every instant of which is itself an eternity of woe. Such is the terrible punishment decreed for those who die in mortal sin by an almighty and a just God.

—Yes, a just God! Men, reasoning always as men, are astonished that God should mete out an everlasting and infinite punishment in

Ritual of the María Lionza cult, Venezuela, 2006. Photograph by Cristina García Rodero.

the fires of hell for a single grievous sin. They reason thus because, blinded by the gross illusion of the flesh and the darkness of human understanding, they are unable to comprehend the hideous malice of mortal sin. They reason thus because they are unable to comprehend that even venial sin is of such a foul and hideous nature that even if the omnipotent Creator could end all the evil and misery in the world—the wars, the diseases, the robberies, the crimes, the deaths, the murders, on condition that he allowed a single venial sin to pass

In the presence of His Glory,
closely watch your heart
so your thoughts won't shame you.
For He sees guilt, opinion, and desire
as plainly as a hair in pure milk.
                              —Rumi, c. 1250

unpunished, a single venial sin, a lie, an angry look, a moment of willful sloth, He, the great omnipotent God could not do so because sin, be it in thought or deed, is a transgression of His law and God would not be God if He did not punish the transgressor.

—A sin, an instant of rebellious pride of the intellect, made Lucifer and a third part of the cohorts of angels fall from their glory. A sin, an instant of folly and weakness, drove Adam and Eve out of Eden and brought death and suffering into the world. To retrieve the consequences of that sin the Only Begotten Son of God came down to earth, lived and suffered and died a most painful death, hanging for three hours on the cross.

—O, my dear little brethren in Christ Jesus, will we then offend that good Redeemer and provoke His anger? Will we trample again upon that torn and mangled corpse? Will we spit upon that face so full of sorrow and love? Will we, too, like the cruel Jews and the brutal soldiers, mock that gentle and compassionate Savior who trod alone for our sake the awful winepress of sorrow? Every word of sin is a wound in His tender side. Every sinful act

is a thorn piercing His head. Every impure thought, deliberately yielded to, is a keen lance transfixing that sacred and loving heart. No, no. It is impossible for any human being to do that which offends so deeply the divine Majesty, that which is punished by an eternity of agony, that which crucifies again the Son of God and makes a mockery of Him.

—I pray to God that my poor words may have availed today to confirm in holiness those who are in a state of grace, to strengthen the wavering, to lead back to the state of grace the poor soul that has strayed if any such be among you. I pray to God, and do you pray with me, that we may repent of our sins. I will ask you now, all of you, to repeat after me the act of contrition, kneeling here in this humble chapel in the presence of God. He is there in the tabernacle burning with love for mankind, ready to comfort the afflicted. Be not afraid. No matter how many or how foul the sins, if only you repent of them they will be forgiven you. Let no worldly shame hold you back. God is still the merciful Lord who wishes not the eternal death of the sinner but rather that he be converted and live.

—He calls you to Him. You are His. He made you out of nothing. He loved you as only a God can love. His arms are open to receive you even though you have sinned against Him. Come to Him, poor sinner, poor vain and erring sinner. Now is the acceptable time. Now is the hour.

The priest rose and turning toward the altar knelt upon the step before the tabernacle in the fallen gloom. He waited till all in the chapel had knelt and every least noise was still. Then, raising his head, he repeated the act of contrition, phrase by phrase, with fervor. The boys answered him phrase by phrase.

James Joyce, *from* A Portrait of the Artist as a Young Man. *In 1904 Joyce halted work on a lengthy novel,* Stephen Hero, *to write the stories later collected in* Dubliners—*three of which appeared under the pseudonym "Stephen Dedalus." He later adapted his semi-autobiographical novel into* A Portrait of the Artist, *casting Stephen Dedalus as its protagonist. Joyce published* Ulysses *in 1922 and* Finnegans Wake *in 1939.*

RESURRECTION

Since I am coming to that holy room,
    Where, with thy choir of saints for evermore,
I shall be made thy music; as I come
    I tune the instrument here at the door,
    And what I must do then, think here before.

Whilst my physicians by their love are grown
    Cosmographers, and I their map, who lie
Flat on this bed, that by them may be shown
    That this is my south-west discovery,
    Per fretum febris, by these straits to die,

I joy, that in these straits I see my west;
    For, though their currents yield return to none,
What shall my west hurt me? As west and east
    In all flat maps (and I am one) are one,
    So death doth touch the resurrection.

Is the Pacific Sea my home? Or are
    The eastern riches? Is Jerusalem?
Anyan, and Magellan, and Gibraltar,
    All straits, and none but straits, are ways to them,
    Whether where Japhet dwelt, or Ham, or Shem.

We think that paradise and Calvary,
    Christ's cross, and Adam's tree, stood in one place;
Look, Lord, and find both Adams met in me;
    As the first Adam's sweat surrounds my face,
    May the last Adam's blood my soul embrace.

So, in his purple wrapp'd, receive me, Lord;
    By these his thorns, give me his other crown;
And as to others' souls I preach'd thy word,
    Be this my text, my sermon to mine own:
"Therefore that he may raise, the Lord throws down."

> **John Donne**, *"Hymn to God, My God, in My Sickness."*
> *As a young man in the 1590s, Donne read law, studied*
> *theology, hunted for Spanish treasure with Sir Walter*
> *Raleigh, and wrote love lyrics. His scandalous marriage in*
> *1602 dashed his hopes for a life in public service and left him*
> *in poverty for a decade. The metaphysical poet was ordained*
> *an Anglican priest in 1615, later becoming a favorite*
> *preacher of kings James I and Charles I.*

Burning Desire from *Esoteric Cosmos*, by Mariko Mori, c. 1996–98.

1982: Utah

JON KRAKAUER AMONG MORMONS

After Dan Lafferty read *The Peace Maker* and resolved to start living the principle of plural marriage, he announced to his wife Matilda that he intended to wed her oldest daughter—his stepdaughter. At the last minute, however, he abandoned that plan and instead married a Romanian immigrant named Ann Randak, who took care of some of Robert Redford's horses on a ranch up Spanish Fork Canyon in the mountains east of the Dream Mine. Ann and Dan had met when he'd borrowed a horse from her to ride in a local parade. She wasn't LDS [Church of Later Day Saints], says Dan, "but she was open to new experiences. Becoming my plural wife was her idea." Ann, he adds, "was a lovely girl. I called her my gypsy bride."

Living according to the strictures laid down in *The Peace Maker* felt good to Dan—it felt *right*, as though this really was the way God intended men and women to live. Inspired, Dan sought out other texts about Mormonism as it was practiced in the early years of the church.

It didn't take him long to discover that polygamy wasn't the only divine principle the modern LDS Church had abandoned in its eagerness to be accepted by American society. Dan learned

that in the nineteenth century, both Joseph Smith and Brigham Young had preached about the righteousness of a sacred doctrine known as "blood atonement"—certain grievous acts committed against Mormons, as Brigham explained it, could be rectified only if the "sinners have their blood spilt upon the ground." And Dan learned that Joseph had taught that the laws of God take precedence over the laws of men.

Legal theory was a subject of particular interest to Dan. His curiosity had first been aroused when he was training to be a chiropractor in California, following a run-in he had with state and county authorities. At the time, he supported his family primarily by running a small sandwich business out of their home. Dan, Matilda, and the oldest kids would get out of bed before dawn every morning in order to make and wrap stacks of "all-natural" vegetarian sandwiches, which Dan would then sell to other chiropractic students during the lunch hour.

"It was a very profitable little hustle," Dan says proudly. "Or it was until the Board of Health closed me down for not following regulations. They claimed I needed a license and that I wasn't paying the required taxes." Just before he was put out of business, Matilda had given birth to a baby boy. Money was tight. Losing their main source of income was problematic. It also proved to be a pivotal event in Dan's passage to fundamentalism.

"After they shut me down," Dan recalls, "I didn't know quite what to do … It didn't seem right to me that the government would penalize me just for being ambitious and trying to support my family—that they would actually force me to go on welfare instead of simply letting me run my little business. It seemed so stupid—the worst kind of government intrusion. In the *Book of Mormon*, Moroni talks about how all of us have an obligation to make sure we have a good and just government, and when I read that, it really got me going. It made me realize that I needed to start getting involved in political issues. And I saw that when it comes right down to it, you can't really separate political issues from religious issues. They're all tied up together."

Upon completing his chiropractic training and returning to Utah, Dan went to work as a chiropractor for his father. The Lafferty parents had sold their farm and bought a house in the old part of downtown Provo; Dan's father ran his practice out of a basement office in this home. In 1981, shortly after Dan started working for Watson Sr., the LDS Church sent both of the elder Laffertys abroad on a two-year mission, at which point Dan and his younger brother Mark (who had graduated from the Los Angeles College of Chiropractic six months after Dan), agreed to take over the practice in their father's absence.

When Dan and Mark started working together in their father's office, the special closeness they had shared in their youth was rekindled. During breaks between patients they engaged in heartfelt discussions about everything that was most important to them—and increasingly what seemed most important concerned religious doctrine and its power to remedy the insidious evils inflicted by the government on its citizens.

Regarding the timing of these heart-to-heart talks, Dan reports, "I began to observe a fascinating phenomenon." Dan and Mark were usually so busy seeing patients that often several days would pass between their religious-political discourses. But on those days when they would

unexpectedly have gaps in the schedule in which to talk at length, says Dan, "rather mysteriously, my younger brothers would show up, unannounced. And we would have some very, very valuable time discussing issues."

Dan usually led the discussions, which inevitably described how the government had far exceeded its constitutionally mandated reach and was dangerously out of control. Buttressing his arguments by quoting scripture from the *Book of Mormon*, he patiently explained to

So long as one believes in God, one has the right to do the Good in order to be moral.
—Jean-Paul Sartre, c. 1950

his brothers that the government had no right to require American citizens to obtain any kind of license, or pay taxes, or submit to the oppressive burden of a Social Security number. "I had come to realize," Dan says, "that a license was simply an agreement with the government to let them have control of your life. And I decided I didn't want them to have control of my life … I already had a basic right to enjoy all of the basic activities of a human being, without their permission."

Although Dan had not yet allied himself with any established fundamentalist church or prophet, his self-directed studies had transformed him into a de facto Mormon fundamentalist—and an exceedingly ardent one. The impetus for most fundamentalist movements—whether Mormon, Catholic, evangelical Christian, Muslim, or Jewish—is a yearning to return to the mythical order and perfection of the original church. Dan Lafferty was moved by this same desire.

The more he studied historical Mormon documents, the more certain Dan became that the LDS Church had blundered off course around 1890, when then-president and prophet Wilford Woodruff was coerced into doing away with the doctrine of plural marriage by the godless government in Washington, DC. The modern LDS Church, Dan had become convinced, was an elaborate fraud.

1904: Heidelberg

WASTE NOT

For the Puritan, waste of time is the first and in principle the deadliest of sins. The span of human life is infinitely short and precious to make sure of one's own election. Loss of time through sociability, idle talk, luxury, even more sleep than is necessary for health—six to at most eight hours—is worthy of absolute moral condemnation. It does not yet hold, with Benjamin Franklin, that time is money, but the proposition is true in a certain spiritual sense. It is infinitely valuable because every hour lost is lost to labor for the glory of God. Thus inactive contemplation is also valueless, or even directly reprehensible if it is at the expense of one's daily work. For it is less pleasing to God than the active performance of His will in a calling. Besides, Sunday is provided for that.

Labor is, on the one hand, an approved ascetic technique, as it always has been in the Western Church, in sharp contrast not only to the East but to almost all monastic rules the world over. It is in particular the specific defense against all those temptations which Puritanism united under the name of the unclean life, whose role for it was by no means small. The sexual asceticism of Puritanism differs only in degree, not in fundamental principle, from that of monasticism; and on account of the Puritan conception of marriage, its practical influence is more far-reaching than that of the latter. For sexual intercourse is permitted, even within marriage, only as the means willed by God for the increase of His glory according to the commandment: "Be fruitful and multiply." Along with a moderate vegetable diet and cold baths, the same prescription is given for all sexual temptations as is used against religious doubts and a sense of moral unworthiness: "Work hard in your calling." But the most important thing was that even beyond that, labor came to be considered in itself the end of life, ordained as such by God. St. Paul's saying, "He who will not work shall not eat" holds unconditionally for everyone. Unwillingness to work is symptomatic of the lack of grace.

Max Weber, *from* The Protestant Work Ethic and the Spirit of Capitalism. *A sociologist and economic theorist who wrote his doctoral dissertation on medieval trading companies, Weber became increasingly interested in the workings of religion late in life, dedicating major works to its role in the societies of China and India.*

Like fundamentalists in other faiths, he was intent on adhering unfailingly to God's "true" commandments, as determined by a rigorously literal interpretation of his church's earliest and most sacred texts. And he was no less intent on adhering to the "true" commandments of his country's earliest and most sacred texts, as well. To Dan, such documents as the *Book of Mormon*, *The Peace Maker*, the United States Constitution, and the Declaration of Independence are all of a piece—they are holy scriptures that provide a direct link to the Almighty. The authority that flows from their divinely inspired sentences is absolute and immutable. And it is the duty of righteous men and women to conduct their lives according to a stringently literal reading of those sentences.

For people like Dan who view existence through the narrow lens of literalism, the language in certain select documents is assumed to possess extraordinary power. Such language is to be taken assiduously at face value, according to a single incontrovertible interpretation that makes no allowance for nuance, ambiguity, or situational contingencies.

After seeking guidance through prayer and receiving confirmation that he was acting in accordance with the Lord's wishes, Dan sent his driver's license back to the state of Utah, revoked his marriage license, and returned his Social Security card. He ignored posted speed limits, which he believed were illegal, and simply drove "wisely and carefully" instead. And he quit paying taxes of any kind—including the sales tax when he shopped in local stores, which provoked frequent confrontations with cashiers.

Energized by the self-evident righteousness of his crusade, in the summer of 1982 Dan declared himself a candidate for sheriff of Utah County and embarked on a lively political campaign, speaking at public forums, writing letters to the Provo newspaper, doing radio interviews, and riding in small-town parades. He promised, if elected, to enforce the laws according to a scrupulously literal interpretation of the U.S. Constitution. As he explained, "My motive in running was to restore the primacy

Dead Christ, by Hans Holbein the Younger, 1521.

of common-law juries and to restore the fundamentals of the Constitution."

On October 4, Dan was driving home after meeting with another candidate for sheriff (the American Fork police chief, with whom Dan had hoped to engage in a public debate), when he was stopped on Interstate 15 by a Utah state trooper for speeding and not having a vehicle-inspection sticker. "I had already had some confrontations with the officer who pulled me over," Dan allows. "He knew I would be driving home from this debate meeting, and he had set a trap for me. They wanted to get a felony against me so I couldn't run for office, and they swarmed me on the freeway. I had just published an important article in the paper—a very important article—which had really unnerved a lot of people, about how the powers of government were being improperly used through improper warrants of arrest—how it was unconstitutional to stop a person on the freeway and arrest them.

"When the officer pulled me over, he told me he had read my article—'I've got it right here in my car,' he said. So I told him, 'Well, if you've read the article, you understand why you can't arrest me right now. If you want to arrest me, go get a warrant from a judge, bring it to my home, and I'll conform to the proper procedures.'" Dan had by now locked the car doors and rolled up all the windows, leaving only a one-inch gap at the top of the driver's window, which, he says, "I figured was narrow enough to keep a hand from reaching in and grabbing me, but would allow me to talk to the officer."

The trooper wasn't amused. He ordered Dan out of the car. "When I refused to get out," says Dan, "the cop did something I hadn't anticipated—he grabbed the top of the window with both hands and pulled hard, pulling the window out of its tracks, and then he tried to reach in and grab me. So I said, 'Well, I gotta go now! See you later!' and took off."

The state troopers gave chase and apprehended Dan a short while later. He was charged with five crimes (including second-degree felony escape, third-degree felony assault by a prisoner, and evading an officer) and locked up in the county jail. At his justice court trial, Dan served as his own attorney and attempted to mount a defense based on several arcane points of constitutional law. The judge repeatedly pointed out, however, that justice courts in Utah are not empowered to hear constitutional matters, which infuriated Dan. He was further angered when the judge overruled his objection to the makeup of the four-woman jury (Dan argued that he was entitled to have at least one male on the jury).

When Dan ignored the judge's instructions and continued to argue his case on constitutional grounds, the exasperated judge declared him in contempt of court—at which point Dan's brothers and several other supporters staged a riot in the courtroom, shouting that they were placing the judge, prosecutor, and court clerk under "citizen's arrest." In the middle of this melee, Dan stood up and loudly admonished the judge, "In the name of Christ, do justice or be struck down!"

From Under the Banner of Heaven. *After his trial, Dan Lafferty was sent to prison for psychiatric evaluation and then jailed. He and his brother Ron were later convicted for the murder of their brother's wife and fifteen-month-old daughter, an act they claimed God had commanded them to do. The author of* Into the Wild *and* Into Thin Air, Krakauer *published* Where Men Win Glory *in 2009.*

c. 166 BC: Judaea

BLOOD ON THE ALTAR

The Seleucid emperor Antiochus came to Jerusalem with his army. Having been admitted within its walls, he treated the inhabitants with great cruelty, sparing not even those who had let him into the city. He dismantled the walls of Jerusalem, burning the finest parts of the city, and stationed a Macedonian garrison in a citadel overlooking the temple. He carried away the golden vessels and treasures of the temple, putting a stop to the sacrifices. He polluted the altar by offering up swine on it, knowing that this was against the Law of Moses. He compelled the Jews to give up their worship of God and to stop circumcising their children. Those who persisted were mutilated, strangled, or crucified, with their children hung from their necks.

At this time there was a Jewish priest named Mattathias who lived in the village of Modin. He had five sons: John who was called Gaddis, Simon called Mathes, Judas called Maccabeus, Eleazar called Auran, and Jonathan called Apphus. Some of the king's men came to Modin to compel the Jews to sacrifice as he had ordered. Because Mattathias was a leader there, they wanted him to be the first to sacrifice, knowing his fellow citizens would follow. Mattathias refused, saying that even if all others obeyed Antiochus' commands, he and his sons never would.

But another Jew sacrificed as Antiochus had commanded. Mattathias and his sons took out broad-bladed knives and cut the man down. After overturning the pagan altar, Mattathias cried out, "Whoever is zealous for the laws of our country and the worship of God, follow me!"

He and his sons then fled to the desert, and many others followed him, and lived there in caves. Marching against them, the Syrians burned them inside their caves on the Sabbath day. Not only did the Jews not resist, they failed even to block the mouths of the caves, and about one thousand suffered. Many, however, escaped with Mattathias, whom they appointed leader. He directed them to fight even on the Sabbath, otherwise the enemy would always choose that day to attack, and they would all be destroyed.

Gathering a large force, Mattathias and his men overturned the pagan altars, killed those who had sacrificed on them, and ordered all their boys circumcised. After he had been in command for a year, however, he became ill. Urging his sons to continue the noble effort he had begun, he told them to choose their brother Simon as paternal adviser and Maccabeus as commander, because of his courage and strength. Then he died and was buried in Modin, greatly mourned by the people.

Judas Maccabeus, with his brothers and followers, drove the enemy from the country. Apollonius, the governor of Samaria, advanced against Judas but was defeated and killed. Next, Seron, governor of Coele-Syria, met the same fate, even though his army greatly outnumbered Judas'.

Lysias, who had been left in charge of Syria while Antiochus was in Persia, now invaded Judaea with an army of sixty thousand infantry and five thousand cavalry and camped at Bethsura. Judas met him with ten thousand, asking God to assist him, and joined battle with the enemy's advance party, killing about five thousand. Alarmed at the desperate spirit of the Jews, Lysias called back his troops and returned to Antioch, where he prepared to invade with an even larger army.

Judas then told his people that after these victories which God had given them, they ought to go up to Jerusalem and purify the temple to offer sacrifices. Rebuilding the altar and restoring the sacred implements, they rekindled the lamp stand and burned incense there, three years to the day since Antiochus defiled the temple. Judas and his men celebrated a great feast which lasted for eight days, and which we continue to observe as the Festival of Lights.

Josephus, *from* A History of the Jewish Wars. *Born into Jerusalem's aristocracy, the historian at the age of sixteen undertook a three-year journey into the wilderness with an ascetic hermit. In 66 he joined a Jewish revolt against Roman rule. Later arrested and led in chains to General Vespasian, Josephus avoided the punishment of death by prophesying that Vespasian would become emperor; three years later, he was.*

Fun, Sun, and Dogma

Summer camps as advertised on their respective websites

The Wilds

Affiliation: Christian
Motto: Whether therefore ye eat, or drink, or whatsoever ye do, do all to the glory of God (1 Corinthians 10:31)
For: Teens who are already growing in their commitment to Christ, and being godly influences in their homes, churches, and schools
Mission: By definition our ministry is: A service organization to the local church, using the out-of-doors to evangelize and edify "all to the glory of God"
Founded: 1969
Locations: North Carolina, New Hampshire
Activities: Biblical guidance and direction, big ball volleyball, God & I Time, waterslides, table tennis, Frisbee golf, lake activities
Cost per week: $250–295
Blurb: "If your desire is to see teens have a passion for God, serve others, and be propelled in their spiritual lives, then this is a must camp for them. The investment in finances is well worth the eternal rewards."
— Jim Ogle, Youth Pastor, Emmanuel Baptist Church, Kings Mountain, NC
www.wilds.org

Camp Quest

Affiliation: Secular Humanist
Motto: It's Beyond Belief!
For: Children of agnostics, atheists, freethinkers, humanists, and others who hold a naturalistic worldview
Mission: Promote among the youth participants a sense of belonging to a large freethought community
Founded: 1996
Locations: California, Florida, Michigan, Minnesota, Ohio, Ontario, Tennessee, United Kingdom
Activities: Astronomy, canoeing, acting out freethought skits, questioning labels about individuals, creating UFO photos, Invisible Unicorn Challenge
Cost per week: $450–575
Blurb: "Camp Quest encourages children to think for themselves, skeptically and rationally. There is no indoctrination, just encouragement to be open-minded, while having fun." — Richard Dawkins, author of *The God Delusion*
www.camp-quest.org

Camp Gilgal

Affiliation: Jews for Jesus
Motto: Providing Jewish children and youth with a Messianic camping experience
For: Children of Jewish believers (even where only one parent is Jewish) to learn about their Messiah and heritage with other children with a similar background
Mission: Though our primary purpose is for the children to grow spiritually and personally, if they haven't had a great time, then we've failed
Founded: 1991
Locations: California, Indiana, Wisconsin, New York
Activities: Horse-back riding, Hebrew, Tabernacle, wall climbing, chill time, swimming
Cost per week: $325
Blurb: "I have always found the ministry of Jews for Jesus and their traveling musicians to be evangelical in their doctrine and appropriately evangelistic in their presentation. They are both creative and biblical in their communication of the gospel." — Mark L. Bailey, Dallas Theological Seminary
www.jewsforjesus.org/join/gilgal

1896: Paris

PROMISED LAND

Anti-Semitism increases day by day and hour by hour among the nations; indeed, it is bound to increase, because the causes of its growth continue to exist and cannot be removed. Its remote cause is our loss of the power of assimilation during the Middle Ages; its immediate cause is our excessive production of mediocre intellects, who cannot find an outlet downward or upward—that is to say, no wholesome outlet in either direction. When we sink, we become a revolutionary proletariat, the subordinate officers of the revolutionary party; when we rise, there rises also our terrible power of the purse.

I do not for a moment wish to imply that I desire assimilation. Our national character is too historically famous, and, in spite of every degradation, too fine to make its annihilation desirable. We might perhaps be able to merge ourselves entirely into surrounding races—if these were to leave us in peace for a space of two generations. But they will not leave us in peace. For a little period they manage to tolerate us, and then their hostility breaks out again and again. The world is provoked by our prosperity, because it has for many centuries been accustomed to consider us as the most contemptible among the poverty stricken. It forgets in its ignorance and narrowness of heart that prosperity weakens our Judaism and extinguishes our peculiarities. It is only pressure that forces us back to the parent stem; it is only hatred encompassing us that makes us strangers once more.

Thus, whether we like it or not, we are now, and shall henceforth remain, a historic group with unmistakable characteristics common to us all.

We are one people—our enemies have made us one in our suffering, as repeatedly happens in history. Distress binds us together, and thus united, we suddenly discover our strength. Yes, we are strong enough to form a state, and a model state. We possess all human and material resources necessary for the purpose.

This is the strictly appropriate place for an account of what has been somewhat rudely termed our human material. But it would not be appreciated till the broad lines of the plan, on which everything depends, had first been marked out.

The whole plan is in its essence perfectly simple, as it must necessarily be if it is to come within the comprehension of all.

Let the sovereignty be granted us over a portion of the globe large enough to satisfy the reasonable requirements of a nation; the rest we shall manage for ourselves.

The creation of a new state is neither ridiculous nor impossible. We have in our day witnessed the process in connection with nations which were not in the bulk of the middle class, but poorer, less educated, and consequently weaker than ourselves. The governments of all countries scourged by anti-Semitism will serve their own interests in assisting us to obtain the sovereignty we want.

We must not imagine the departure of the Jews to be a sudden one. It will be gradual, continuous, and will cover many decades. The poorest will go first to cultivate the soil. In accordance with a preconcerted plan, they will construct roads, bridges, railways, and telegraphs, regulate rivers, and build their own habitations. Their labor will create trade, trade will create markets, and markets will attract new settlers—for every man will go voluntarily, at his own expense and his own risk. The labor expended on the land will enhance its value, and the Jews will soon perceive that a new and permanent sphere of operation is opening here for that spirit of enterprise which has heretofore met only with hatred and obloquy.

Theodor Herzl, *from* The Jewish State. *Herzl in later years attributed his conversion to Zionism to the prevalence of French anti-Semitism during the Dreyfus Affair, which he encountered while serving as the Paris correspondent for a Viennese newspaper. He helped organize the First Zionist Congress in 1897 in Basel, writing in his diary, "At Basel I founded the Jewish state … Perhaps in five years and certainly in fifty, everyone will know it."*

1527: Hindustan

THE GATES OF REPENTANCE

Let us praise the Merciful One, who loves the penitent and who loves the cleansers of themselves, and let thanks be rendered to the Gracious One who absolves His debtors, and forgives those who seek forgiveness. Blessings be on Muhammad, the Lord of creatures, on the Holy family, on the pure Companions—and on the mirrors of the glorious congregation, to wit, the Masters of wisdom who are treasure houses of the pearls of purity and who bear the impress of the sparkling jewels of this purport—that the nature of man is prone to evil, and that the abandonment of sinful appetites is only feasible by divine aid and the help that comes from on high.

All of us, from the Shah to the soldier, in the heyday of our youth, have transgressed and done what we ought not to have done. After some days of sorrow and repentance, we abandoned evil practices one by one, and the gates of retrogression became closed. But the renunciation of wine, the greatest and most indispensable of renunciations, remained under a veil in the chamber of deeds pledged to appear in due season and did not show its countenance until the glorious hour when we had put on the garb of the holy warrior and had encamped with the army of Islam. On this occasion I received a secret inspiration and heard an infallible voice say, "Is not time that the hearts of those who believe should be humbled to the remembrance of God and the truth which be has sent down?" Thereupon we set ourselves to extirpate the things of wickedness, and we earnestly knocked at the gates of repentance. The Guide of Help assisted us according to the saying "Whoever knocks and re-knocks to him the door will be opened."

St. Francis preaching to the birds, from *St. Francis Receiving the Stigmata*, by Giotto di Bondone, c. 1295–1300.

And an order was given that with the jihad there should begin the still greater jihad which has to be waged against sensuality. In short, we declared with sincerity that we would subjugate our passions, and I engraved on the tablet of my heart, "I repent to Thee; I am the first of the believers." And I made public the resolution to abstain from wine, which had been hidden in the treasury of my breast. The victorious servants, in accordance with the illustrious order, dashed upon the earth of contempt and destruction the flagons and the cups, and the other utensils in gold and silver, which in their number and their brilliance were like the stars of the firmament. They dashed them in pieces. They distributed the fragments among the poor and needy. By the blessing of this acceptable repentance, many of the courtiers, by virtue of the saying "Men follow the religion of their kings," embraced abstinence at the same assemblage, and entirely renounced the use of wine. Up till now crowds of our subjects hourly

c. 1880: England

WHO KNOWS WHY?

Glory be to God for dappled things—
For skies of couple-colour as a brinded cow;
For rose-moles all in stipple upon trout that
    swim;
Fresh-firecoal chestnut-falls; finches' wings;
Landscape plotted and pieced—fold, fallow,
    and plough;
And all trades, their gear and tackle and
    trim.

All things counter, original, spare, strange;
Whatever is fickle, freckled (who knows
    how?)
With swift, slow; sweet, sour; adazzle, dim;
He fathers-forth whose beauty is past
    change: Praise him.

Gerard Manley Hopkins, *"Pied Beauty." John Henry Newman received Hopkins into the Roman Catholic Church in 1866, after the young man had read the Cardinal's account of his own conversion. Entering into the Jesuit novitiate two years later, Hopkins burned his youthful verse. His poetic silence lasted seven years, until, prompted by the drowning of five Franciscan nuns, he composed "The Wreck of the Deutschland."*

attain this auspicious happiness. I hope that in accordance with the saying, "He who incites to good deeds has the same reward as he who does them," the benefit of this action will react on the royal fortune and increase it daily by victories.

After carrying out this design, a universal decree was issued that in the imperial dominions—may God protect them from danger and calamity—no one shall partake of strong drink or engage in its manufacture, nor sell it nor buy it or possess it, nor convey it or fetch it.

In thanks for these great victories over self, and as a thanksgiving for God's acceptance of repentance and sorrow, the ocean of the royal munificence became unsettled, and those waves of kindness, which are the cause of the civilization of the world and of the glory of the sons of Adam, were displayed, and throughout all the territories the tax on Muslims was abolished— though its yield was more than the dreams of avarice, and though it had been established and maintained by former rulers—for it is a practice outside of the edicts of the Prince of apostles, Muhammad. So a decree was passed that in no city, town, road, ferry, pass, or port, should the tax be levied or exacted. No alteration whatsoever of this order is permitted. "Then if any man changes it after hearing it, the sin shall rest upon those who change it."

The correct path of Allah for all who shelter under the shade of the royal benevolence, whether they be Turk, Tajik, Arab, Hindustani, or Persian, peasants or soldiers, of every nation or tribe of the sons of Adam, is to strengthen themselves by the tenet of religion, and to be full of hope and prayer for the dynast, which is linked with eternity, and to adhere to these ordinances, and not in any way to transgress them. It behooves all to act according to this decree.

Babur, *from* The Baburnama. *The founder of the Mughal Dynasty was the fifth in male succession from the Turkic conqueror Tamerlane and thirteenth through the female line from Genghis Khan. A noted poet and brilliant military strategist, Babur also loved gardens; he personally selected sites for them around his empire and requested to be buried in his garden in Kabul.*

1978: Tel Aviv

PHILIP ROTH VISITS THE AMERICAN-JEWISH AUSTRALIA

"What the hell *are* you doing in a place like this?" Shuki asked.

"I'm here to see my brother. He's made aliyah."

"You've got a brother who's emigrated to Israel? What is he, a religious nut?"

"No, a successful dentist. Or he was. He's living in a little frontier settlement on the West Bank. He's learning Hebrew there."

"You're making this up. This is another of your hilarious ideas."

"My sister-in-law Carol wishes it were. No, Henry's made it up. Henry appears to have left his wife, his kids, and his mistress to come to Israel to become an authentic Jew."

"Why would he want to be something like that?"

"That's what I'm here to find out."

"Which settlement is it?"

"Not far from Hebron, in the Judaean hills. It's called Agor. His wife says he's found a hero there—a man named Mordecai Lippman."

"Oh, has he?"

"You know Lippman?"

"Nathan, I can't talk about these things. It's too painful for me. I mean this. Your brother is a follower of Lippman's?"

"Carol says that when Henry calls to speak to the kids, Lippman's all he talks about."

"Yes? He's so impressed? Well, when you see Henry, tell him all he has to do is go to the jail and he can meet plenty of little gangsters just as impressive."

"He intends to stay on at Agor after he's finished his Hebrew course, *because* of Lippman."

"Well, that's wonderful. Lippman drives into Hebron with his pistol and tells the Arabs in the market how the Jews and Arabs can live happily side by side as long as the Jews are on top. He's

dying for somebody to throw a Molotov cocktail. Then his thugs can really go to town."

"Carol mentioned Lippman's pistol. Henry told the kids all about it."

"Of course. Henry must find it very romantic," Shuki said. "The American Jews get a big thrill from the guns. They see Jews walking around with guns and they think they're in paradise. Reasonable people with a civilized repugnance for violence and blood, they come on tour from America, and they see the guns and they see the beards, and they take leave

Goddess with an offering,
terracotta drinking cup, Greece, c. 470 BC.

of their senses. The beards to remind them of saintly Yiddish weakness and the guns to reassure them of heroic Hebrew force. Jews ignorant of history, Hebrew, Bible, ignorant of Islam and the Middle East, they see the guns and they see the beards, and out of them flows every sentimental emotion that wish fulfillment can produce. A regular pudding of emotions. The fantasies about this place make me sick. And what *about* the beards? Is your brother as thrilled by the religion as by the explosives? These settlers, you know, are our great believing messianic Jews. The Bible is their *bible*—these idiots take it seriously. I tell you, all the madness of the human race is in the sanctification of that book. Everything going wrong with this country is in the first five books of the Old

Noah's Ark, Senegalese glass painting, c. 1990.

Testament. Smite the enemy, sacrifice your son, the desert is yours and nobody else's all the way to the Euphrates. A body count of dead Philistines on every other page—that's the wisdom of their wonderful Torah. If you're going out there, go tomorrow for the Friday night service and watch them sitting around kissing God's ass, telling him how big and wonderful he is—telling the rest of us how wonderful *they* are, bravely doing his work as courageous pioneers in biblical Judaea. Pioneers! They work all day in government jobs in Jerusalem and drive home to biblical Judaea for dinner at night. Only eating chopped chicken liver at the biblical source, only going to bed on the biblical sites, can a Jew find true Judaism. Well, if they want so much to sleep at the biblical source because that is where Abraham tied his shoelaces, then they can sleep there under Arab rule! Please, don't talk to me

about what these people are up to. It makes me too crazy."

"Tell me more about my brother's hero."

"Lippman? I smell fascism on people like Lippman."

"What's that smell like here?"

"It smells the same here as it does everywhere. The situation gets so complicated that it seems to require a simple solution, and that's where Lippman comes in. His racket is to play upon Jewish insecurity—he says to the Jews, 'I have the solution to our problem of fear.' Of course there's a long history of these people. Mordecai Lippman doesn't come from nowhere. In every Jewish community there was always such a person. What could the rabbi do for their fears? The rabbi looks like you, Nathan—the rabbi is tall, he is thin, he is introverted and ascetic, always over his books, and usually he's also ill. He is not a person who can deal with the goyim. So in every community there is a butcher, a teamster, a porter, he is big, he is healthy—you sleep with one, two, maybe three women, he sleeps with twenty-seven, and all at the same time. *He* deals with the fear. He marches off at night with the other butcher and when he comes back, there are a hundred goyim you don't ever have to worry about again. There was even a name for him: the *shlayger*. The whipper. The only difference between the Old Country *shlayger* and Mordecai Lippman is that on a superficial level Mr. Lippman is very deep. He hasn't only a Jewish gun, he has a Jewish mouth—remnants even of a Jewish brain. There is now so much antagonism between Arab and Jew that even a child would understand that the best thing is to keep them apart—so Mr. Lippman drives into Arab Hebron wearing his pistol. Hebron! This state was not established for Jews to police Nablus and Hebron! This was not the Zionist idea! Look, I have no illusions about Arabs and I have no illusions about Jews. I just don't want to live in a country that's *completely* crazy. It excites you to hear me going on like this—I can see it.

"You envy me—you think, 'Craziness and dangerousness; that sounds like fun!' But believe me, when you have so much of it over so many years that even craziness and dangerousness become tedious and boring, then it's *really* dangerous. People are frightened here for thirty-five years—when will there be another war? The Arabs can lose and lose and lose, and we can lose only once. All that is true. But what is the result? Onto the stage comes Menachem Begin—and the logical step after Begin, a gangster like Mordecai Lippman, who tells them, 'I have the solution to our Jewish problem of fear.' And the worse Lippman is, the better. He's right, they say, that's the kind of world we live in. If the humane approach fails, try brutality."

"And yet my little brother likes him."

"Ask your little brother, then, 'What are the consequences of this delightful man?' The destruction of the country! Who comes to this country now to settle and live? The intellectual Jew? The humane Jew? The beautiful Jew? No,

not the Jew from Buenos Aires, or Rio, or Manhattan. The ones who come from America are either religious or crazy or both. This place has become the American-Jewish Australia. Now who we get is the Oriental Jew and the Russian Jew and the social misfits like your brother, roughnecks in yarmulkes from Brooklyn."

"My brother's from suburban New Jersey. You couldn't possibly describe him as a misfit. The problem that brought him here may have been the opposite: he fit all too well into his comfortable existence."

An irreligious man is not one who denies the gods of the majority, but one who applies to the gods the opinions of the majority. For what most men say about the gods are not ideas derived from sensation, but false opinions, according to which the greatest evils come to the wicked, and the greatest blessings come to the good from the gods. —*Epicurus, c. 250 BC*

"So what did he come for? The pressure? The tensions? The problems? The danger? Then he's really meshuggah. You're the only smart one—you, of all people, are the only normal Jew, living in London with an English Gentile wife and thinking you won't even bother to circumcise your son. You, who say, 'I live in this time, I live in this world, and out of that I form my life.' This, you understand, was supposed to be the place where to become a normal Jew was the *goal*. Instead we have become the Jewish obsessional prison par excellence! Instead it has become the breeding ground for every brand of madness that Jewish genius can devise!"

From The Counterlife. *Roth's first short-story collection,* Goodbye, Columbus, *won him the respect of many literary critics as well as the enmity of various rabbis; both responses recurred ten years later when he published* Portnoy's Complaint. *The Pulitzer Prize-winning author said in 1984 that the Jewish quality of his writing was derived from "the nervousness, the excitability, the arguing, the dramatizing, the indignation, the obsessiveness, the touchiness, the play acting—above all the* talking."

CRISES OF FAITH

c. 1990: **Kars**

ORHAN PAMUK SEES A SNOWFLAKE

Ka made his way along the train track, past the snow-covered silo that loomed overhead like a great white cloud, and was soon inside the station. As he passed through the empty, dirty building, he saw a dog approaching, wagging its curly tail in a friendly way. It was a black dog with a round white patch on its forehead. As he looked across the filthy waiting hall, Ka saw three teenage boys who were beckoning the dog with sesame rolls. One of them was Necip; he broke away from his friends and ran toward Ka.

"On no account are you to let my classmates know how I knew you'd be coming through here," he said. "My best friend Fazil has a very important question to ask you. If you can give him a moment of your time, he'll be very happy."

"All right," said Ka, and he walked over to the bench where the other teenagers were sitting.

One poster on the wall behind them urgently reminded travelers how important the railroads were to Atatürk; another sought to strike fear in the heart of any girl contemplating suicide. The boys rose to their feet to shake Ka's hand, but then shyness overtook them.

"Before Fazil asks his question, Mesut would like to tell you a story he's heard," said Necip.

"No, I can't tell it myself," said Mesut, hardly containing his excitement. "Please—could you tell the story for me?"

While Necip told the story, Ka watched the black dog frolicking about the half-lit station.

"The story takes place in a religious high school in Istanbul, or that's what I heard," Necip began. "A typical slapdash place in a suburb on the edge of the city. The director of this school had an appointment with a city official in one of those new Istanbul skyscrapers we've seen on television. He got into this enormous elevator and began to go up. There was another man in the elevator, a tall man younger than he; this man showed the director the book in his hand, and as some of its pages were still uncut he took out a knife with a mother-of-pearl handle while he recited a few lines. When the elevator stopped on the nineteenth floor, the director got out.

Religion is by no means a proper subject of conversation in mixed company.
—*Philip Dormer Stanhope, 1754*

"During the days that followed, he began to feel very strange. He became obsessed with death, he couldn't find the will to do anything, and he couldn't stop thinking about the man in the elevator. The school director was a devout man, so he went to see some Cerrahi dervishes, hoping to find solace and guidance. He sat there until morning, pouring out all his woes, and after he had done this, the celebrated sheikh made the following diagnosis: 'It seems you've lost your faith in God,' he said. 'What's worse, you don't even know it—and as if that weren't bad enough, you're even proud of not knowing it! You contracted this disease from the man in the elevator. He's turned you into an atheist.' The director rose to his feet in tears to deny what the illustrious sheikh had said, but there was still one part of his heart that was pure and honest, and this part assured him that the sheikh was telling the truth.

"Infected by the disease of atheism, the director began to put unreasonable pressure on his lovely little pupils; he tried to spend time alone with their mothers; he stole money from another teacher whom he envied. And the worst of it was, he felt proud for having committed these sins. He would assemble the whole school to accuse them of blind faith; he told them their traditions made no sense and asked why they couldn't be free as he was; he couldn't utter a sentence without stuffing it with French words; he spent the money he had stolen on the latest European fashions. And wherever he went, he made sure to let people know how much he despised them for being 'backward.'

"Before long, the school had descended into anarchy. One group of pupils raped a beautiful classmate, another group beat up an elderly Qur'an teacher, and the whole place was on the brink of revolt. The director would go home in tears contemplating suicide, but because he lacked the courage to follow through, he kept hoping that someone else would kill him. To make this happen, he—God forbid—cursed His Excellency the Prophet Muhammad in front of one of his most God-fearing pupils. But knowing by now that he had lost his mind, his pupils didn't lay a finger on him. He took to the streets to proclaim—God forbid—that God did not exist, that mosques should be turned into discotheques, and that we'd only become as rich as people in the West if we all converted to Christianity. But now that the young Islamists wanted to kill him, he lost his resolve and hid from them.

"Hopeless and unable to find any way to satisfy his death wish, the director returned to the same fateful skyscraper in Istanbul and, stepping into the same elevator car, found himself face-to-face once again with the tall man who had first exposed him to atheism. The man smiled in a way to indicate that he knew the director's whole story, and then he presented the book as he had the time before—the cure for atheism was to be found in it too. As the director stretched out a trembling hand, the man took out the knife with the mother-of-pearl handle, as if preparing to cut the pages of the book, but with the elevator still moving, he plunged it into the director's heart."

When Necip finished the story, Ka realized that he'd heard it before, from Islamist Turks in Germany. In Necip's version, the mysterious book at the end of the story remained unnamed, but Mesut now named one or two Jewish writ-

Witches' Sabbath (Aquelarre), by Francisco de Goya y Lucientes, c. 1820–23.

ers known to be agents of atheism, as well as a number of columnists who had led the media campaign against political Islam—one of these would be assassinated three years later.

"The director is not alone in his anguish—there are many atheists in our midst. They've been seduced by the devil and now roam among us, desperate for peace and happiness," said Mesut. "Do you share this view?"

"I don't know."

"What do you mean, you don't know?" Mesut asked, with some annoyance. "Aren't you an atheist too?"

"I don't know," said Ka.

"Then tell me this: do you or don't you believe that God Almighty created the universe and everything in it, even the snow that is swirling down from the sky?"

"The snow reminds me of God," said Ka.

"Yes, but do you believe that God created snow?" Mesut insisted.

There was a silence. Ka watched the black dog run through the door to the platform to frolic in the snow under the dim halo of neon light.

"You're not giving me an answer," said Mesut. "If a person knows and loves God, he never doubts God's existence. It seems to me that you're not giving me an answer because you're too timid to admit that you're an atheist. But we knew this already. That's why I wanted to ask you a question on my friend Fazil's behalf. Do you suffer the same terrible pangs as the poor atheist in the story? Do you want to kill yourself?"

"No matter how unhappy I was, I'd still find suicide terrifying," said Ka.

"But why?" asked Fazil. "Is it because it's against the law? But when the state talks about the sanctity of human life, they get it all wrong. Why are you afraid of committing suicide? Explain this."

"Please don't take offense at my friend's insistence," said Necip. "Fazil's asking you this question for a reason—a very special reason."

"What I wanted to ask," said Fazil, "is this: aren't you so troubled and unhappy that you want to commit suicide?"

"No," said Ka. He was beginning to get annoyed.

"Please, don't try to hide anything from us," said Mesut. "We won't do anything bad to you just because you're an atheist."

There was a tense silence. Ka rose to his feet. He had no desire to let them see how he felt. He started walking.

"Where are you going? Please don't go," said Fazil. Ka stopped in his tracks but said nothing.

"Maybe I should speak instead," said Necip. "The three of us are in love with girls who have put everything at risk for the sake of their faith. The secular press calls them "covered girls." For us they are simply Muslim girls, and what they do to defend their faith is what all Muslim girls must do."

"And men too," said Fazil.

"Of course," said Necip. "I'm in love with Hicran. Mesut is in love with Hande. Fazil was in love with Teslime, but now she's dead.

Or she committed suicide. But we can't bring ourselves to believe that a Muslim girl ready to sacrifice everything for her faith would be capable of suicide."

"Perhaps she could no longer bear her suffering," Ka suggested. "After all, she'd been thrown out of school, and her family was putting pressure on her to take off her headscarf."

"No amount of suffering can justify a believer's committing this sin," Necip said excitedly. "If we even forget or miss our morning prayers, we're so worried about our sinful state

Eve and the Apple, by Giuseppe Arcimboldo, 1578.

that we can hardly sleep at night. The more it happens, the earlier we run back to the mosque. When someone's faith is this strong, he'll do anything to keep from committing such a sin—even submit to a life of torture."

"We know that you went to see Teslime's family," Fazil said. "Do they think she committed suicide?"

"They do. She watched *Marianna* on TV with her parents, washed herself, and said her prayers."

"Teslime never watched soap operas," Fazil said, in a soft voice.

"How well did you know her?" Ka asked.

"I didn't know her personally; we never actually spoke," said Fazil, with some embarrassment. "I saw her once from far away, and she was pretty well covered. But as a soulmate, of course I knew her very well—when you love someone above all others, you know everything there is to know about her. The Teslime I knew would never have committed suicide."

"Maybe you didn't know her well enough."

"And maybe the westerners sent you here to cover up Teslime's murder," said Mesut with a swagger.

"No, no, we trust you," said Necip. "Our leaders say you're a recluse, a poet. It's because we trust you that we wanted to talk to you about something that's making us very unhappy. Fazil would like to apologize for what Mesut has just said."

"I apologize," said Fazil. His face was beet red. Tears were forming in his eyes.

Mesut remained silent as peace was restored.

"Fazil and I are blood brothers," said Necip. "Most of the time we think the same things; we can read each other's thoughts. Unlike me, Fazil has no interest in politics. Now we'd like to know if you could do us both a favor. The thing is, we can both accept that Teslime might have been driven to the sin of suicide by the pressures from her parents and the state. It's very painful; Fazil can't stop thinking that the girl he loved committed the sin of suicide. But if Teslime was a secret atheist like the one in the story, if she was one of those unlucky souls who don't even know they are atheists, or if she committed suicide because she was an atheist, for Fazil this is a catastrophe—it means he was in love with an atheist.

"You're the only one who can answer this terrible suspicion that's plaguing us. You're the only one who can offer Fazil comfort. Do you understand what we're thinking?"

"Are you an atheist?" asked Fazil, with imploring eyes. "And if you are an atheist, do you want to kill yourself?"

"Even on days when I am most certain that I'm an atheist, I feel no urge to commit suicide," said Ka.

"Thank you for giving us a straight answer to our question," said Fazil. He looked calmer now. "Your heart is full of goodness, but you're afraid of believing in God."

Seeing that Mesut was still glaring at him, Ka was eager to put some distance between them. His mind was already far, far away. He felt a desire stirring inside him and a dream connected to that desire, but at the same time he was unable to give himself over to this dream on account of the activity around him. Later, when he could think carefully, he would understand that this dream rose from his yearning for Ipek as well as from his fear of dying and his failure to believe in God. And at the last moment, Mesut added something else.

"Please don't misunderstand us," said Necip. "We have no objection to someone's becoming an atheist. There's always room for atheists in Muslim societies."

"Except that the cemeteries have to be kept separate," said Mesut. "It would bring disquiet to the souls of believers to lie in the same cemeteries as the godless. When people go through life concealing their lack of faith, they bring turbulence not only to the land of the living but also to cemeteries. It's not just the torment of having to lie beside the godless till Judgment Day; the worst horror would be to rise up on Judgment Day only to find oneself face-to-face with a luckless atheist … Mr. Poet, Ka Bey, you've made no secret of the fact that you were once an atheist. Maybe you still are one. So tell us, who makes the snow fall from the sky? What is the snow's secret?"

For a moment they all looked outside to watch the snow falling onto the empty tracks.

God gave man an upright countenance to survey the heavens, and to look upward to the stars.
—Ovid, c. 8

What am I doing in this world? Ka asked himself. How miserable these snowflakes look from this perspective, how miserable my life is. A man lives his life, then he falls apart, and soon there is nothing left. Ka felt as if half his soul had just abandoned him but still the other half remained; he still had love in him. Like a snowflake, he would fall as he was meant to fall; he would devote himself heart and soul to the melancholy course on which his life was set. His father had a certain smell after shaving, and now this smell came back to him. He thought of his mother making breakfast, her feet aching inside her slippers on the cold kitchen floor; he had a vision of a hairbrush; he remembered his mother giving him sugary pink syrup when he woke up coughing in the night, he felt the spoon in his mouth, and as he gave his mind over to all the other little things that make up a life and realized how they all added up to a unified whole, he saw a snowflake …

From Snow. *Pamuk received a degree in journalism from the University of Istanbul in 1977. He first won international acclaim for his third novel,* The White Castle, *published in 1985. After making statements about his country's massacre of Armenians and Kurds, the novelist was put on trial in 2005 for "denigrating Turkishness." The following year he was awarded the Nobel Prize for Literature.*

1879: Yasnaya Polyana

SEARCHING FOR GOD

This is what happened to me: in the course of a whole year, when almost every minute I was asking myself whether I should end it all with a rope or a bullet, my heart was tormented with an agonizing feeling. This feeling I can only describe as a search for God.

This search for God was born not of reason but of an emotion, because it was a search that arose not from my thought process—indeed, it was in direct opposition to my thinking—but from my heart. It was a feeling of dread, of loneliness, of forlornness in the midst of all that was alien to me—and it was a feeling of hope for someone's help.

The nature of God is a circle, of which the center is everywhere and the circumference is nowhere. —Empedocles, c. 450 BC

In spite of the fact that I was convinced of the impossibility of proving the existence of God (Kant had shown me, and I had fully understood him, that there can be no such proof), I nonetheless searched for God in the hope that I might find him, and according to an old habit of prayer, I addressed the one for whom I searched and could not find. In my mind I would go over the conclusions of Kant and Schopenhauer regarding the impossibility of proving the existence of God, and I would try to refute them. Causation, I would say to myself, is not in the same category of thought as space and time. If I exist, then there is something that causes me to exist, the cause of all causes. And this cause of all that exists is called God, and I dwelled on this thought and tried with all my being to recognize the presence of this cause. As soon as I was conscious of the existence of such a power over me, I felt the possibility of life. But I asked myself, "What is this cause, this power? How am I to think about it? What is my relation to this thing I call God?" And

only the answer that was familiar to me came into my head: "He is the creator, the provider of all things." I was not satisfied with this answer, and I felt that the thing I needed in order to live was still missing. I was overcome with horror, and I began to pray to the one whom I sought, that he might help me. And the more I prayed, the more clear it became to me that he did not hear me and that there was absolutely no one I could turn to. My heart full of despair over the fact that there is no God, I cried, "Lord, have mercy on me, save me! O Lord my God, show me the way!" But no one had mercy on me, and I felt that my life had come to a stop.

But again and again and from various directions I kept coming back to the conviction that I could not have come into the world without any motive, cause, or meaning, that I could not be the fledgling fallen from a nest that I felt myself to be. If I lie on my back in the tall grass and cry out like a fallen fledgling, it is because my mother brought me into the world, kept me warm, fed me, and loved me. But where is my mother now? If I have been cast out, then who has cast me out? I cannot help but feel that someone who loved me gave birth to me. Who is this someone? Again, God.

"He sees and knows of my search, my despair, my struggle," I would say to myself. "He exists." And as soon as I acknowledged this for an instant, life immediately rose up within me, and I could sense the possibility and even the joy of being. But again I would shift from the acknowledgment of the existence of God to a consideration of my relation to him, and again there arose before me the God who is our creator, the God of the Trinity, who sent his son, our redeemer. And again, isolated from me and from the world, God would melt away before my eyes like a piece of ice; again nothing remained, again the source of life withered away. I was overcome with despair and felt that there was nothing for me to do but kill myself. And worst of all, I felt that I could not bring myself to go through with it.

I slipped into these situations not two or three times but tens and hundreds of times—

now joy and vitality, now despair and a consciousness of the impossibility of life.

I remember one day in early spring when I was alone in the forest listening to the sounds of the woods. I listened and thought about the one thing that had constantly occupied me for the last three years. Again I was searching for God.

"Very well," I said to myself. "So there is no God like the one I have imagined—the only reality is my life. There is no such God. And nothing, no miracle of any kind, can prove there is, because miracles exist only in my irrational imagination."

"But where does my notion of God, of the one whom I seek, come from?" I asked myself. And again with this thought there arose in me joyous waves of life. Everything around me came to life, full of meaning. But my joy did not last long. My mind continued its work. "The concept of God," I told myself, "is not God. A concept is something that occurs within me; the concept of God is something I can conjure up inside myself at will. This is not what I seek. I am seeking that without which there could be no life." Once again everything within me and around me began to die—again I felt the longing to kill myself.

But at that point I took a closer look at myself and at what had been happening within me, and I remembered the hundreds of times I had gone through these deaths and revivals. I remembered that I had lived only when I believed in God. Then as now, I said to myself, "As long as I know God, I live; when I forget, when I do not believe in him, I die." What are these deaths and revivals? It is clear that I do not live whenever I lose my faith in the existence of God, and I would have killed myself long ago if I did not have some vague hope of finding God. I truly live only whenever I am conscious of him and seek him. "What, then, do I seek?" a voice cried out within me. "He is there, the one without whom there could be no life." To know God and to live come to one and the same thing. God is life.

Leo Tolstoy, *from* Confession. *Tolstoy's spiritual crisis led him to develop his own version of Christianity, writing a gospel and rejecting the Trinity. He inspired numerous followers and was excommunicated from the Russian Orthodox Church in 1901. After years of marital discord, the author of* War and Peace *ran away from his home in 1910, dying in a small-town train station at the age of eighty-two.*

Worshippers at a mosque, Jakarta, Indonesia, 1993. Photograph by Bruno Barbey.

c. 110: Bithynia

GOVERNMENT POLICY

To Trajan,

It is with me, sir, an established custom to refer to you all matters on which I am in doubt. Who indeed is better able either to direct my scruples or to instruct my ignorance?

I have never been present at trials of Christians and consequently do not know for what reasons or how far punishment is usually inflicted or inquiry made in their case. Nor have my hesitations been slight: as to whether any distinction of age should be made, or persons however tender in years should be viewed as differing in no respect from the full-grown; whether pardon should be accorded to repentance, or he who has once been a Christian should gain nothing by having ceased to be one—whether the very profession itself, if unattended by crime, or else the crimes necessarily attaching to the profession, should be made the subject of punishment.

Meanwhile, in the case of those who have been brought before me in the character of Christians, my course has been as follows: I put it to themselves whether they were or were not Christians. To those that professed they were, I put the inquiry a second and a third time, threatening them with the supreme penalty.

Those who persisted, I ordered to execution. For indeed, I could not doubt, whatever might be the nature of that which they professed, that their pertinacity, at any rate, and inflexible obstinacy, ought to be punished. There were others afflicted with like madness, with regard to whom, as they were Roman citizens, I made a memorandum that they were to be sent for judgment to Rome. Soon, the very handling of this matter caused, as often happens, the area of the charge to spread, and many fresh examples occurred. An anonymous paper was put forth containing the names of many persons. Those who denied that they either were or had been Christians, upon their calling on the gods after me and upon their offering wine and incense before your statue, which for this purpose I had ordered to be introduced in company with the images of the gods, moreover upon their reviling Christ—none of which things it is said can such as are really and truly Christians be compelled to do—these I deemed it proper to dismiss. Others named by the informant admitted that they were Christians and then shortly afterward denied it, adding that they had been Christians, but had ceased to be so, some three years, some many years, more than one of them as much as twenty years, before. All these, too, not only honored your image and the effigies of the gods, but also reviled Christ. They affirmed, however, that this had been the sum, whether

1773: Boston

ABOARD THE ANGELIC TRAIN

'Twas mercy brought me from my pagan land,
Taught my benighted soul to understand
That there's a God—that there's a savior too:
Once I redemption neither sought nor knew.
Some view our sable race with scornful eye—
"Their color is a diabolic dye."
Remember, Christians, Negroes black as Cain
May be refined, and join the angelic train.

Phillis Wheatley, *"On Being Brought from Africa to America." Wheatley was kidnapped by slave traders in 1761 and taken by ship to Boston, where she was bought by a tailor. After mastering English, she learned Greek and Latin, translating a tale by Ovid, a feat which shocked the local scholars. Her* Poems on Various Subjects, Religious and Moral *was published in 1773; shortly thereafter, she was awarded her freedom.*

of their crime or their delusion; they had been in the habit of meeting together on a stated day before sunrise, and of offering in turns a form of invocation to Christ, as to a god—also of binding themselves by an oath, *not* for any guilty purpose, but not to commit thefts, robberies, or adulteries, not to break their word, not to repudiate deposits when called upon. These ceremonies having been gone through, they had been in the habit of separating, and again meeting together for the purpose of taking food—food, that is, of an ordinary and innocent kind. They had, however, ceased from doing even this after my edict, in which, following your orders, I had forbidden the existence of fraternities. This made me think it all the more necessary to inquire—even by torture—of two maid servants

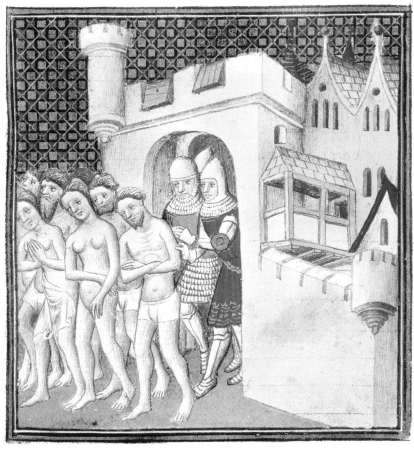

Expulsion of Albigensian heretics from Carcassonne in 1209 during the Albigensian Crusade, from *Les Grandes chroniques de France*, c. 1350.

who were styled deaconesses what the truth was. I could discover nothing else than a vicious and extravagant superstition; consequently, having adjourned the inquiry, I have had recourse to your counsels. Indeed, the matter seemed to me a proper one for consultation, chiefly on account of the number of persons imperilled. For many of all ages and all ranks, even of both sexes, are being called—and will be called—into danger. Nor are cities only permeated by the contagion of this superstition, but villages and country parts as well; yet it seems possible to stop it and cure it. It is in truth sufficiently

evident that the temples, which were almost entirely deserted, have begun to be frequented, that the customary religious rites which had long been interrupted are being resumed, and that there is a sale for the food of sacrificial beasts, for which hitherto very few buyers indeed could be found. From all this it is easy to form an opinion as to the great number of persons who may be reclaimed, if only room be granted for penitence.

Pliny the Younger, *from a letter to Emperor Trajan. Raised in a wealthy family, Pliny was practicing law at the age of eighteen and eventually reached the high ranks of praetor and consul. He is well regarded for his collections of letters, which combine aspects of poetic and oratorical style, and contain his account of the eruption of Mt. Vesuvius in 79, during which his uncle, Pliny the Elder, perished.*

1925: Dayton, TN

H. L. MENCKEN UNEASY IN ZION

Life down here in the Cumberland Mountains realizes almost perfectly the ideal of righteous and devoted men. That is to say, evangelical Christianity is 100 percent triumphant. There is, of course, a certain subterranean heresy, but

> *When we say God is a spirit, we know what we mean as well as we do when we say that the pyramids of Egypt are matter. Let us be content therefore to believe him to be a spirit, that is, an essence that we know nothing of, in which originally and necessarily reside all energy, all power, all capacity, all activity, all wisdom, all goodness.* —*John Adams, 1820*

it is so cowed that it is almost inarticulate, and at its worst it would pass for the strictest orthodoxy in such Sodoms of infidelity as Baltimore. It may seem fabulous, but it is a sober fact that a sound Episcopalian or even a Northern Methodist would be regarded as virtually an atheist in Dayton. Here the only genuine conflict is between true believers. Of a given text in Holy Writ one faction may say this thing and another that, but both agree unreservedly that the text itself is impeccable, and neither in the midst of the most violent disputation would venture to accuse the other of doubt.

To call a man a doubter in these parts is equal to accusing him of cannibalism. Even the infidel John Scopes himself is not charged with any such infamy. What they say of him, at worst, is that he permitted himself to be used as a cat's paw by scoundrels eager to destroy the anti-evolution law for their own dark and hellish ends. There is, it appears, a conspiracy of scientists afoot. Their purpose is to break down religion, propagate immorality, and so reduce mankind to the level of the brutes. They are the sworn and sinister agents of Beelzebub, who yearns to conquer the world—and has his eye

especially upon Tennessee. Scopes is thus an agent of Beelzebub once removed, but that is as far as any fair man goes in condemning him. He is young and yet full of folly. When the secular arm has done execution upon him, the pastors will tackle him and he will be saved.

The selection of a jury to try him, which went on all yesterday afternoon in the atmosphere of a blast furnace, showed to what extreme lengths the salvation of the local primates has been pushed. It was obvious after a few rounds that the jury would be unanimously hot for Genesis [*Moriah*, page 111]. The most that Mr. Clarence Darrow could hope for was to sneak in a few men bold enough to declare publicly that they would have to hear the evidence against Scopes before condemning him. The slightest sign of anything further brought forth a peremptory challenge from the State. Once a man was challenged without examination for simply admitting that he did not belong formally to any church. Another time a panel man who confessed that he was prejudiced against evolution got a hearty round of applause from the crowd.

The whole process quickly took on an air of strange unreality, at least to a stranger from heathen parts. The desire of the judge to be fair to the defense, and even polite and helpful, was obvious enough—in fact, he more than once stretched the local rules of procedure in order to give Darrow a hand. But it was equally obvious that the whole thing was resolving itself into the trial of a man by his sworn enemies. A local pastor led off with a prayer calling on God to put down heresy; the judge himself charged the grand jury to protect the schools against subversive ideas. And when the candidates for the petit jury came up, Darrow had to pass fundamentalist after fundamentalist into the box—some of them glaring at him as if they expected him to go off with a sulphurous bang every time he mopped his bald head.

In brief, this is a strictly Christian community, and such is its notion of fairness, justice, and due process of law. Its people are simply unable to imagine a man who rejects the literal authority of the Bible. The most they can conjure up, straining until they are red in the face, is a man who is in error about the meaning of this or that text. Thus one accused of heresy among them is like one accused of boiling his grandmother to make soap in Maryland. He must resign himself to being tried by a jury wholly innocent of any suspicion of the crime he is charged with and unanimously convinced that it is infamous. Such a jury, in the legal sense, may be fair. That is, it may be willing to hear the evidence against him before bumping him off. But it would certainly be spitting into the eye of reason to call it impartial.

The trial indeed takes on, for all its legal forms, something of the air of a religious orgy. Judge Raulston rapped it down and threatened to clear the room if it was repeated, but he was quite unable to still its echoes under his very windows. The courthouse is surrounded by a large lawn, and it is peppered day and night with evangelists. One and all they are fundamentalists, and their yells and bawlings fill the air with orthodoxy. I have listened to twenty of them and had private discourse with a dozen, and I have yet to find one who doubted so much as the typographical errors in Holy Writ. They dispute raucously and far into the night, but they begin and end on the common ground of complete faith. One of these holy men wears a sign on his back announcing that he is the Bible champion of the world. He told me today that he had

Ascent to Heaven from *Visions of the Hereafter*, by Hieronymous Bosch, c. 1500.

Most of the participants in such recondite combats, of course, are yokels from the hills, where no sound is heard after sundown save the roar of the catamount and the wailing of departed spirits, and a man thus has time to ponder the divine mysteries. But it is an amazing thing that the more polished classes also participate actively. The professor who challenged the Bible champion was indistinguishable to the eye from a bond salesman or city bootlegger. He had on a natty Palm Beach suit and a fashionable soft collar, and he used excellent English. Obviously, he was one who had been through the local high school and perhaps a country college. Yet he was so-far uncontaminated by infidelity that he stood in the hot sun for a whole hour debating a point that even bishops might be excused for dodging, winter as well as summer.

The Bible champion is matched and rivaled by whole herds of other metaphysicians, and all of them attract good houses and have to defend themselves against constant attack. The Seventh Day Adventists, the Campbellites, the Holy Rollers, and a dozen other occult sects have field agents on the ground. They follow the traveling judges through all this country. Everywhere they go, I am told, they find the natives ready to hear them and dispute with them. They find highly accomplished theologians in every village, but even in the county towns they never encounter a genuine skeptic. If a man has doubts in this immensely pious country, he keeps them to himself.

The Adoration of the Calf, by Francis Picabia, c. 1941–42.

studied the Bible four hours a day for thirty-three years, and that he had devised a plan of salvation that would save the worst sinner ever heard of—even a scientist, a theater actor, or a pirate on the high seas—in forty days. This gentleman denounced the hard-shell Baptists as swindlers. He admitted freely that their sorcerers were powerful preachers and could save any ordinary man from sin, but he said that they were impotent against iniquity. The distinction is unknown to city theologians but is as real down here as that between sanctification and salvation. The local experts, in fact, debate it daily. The Bible champion, just as I left him, was challenged by one such professor, and the two were still hard at it an hour later.

From A Religious Orgy in Tennessee. *For the* Baltimore Sun, *Mencken covered the Scopes Trial, in which a Tennessee high-school teacher was charged with teaching evolution. He wrote for the* Sun *regularly from 1906 until his death in 1956. The newspaperman once described the puritanical mind frame as, "the haunting fear that someone, somewhere, may be happy."*

c. 1177: Neyshabur

BURNING DISCONTENT

Sheikh Nasrabad made Mecca's pilgrimage
Twice twenty times, yet this could not assuage
His yearning heart. This white-haired sheikh became
A pilgrim of the pagans' sacred flame,
A naked beggar in whose heart their fire
Was mirrored by the blaze of his desire.
A passerby said, "Shame on you, O sheikh,
Shame on these wretched orisons you make;
Have you performed the Muslims' pilgrimage
To be an infidel in your old age?
This is mere childishness; such blasphemy
Can only bring the Sufis infamy.
What sheikh has followed this perverted way?
What is this pagan fire to which you pray?"
The sheikh said, "I have suffered from this flame,
Which burnt my clothes, my house, my noble name,
The harvest of my life, all that I knew,
My learning, wisdom, reputation too—
And what is left to me?—Bewilderment,
The knowledge of my burning discontent;
All thoughts of reputation soon depart
When such fierce conflagrations fire the heart.
In my despair I turn with equal hate
Both from the Kaaba and this temple's gate—
If this bewilderment should come to you
Then you will grieve, as I am forced to do."

Farid ud-Din Attar, *from* The Conference of the Birds. *The Persian poet traveled throughout the Middle East and Central Asia before returning to his native Neyshabur in northeastern Iran. In addition to his allegorical poem about birds searching for their king, Attar composed at least 45,000 couplets, drawing upon the sayings of famous Sufis that he had collected over the course of his life.*

1882: Sils-Maria

OBITUARY NOTICE

In the horizon of the infinite. We have left the land and have embarked. We have burned our bridges behind us—indeed, we have gone further and destroyed the land behind us. Now, little ship, look out! Beside you is the ocean: to be sure, it does not always roar, and at times it lies spread out like silk and gold and reveries of graciousness. But hours will come when you will realize that it is infinite and that there is nothing more awesome than infinity. Oh, the poor bird that felt free and now strikes the walls of this cage! Woe, when you feel homesick for the land as if it had offered more *freedom*—and there is no longer any "land."

The madman. Have you not heard of that madman who lit a lantern in the bright morning hours, ran to the marketplace, and cried incessantly, "I seek God! I seek God!" As many of those who did not believe in God were standing around just then, he provoked much laughter. Has he got lost? asked one. Did he lose his way like a child? asked another. Or is he hiding? Is he afraid of us? Has he gone on a voyage? Emigrated?—Thus they yelled and laughed.

The madman jumped into their midst and pierced them with his eyes. "Where is God?" he cried. "I will tell you. *We have killed him*— you and I. All of us are his murderers. But how did we do this? How could we drink up the sea? Who gave us the sponge to wipe away the entire horizon? What were we doing when we unchained this earth from its sun? Where is it moving now? Where are we moving? Away from all suns? Are we not plunging continually? Backward, sideward, forward—in all directions? Is there still any up or down? Are we not straying as through an infinite nothing? Do we not feel the breath of empty space? Has it not become colder? Is not night continually closing in on us? Do we not need to light lanterns in the morning? Do we hear nothing as yet of the noise of the gravediggers who are burying God? Do we smell nothing as yet of the divine decomposition? Gods, too, decompose. God is dead. God remains dead. And we have killed him.

"How shall we comfort ourselves, the murderers of all murderers? What was holiest and mightiest of all that the world has yet owned has bled to death under our knives—who will wipe this blood off us? What water is there for us to clean ourselves? What festivals of atonement, what sacred games shall we have to invent? Is not the greatness of this deed too great for us? Must we ourselves not become gods simply to appear worthy of it? There has never been a greater deed, and whoever is born after us—for the sake of this deed he will belong to a higher history than all history hitherto."

Here the madman fell silent and looked again at his listeners, and they, too, were silent and stared at him in astonishment. At last he threw his lantern on the ground, and it broke into pieces and went out. "I have come too early," he said then. "My time is not yet. This tremendous event is still on its way, still wandering—it has not yet reached the ears of men. Lightning and thunder require time; the light of the stars requires time; deeds, though done, still require time to be seen and heard. This deed is still more distant from them than the most distant stars—*and yet they have done it themselves.*"

It has been related further that on the same day the madman forced his way into several churches and there struck up his *requeim aeternam deo.* Led out and called to account, he is said always to have replied nothing but, "What after all are these churches now if they are not the tombs and sepulchers of God?"

Friedrich Nietzsche, *from* The Gay Science. *Between 1879 and 1889, Nietzsche published almost a dozen books, among them* Twilight of the Idols, The Antichrist, *and* Ecce Homo. *The last of these works included chapters entitled "Why I Am So Clever" and "Why I Write Such Good Books." The philosopher and philologist was plagued with illness for most of his adult life, spending his final decade both in an asylum and in his mother's care.*

c. 1923: Seattle

MARY MCCARTHY LOSES HER FAITH

People are always asking me how I came to lose my faith, imagining a period of deep inward struggle. The truth is the whole momentous project simply jumped at me, ready-made, out of one of Mme MacIllvra's discourses. I had decided to do it before I knew what it was, when it was merely an interweaving of words, lose-your-faith, like the ladder made of sheets on which the daring girl had descended into the arms of her Romeo. "Say you've lost your faith," the devil prompted, assuring me that there was no risk if I chose my moment carefully. Starting Monday morning, we were going to have a retreat, to be preached by a stirring Jesuit. If I lost my faith on, say, Sunday, I could regain it during the three days of retreat, in time for Wednesday confessions. Thus there would be only four days in which my soul would be in danger if I should happen to die suddenly. The only real sacrifice would be forgoing Com-

munion on Sunday. He who hesitates is lost; *qui ne risque rien n'a rien* [he who risks nothing gains nothing], observed the devil, lapsing into French, as is his wont. If I did not do it, someone else might. It was a miracle that someone had not thought of it already, the idea seemed so obvious, like a store waiting to be robbed.

Surprised looks were bent on me Sunday morning in the chapel when the line formed for Communion and I knelt unmoving in my pew. I was always an ostentatious communicant. Now girls clambered over me, somebody gave me a poke, but I shook my head sorrowfully, signifying by my expression that I was in a state of mortal sin and dared not approach the table. At lunch, eating little, I was already a center of attention at my table. I maintained a mournful silence, rehearsing what I would say to Mme MacIllvra in her office as soon as the meal was over. Having put in my request for an appointment, I was beginning to be slightly frightened. After lunch, as I stood waiting outside her door, I kept licking my lips. Yet this fear, I argued, was a token of

Potala Palace, former residence and burial site of past Dalai Lamas, Tibet. Photograph by Gilles Mermet.

sincerity; naturally you would be frightened if you had just lost your faith.

"*Ma Mère*, I have lost my faith." At her rolltop desk, Mme MacIllvra started; one plump white hand fluttered to her heart. She gave me a single searching look. Evidently, my high standing in my studies had prepared her for this catastrophe, for she did not ransack me further as I stood there quaking and bowing and trying to repress a foolish giveaway grin. I had been expecting a long questioning, but she

Man sacrificed by feline, Moche artifact, Peru, c. 350.

reached, sighing, for the telephone, as though I had appendicitis or the measles.

"Pray, my child," she murmured as she summoned Father Dennis, our chaplain, from the neighboring Jesuit college. "I can't pray," I promptly responded. A classical symptom of unbelief was the inability to pray, as I knew from her own lectures. Mme MacIllvra nodded, turning a shade paler; she glanced at the watch in her bosom. "Go to your room," she said perturbedly. "You are not to speak to anyone. You will be sent for when Father Dennis comes. I will pray for you myself."

Some of her alarm had communicated itself to me. I had not realized that what I had said was so serious. I felt quite frightened now

by what I had done and by the prospect of a talk with Father Dennis, who was an old, dry, forbidding man, very different from the handsome missionary father who was going to preach our retreat. The idea of backing down presented itself with more and more attraction, but I did not see how I could do this without being convicted of shallowness. Moreover, I doubted very much that Mme MacIllvra would believe me if I said now that I had got my faith back all at once. She would make me talk to Father Dennis anyway. Once the convent machinery had got into motion, there was no way of stopping it, as I knew from horrendous experience. It was like the mills of the gods.

By the time I reached my cubicle, I was thoroughly scared. I saw that I was going to have to go through with this or be exposed before them all as a liar, and for the first time it occurred to me that I would have to have arguments to make my doubts sound real. At the same shaken moment, I realized that I knew nothing whatever of atheism. If I were out in the world, I could consult the books that had been written on the subject, but here in the convent, obviously, there could be no access to atheistic literature. From the playground outside floated the voices of the girls, laughing. I went to the window and looked down at them, feeling utterly cut off and imprisoned within my own emptiness. There was no one to turn to but God, yet this was one occasion when prayer would be unavailing. A prayer for atheistic arguments (surely?) would only bring out the stern side of God. What was I going to do?

I sat down on my bed and tried to count my resources. After all, I said to myself suddenly, I did know something about skepticism, thanks to Mme MacIllvra herself. The skeptics' arguments were based on science—false science, said Mme MacIllvra—which reasoned that there was no God because you could not see Him. This was a silly materialistic "proof," to which, unfortunately, I knew the answer. Could you see the wind? And yet its touch was everywhere, like God's invisible grace blowing on our souls. Skeptics denied the life after death and said there was

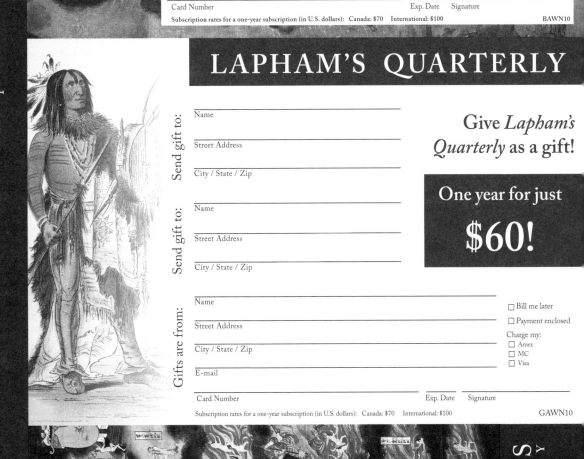

BUSINESS REPLY MAIL
FIRST-CLASS MAIL   PERMIT NO. 19   DENVILLE NJ

POSTAGE WILL BE PAID BY ADDRESSEE

LAPHAM'S QUARTERLY
PO BOX 3000
DENVILLE NJ 07834-9807

BUSINESS REPLY MAIL
FIRST-CLASS MAIL   PERMIT NO. 19   DENVILLE NJ

POSTAGE WILL BE PAID BY ADDRESSEE

NO POSTAGE
NECESSARY
IF MAILED
IN THE
UNITED STATES

LAPHAM'S QUARTERLY
PO BOX 3000
DENVILLE NJ 07834-9807

Visit us online at:

www.laphamsquarterly.org

no heaven, only the blue of space in the celestial vault. Science proved that, they said, and science proved too that there was no hell burning under the earth. We had had the answer to that one, only last week in Christian doctrine, in St. Paul's steely words which we had had to memorize: "That eye hath not seen, nor ear heard, neither hath it entered into the heart of man, what things God hath prepared for them that love Him." I sank into a dull despair. Was I going to have to offer "proofs" that any fool could see through? Any fool knew that man's scientific calipers could not grasp God directly. Hell and heaven were not contradictory to science but something different altogether, beyond science. But what about miracles?

I sat up suddenly. Miracles were not invisible. They were supposed to happen right here on earth, today. They were attested in the photographs of Lourdes by all the crutches hanging up in token of thankfulness for cures. Nevertheless, I said to myself delightedly, *I* had never seen a miracle, and perhaps all these people were lying or deluded. Christian Science claimed cures, too, and we knew that that was just imagination. Voltaire [*Ferney*, page 109] was an intelligent man and he had laughed at miracles. Why not I?

As I sat there searching my memory, doubts that I had hurriedly stowed away like contraband in a bureau drawer came back to me reassuringly. I found that I had always been a little suspicious of the life after death. Perhaps it was really true that the dead just rotted and I would never rejoin my parents in heaven? I scratched a spot on my uniform, watching it turn white under my thumbnail. Another memory was tapping at my consciousness: the question of the Resurrection of the Body. At the last trump, all the bodies of men from Adam onward were supposed to leap from their graves and rejoin the souls that had left them—this was why the Church forbade cremation. But somewhere not so long ago I had heard a priest quote scornfully a materialistic argument against this. The materialist said (yes, that was it!) that people rotted and turned into fertilizer, which went into vegetables, and then other people ate the vegetables, so that when the Resurrection came there would not be enough bodies to go around. The priest answered that for God, anything was possible; if God made man from clay, He could certainly make some extra bodies. But in that case, I thought, pouncing, why did He object to cremation? And in any case they would not be the *same* bodies, which was the whole point. And I could think of an even stronger instance: what about cannibals? If God divided the cannibal into the component bodies he had digested, what would become of the cannibal? God

I count religion but a childish toy
And hold there is no sin but ignorance.
                    —*Christopher Marlowe, 1592*

could start with whatever flesh the cannibal had had when he was a baby—before he began eating missionaries—but if his father and mother had been cannibals, too, what flesh would he really have that he could call his own?

At that time, I did not know that this problem had been treated by Aquinas, and with a child's pertinacity, I mined away at the foundations of the fortress rock. Elation had replaced fear. I could hardly wait now to meet Father Dennis and confront him with these doubts, so remarkable in one of my years. Parallels with the young Jesus discoursing with the scribes and doctors bounded through my head. "And all that heard Him were astonished at His wisdom and His answers." No one now, I felt certain, would dare accuse me of faking. I strolled along proudly with the messenger who had come to fetch me; just as her knock sounded, I had reached the stage of doubting the divinity of Christ.

From Memories of a Catholic Girlhood. *The novelist, essayist, and literary critic was orphaned at the age of six after her parents were killed by the influenza epidemic of 1918. In the 1930s McCarthy published a series of essays on the state of criticism;* Time *magazine called her effort the "St. Valentine's massacre of reviewers and critics," and she soon emerged as one of the era's leading intellectuals.*

c. 987: Kiev

THE DEVIL VANQUISHED

Prince Vladimir summoned together his boyars and the city elders and said to them, "Behold, the Bulgarians came before me urging me to accept their religion. Then came the Germans and praised their own faith, and after them came the Jews. Finally the Greeks appeared, criticizing all other faiths but commending their own, and they spoke at length, telling the history of the whole world from its beginning. Their words were artful, and it was wondrous to listen and

The freedom or immunity from coercion in matters religious, which is the endowment of persons as individuals, is also to be recognized as their right when they act in community. Religious communities are a requirement of the social nature both of man and of religion itself.
—Pope Paul VI, 1965

pleasant to hear them. They preach the existence of another world. 'Whoever adopts our religion and then dies shall arise and live forever. But whosoever embraces another faith, shall be consumed with fire in the next world.' What is your opinion on this subject, and what do you answer?" The boyars and the elders replied: "You know, O prince, that no man condemns his own possessions, but praises them instead. If you desire to make certain, you have servants at your disposal. Send them to inquire about the ritual of each and how he worships God."

Their counsel pleased the prince and all the people, so that they chose good and wise men to the number of ten, and directed them to go first among the Bulgarians and inspect their faith. The emissaries went their way, and when they arrived at their destination they beheld the disgraceful actions of the Bulgarians and their worship in the mosque; then they returned to their own country. Vladimir then instructed them to go likewise among the Germans and examine their faith, and finally

to visit the Greeks. They thus went into Germany, and after viewing the German ceremonial, they proceeded to Constantinople where they appeared before the emperor. He inquired on what mission they had come, and they reported to him all that had occurred. When the emperor heard their words, he rejoiced and did them great honor on that very day.

The next day, the emperor sent a message to the patriarch to inform him that a Russian delegation had arrived to examine the Greek faith, directed him to prepare the church and the clergy, and to array himself in his sacerdotal robes so that the Russians might behold the glory of the God of the Greeks. When the patriarch received these commands, he bade the clergy assemble, and they performed the customary rites. They burned incense, and the choirs sang hymns. The emperor accompanied the Russians to the church and placed them in a wide space, calling their attention to the beauty of the edifice, the chanting, and the offices of the archpriest and the ministry of the deacons, while he explained to them the worship of his God. The Russians were astonished, and in their wonder praised the Greek ceremonial. Then the emperors Basil II and Constantine VIII invited the envoys to their presence, and said, "Go hence to your native country," and thus dismissed them with valuable presents and great honor.

Thus they returned to their own country, and the prince called together his boyars and the elders. Vladimir then announced the return of the envoys who had been sent out, and suggested that their report be heard. He thus commanded them to speak out before his vassals. The envoys reported, "When we journeyed among the Bulgarians, we beheld how they worship in their temple, called a mosque, while they stand slack. The Bulgarian bows, sits down, looks hither and thither like one possessed, and there is no happiness among them, but instead only sorrow and a dreadful stench. Their religion is not good. Then we went among the Germans and saw them performing many ceremonies in their temples—but we beheld no glory there. Then we went on to Greece, and the Greeks led

Satan devouring the damned, from *Last Judgment* (detail), by Fra Angelico, c. 1432–35.

us to the edifices where they worship their God, and we knew not whether we were in heaven or on earth. For on earth there is no such splendor or such beauty, and we are at a loss how to describe it. We know only that God dwells there among men, and their service is fairer than the ceremonies of other nations. For we cannot forget that beauty. Every man, after tasting something sweet, is afterward unwilling to accept that which is bitter, and therefore we cannot dwell longer here." Vladimir then inquired where they should all accept baptism, and they replied that the decision rested with him.

After a year had passed, Vladimir marched with an armed force against Kherson, a Greek city, and the people of Kherson barricaded themselves therein. Vladimir halted at the farther side of the city beside the bay, a bowshot from the town, and the inhabitants resisted energetically while Vladimir besieged the town.

Eventually, however, they became exhausted, and Vladimir warned them that if they did not surrender, he would remain on the spot for three years. When they failed to heed this threat, Vladimir marshaled his troops and ordered the construction of an earthwork in the direction of the city. While this work was under construction, the inhabitants dug a tunnel under the city wall, stole the heaped-up earth, and carried it into the city, where they piled it up in the center of the town. But the soldiers kept on building, and Vladimir persisted. Then a man of Kherson, Anastasius by name, shot into the Russian camp an arrow on which he had written: "There are springs behind you to the east, from which water flows in pipes. Dig down and cut them off." When Vladimir received this information, he raised his eyes to heaven and vowed that if this hope was realized, he would be baptized. He gave orders straightway to dig down above the pipes, and the water supply was thus cut off. The inhabitants were accordingly overcome by thirst, and surrendered.

Vladimir and his retinue entered the city, and he sent messages to the emperors Basil and Constantine, saying, "Behold, I have captured your glorious city. I have also heard that you have an unwedded sister. Unless you give her to me to wife, I shall deal with your own city as I have with Kherson." When the emperors heard this message, they were troubled, and replied, "It is not proper for Christians to give in marriage to pagans. If you are baptized, you shall have her to wife, inherit the kingdom of God, and be our companion in the faith. Unless you do so, however, we cannot give you our sister in marriage." When Vladimir learned their response, he directed the envoys of the emperors to report to the latter that he was willing to accept baptism, having already given some study to their

1862: Washington, DC

GOD WILLS IT

The will of God prevails. In great contests each party claims to act in accordance with the will of God. Both may be, and one must be, wrong. God cannot be for and against the same thing at the same time. In the present civil war it is quite possible that God's purpose is something different from the purpose of either party—and yet the human instrumentalities, working just as they do, are of the best adaptation to effect his purpose. I am almost ready to say that this is probably true, that God wills this contest, and wills that it shall not end yet. By his mere great power on the minds of the now contestants, he could have either saved or destroyed the Union without a human contest. Yet the contest began. And having begun, he could give the final victory to either side any day. Yet the contest proceeds.

Abraham Lincoln, *"Meditation on the Divine Will." Composed during the second year of the Civil War—only weeks before the battle of Antietam claimed more than 23,000 American lives—the fragment was preserved by one of the president's White House secretaries, who said it was "not written to be seen of men."*

religion, and that the Greek faith and ritual as described by the emissaries sent to examine it had pleased him well. When the emperors heard this report, they rejoiced and persuaded their sister Anna to consent to the match. They then requested Vladimir to submit to baptism before they should send their sister to him, but Vladimir desired that the princess should herself bring priests to baptize him. The emperors complied with his request, and sent forth their sister, accompanied by some dignitaries and priests. Anna, however, departed with reluctance. "It is as if I were setting out into captivity," she lamented. "Better were it for me to die here." But her brothers protested, "Through your agency God turns the Russian land to repentance, and you will relieve Greece from the danger of grievous war. Do you not see how much evil the Russians have already brought upon the Greeks? If you do not set out, they may bring on us the same misfortunes." It was thus that they overcame her hesitation only with great difficulty. The princess embarked upon a ship, and after tearfully embracing her kinfolk, she set forth across the sea and arrived at Kherson. The natives came forth to greet her and conducted her into the city, where they settled her in the palace.

By divine agency, Vladimir was suffering at that moment from a disease of the eyes and could see nothing, being in great distress. The princess declared to him that if he desired to be relieved of this disease, he should be baptized with all speed, otherwise it could not be cured. When Vladimir heard her message, he said, "If this proves true, then of a surety is the God of the Christians great," and gave order that he should be baptized. The Bishop of Kherson, together with the princess' priests, after announcing the tidings, baptized Vladimir, and as the bishop laid his hand upon him, he straightway received his sight. Upon experiencing this miraculous cure, Vladimir glorified God, saying, "I have now perceived the one true God." When his followers beheld this miracle, many of them were also baptized.

Vladimir was baptized in the Church of St. Basil, which stands at Kherson upon a square

Various poses during Muslim prayer, from the album of Jean Baptiste Joseph Gentil, India, 1774.

in the center of the city, where the Khersonians trade. The palace of Vladimir stands beside this church to this day, and the palace of the princess is behind the altar. After his baptism, Vladimir took the princess in marriage. As a wedding present for the princess, he gave Kherson over to the Greeks again, and then departed for Kiev.

When the prince arrived at his capital, he directed that the idols should be overthrown and that some should be cut to pieces and others burned with fire. He thus ordered that the idol of the god Perun should be bound to a horse's tail and dragged along Borichev to the river. He appointed twelve men to beat the idol with sticks, not because he thought the wood was sensitive, but to affront the demon who had deceived man in this guise, that he might receive chastisement at the hands of men. Great art thou, O Lord, and marvelous are thy works!

Thereafter Vladimir sent heralds throughout the whole city to proclaim that if any inhabitant, rich or poor, did not betake himself to the river, he would risk the prince's displeasure. When the people heard these words, they wept for joy, and exclaimed in their enthusiasm, "If this were not good, the prince and his bo-

yars would not have accepted it." The next day the prince went forth to the Dnieper with the priests of the princess and those from Kherson, and a countless multitude assembled. They all went into the water—some stood up to their necks, others to their breasts, the younger near the bank, some of them holding children in their arms, while the adults waded farther out. The priests stood by and offered prayers. There was joy in heaven and upon earth to behold so many souls saved. But the devil groaned, lamenting, "Woe is me! How am I driven out hence! For I thought to have my dwelling place here, since the apostolic teachings do not abide in this land. Nor did this people know God, but I rejoiced in the service they rendered unto me. But now I am vanquished by the ignorant, not by apostles and martyrs, and my reign in these regions is at an end."

From The Primary Russian Chronicle. *The history of the early Russian peoples was compiled around 1113 from oral sagas, official documents, Byzantine chronicles, and Slavonic literature. Before Prince Vladimir converted to Christianity and became the first Christian ruler of Kievan Rus, he had multiple wives and was said to conduct human sacrifices.*

1805: Buffalo Grove, NY

POINT OF ORDER

Friend and brother: It was the will of the Great Spirit that we should meet together this day. He orders all things and has given us a fine day for our council. He has taken His garment from before the sun and caused it to shine with brightness upon us. Our eyes are opened that we see clearly; our ears are unstopped that we have been able to hear distinctly the words you have spoken. For all these favors we thank the Great Spirit, and Him only.

Brother, listen to what we say. There was a time when our forefathers owned this great island. Their seats extended from the rising to the setting sun. The Great Spirit had made it for the use of Indians. He had created the buffalo, the deer, and other animals for food. He had made the bear and the beaver. Their skins served us for clothing. He had scattered them over the country and taught us how to take them. He had caused the earth to produce corn for bread. All this He had done for His red children because He loved them. If we had some disputes about our hunting ground, they were generally settled without the shedding of much blood.

But an evil day came upon us. Your forefathers crossed the great water and landed on this island. Their numbers were small. They found friends and not enemies. They told us they had fled from their own country for fear of wicked men and had come here to enjoy their religion. They asked for a small seat. We took pity on them, granted their request, and they sat down among us. We gave them corn and meat; they gave us poison in return.

The white people, brother, had now found our country. Tidings were carried back and more came among us. Yet we did not fear them. We took them to be friends. They called us brothers. We believed them and gave them a larger seat. At length their numbers had greatly increased. They wanted more land; they wanted our country. Our eyes were opened and our minds became uneasy. Wars took place. Indi-ans were hired to fight against Indians, and many of our people were destroyed. They also brought strong liquor among us. It was strong and powerful and has slain thousands.

Brother, our seats were once large and yours were small. You have now become a great people, and we have scarcely a place left to spread our blankets. You have got our country, but are not satisfied: you want to force your religion upon us.

Brother, continue to listen. You say that you are sent to instruct us how to worship the Great Spirit agreeably to His mind; and, if we do not take hold of the religion which you white people teach, we shall be unhappy hereafter. You say that you are right and we are lost. How do we know this to be true? We understand that your religion is written in a book. If it was intended for us as well as you why has not the Great Spirit given to us, and not only to us, but why did He not give to our forefathers the knowledge of that book, with the means of understanding it right-ly. We only know what you tell us about it. How shall we know when to believe, being so often deceived by the white people?

Brother, you say there is but one way to worship and serve the Great Spirit. If there is but one religion, why do you white people dif-fer so much about it? Why not all agreed, as you can all read the book?

Brother, we do not understand these things. We are told that your religion was given to your forefathers and has been handed down from fa-ther to son. We also have a religion which was given to our forefathers and has been handed down to us, their children. We worship in that way. It teaches us to be thankful for all the fa-vors we receive, to love each other, and to be united. We never quarrel about religion.

Brother, the Great Spirit has made us all, but He has made a great difference between His white and His red children. He has given us different complexions and different customs. To you He has given the arts. To these He has not opened our eyes. We know these things to be true. Since He has made so great a differ-ence between us in other things, why may we not conclude that He has given us a different religion according to our understanding? The Great Spirit does right. He knows what is best for His children; we are satisfied.

Brother, we do not wish to destroy your religion or take it from you. We only want to enjoy our own.

Brother, you say you have not come to get our land or our money, but to enlighten our minds. I will now tell you that I have been at your meetings and saw you collect money from the meeting. I cannot tell what this money was intended for, but suppose that it was for your minister, and if we should conform to your way of thinking, perhaps you may want some from us.

Brother, we are told that you have been preaching to the white people in this place. These people are our neighbors. We are acquainted with them. We will wait a little while and see what effect your preaching has upon them. If we find it does them good, makes them honest and less disposed to cheat Indians, we will then consider again of what you have said.

> **Red Jacket**, *from a speech. The Seneca chief opposed attempts to spread Christianity among his people, as well as the rise of a new Seneca prophet, Handsome Lake, who responded by charging Red Jacket with, among other things, witchcraft. His own family eventually converted to Christianity, and when he died in 1830, his wife buried him in a Christian cemetery.*

Sacrifice of Isaac, by Marc Chagall, c. 1960–66.

1516: Utopia

THOMAS MORE POSES AN ALTERNATIVE

There are several different religions on the island of Utopia, and indeed in each town. There are sun worshippers, moon worshippers, and worshippers of various other planets. There are people who regard some great or good man of the past not merely as a god, but as the supreme god. However, the vast majority take the much more sensible view that there is a single divine power, unknown, eternal, infinite, inexplicable, and quite beyond the grasp of the human mind, diffused throughout this universe of ours, not as a physical substance, but as an active force. This power they call "The Parent." They give him credit for everything that happens to everything, for all beginnings and ends, all growth, development, and change. Nor do they recognize any other form of deity.

On this point, indeed, all the different sects agree—that there is one supreme being, who is responsible for the creation and management of the universe, and they all use the same Utopian word to describe him: Mythras. What they disagree about is who Mythras is. Some say one thing, some another—but everyone claims that *his* supreme being is identical with Nature, that tremendous power which is internationally acknowledged to be the sole cause of everything. However, people are gradually tending to drift away from all these inferior creeds and to unite in adopting what seems to be the most reasonable religion. And doubtless the others would have died out long ago if it weren't for the superstitious tendency to interpret any bad luck, when one is thinking of changing one's religion, not as a coincidence, but as a judgment from heaven—as though the discarded god were punishing one's disloyalty.

But when we told them about Christ, His teaching, His character, His miracles, and the no less miraculous devotion of all the martyrs who, by voluntarily shedding their blood, converted so many nations to the Christian faith, you've no idea how easy it was to convert them too.

Of course many Utopians refuse to accept Christianity, but even they make no attempt to discourage other people from adopting it, or to attack those who do—though there was one member of our congregation who got into trouble while I was there. Immediately after his baptism, in spite of all our advice to the contrary, this man started giving public lectures on the Christian faith, in which he showed rather more zeal than discretion. Eventually he got so worked up that, not content with asserting the superiority of our religion, he went so far as to condemn all others. He kept shouting at the top of his voice that they were all vile superstitions, and that all who believed in them were monsters of impiety, destined to be punished in hellfire forever. When he'd been going on like this for some time, he was arrested and charged, not with blasphemy, but with disturbance of the peace. He was duly convicted and sentenced to exile—for one of the most ancient principles of their constitution is religious toleration.

This principle dates right back to the time of the conquest. Up till then there'd been constant quarrels about religion, and the various warring sects had refused to cooperate in the defense of their country. When Utopos, the founder of Utopia, heard how they'd behaved, he realized that this was why he'd been able to conquer the whole lot of them. So immediately after his victory he made a law by which everyone was free to practice what religion he liked—and to try and convert other people to his own faith—provided he did it quietly and politely, by rational argument. But if he failed to convince them, he was not allowed to make bitter attacks on other religions, nor to employ violence or personal abuse. The normal penalty for being too aggressive in religious controversy is either exile or slavery.

Utopos made this law, not only to preserve the peace, which he saw being completely destroyed by endless disputes and implacable feuds, but also because he thought it was in the best interests of religion itself. He didn't presume to say which creed was right. Apparently he considered it possible that God made different people believe different things, because He wanted to be

Trading Places
Twentieth-century conversions

Who and When	Raised		Became
Buffalo Bill, 1917, while nearing death	Methodist	┈▶	Roman Catholic
T. S. Eliot, 1927, while experiencing turmoil in his relationship with wife Vivien Haigh-Wood	Unitarian	┈▶	Anglo-Catholic
Chiang Kai-Shek, 1930, after prayer in battle was answered with snowstorm that hindered enemy forces	Buddhist	┈▶	Methodist
Dwight D. Eisenhower, 1953, second Sunday after becoming thirty-fourth president of the United States	Mennonite	┈▶	Presbyterian
Elizabeth Taylor, 1959, two years after marrying grandson of a Polish rabbi	Christian Scientist	┈▶	Jewish
Yusuf Islam (formerly Cat Stevens), 1977, after spiritual search, prompted in part by near-drowning experience	Christian	┈▶	Muslim

worshipped in many different ways. But he was evidently quite certain that it was stupid and arrogant to bully everyone else into adopting one's own particular creed. It seemed to him perfectly obvious that, even if there was only one true religion, and all the rest were nonsense, truth would eventually prevail of its own accord—as long as the matter was discussed calmly and reasonably. But if it was decided by force of arms, the best and most spiritual type of religion would go down before the silliest forms of superstition, just as corn is liable to be overgrown by thorns and brambles—for the worst people are always the most obstinate.

So he left the choice of creed an open question, to be decided by the individual according to his own ideas—except that he strictly and solemnly forbade his people to believe anything so incompatible with human dignity as the doctrine that the soul dies with the body, and the universe functions aimlessly, without any controlling providence. That's why they feel so sure that there must be rewards and punishments after death. Anyone who thinks differently has, in their view, forfeited his right to be classed as a human being, by degrading his immortal soul to the level of an animal's body. Still less do they regard him as a Utopian citizen. They say a person like that doesn't really care a damn for the Utopian way of life—only he's

too frightened to say so. For it stands to reason, if you're not afraid of anything but prosecution and have no hopes of anything after you're dead, you'll always be trying to evade or break the laws of your country in order to gain your own private ends. So nobody who subscribes to this doctrine is allowed to receive any public honor, hold any public appointment, or work in any public service. In fact such people are generally regarded as utterly contemptible.

They're not punished in any way, though, for no one is held responsible for what he believes. Nor are they terrorized into concealing their views, because Utopians simply can't stand hypocrisy, which they consider practically equivalent to fraud. Admittedly, it's illegal for any such person to argue in defense of his beliefs, but that's only in public. In private discussions with priests or other serious-minded characters, he's not merely allowed but positively encouraged to do so, for everyone's convinced that this type of delusion will eventually yield to reason.

From Utopia. *While on a diplomatic mission to Antwerp in 1515, More began his magnum opus and completed it upon his return to London;* Utopia *was an immediate success. A one-time monk, committed Catholic, and chancellor of England, More opposed King Henry VIII's divorce from Catherine of Aragon, a position for which he was beheaded in 1535 and canonized as a Roman Catholic saint in 1935.*

1947: Amritsar

SAADAT HASAN MANTO
IN THE TIME OF TROUBLES

Beginning with isolated incidents of stabbing, it had now developed into full-scale communal violence, with no holds barred. Even homemade bombs were being used.

The general view in Amritsar was that the riots could not last long. They were seen as no more than a manifestation of temporarily inflamed political passions which were bound to cool down before long. After all, these were not the first communal riots the city had known.

Throw away thy rod,
Throw away thy wrath;
O my God,
Take the gentle path.
　　　　　　　—George Herbert, c. 1620

There had been so many of them in the past. They never lasted long. The pattern was familiar. Two weeks or so of unrest and then business as usual. On the basis of experience, therefore, the people were quite justified in believing that the current troubles would also run their course in a few days. But this did not happen. They not only continued, but grew in intensity.

Muslims living in Hindu localities began to leave for safer places, and Hindus in Muslim-majority areas followed suit. However, everyone saw these adjustments as strictly temporary. The atmosphere would soon be clear of this communal madness, they told themselves.

Retired judge Mian Abdul Hai was absolutely confident that things would return to normal soon, which was why he wasn't worried. He had two children, a boy of eleven and a girl of seventeen. In addition, there was an old servant who was now pushing seventy. It was a small family. When the troubles started, Mian sahib, being an extra cautious man, stocked up on food … just in case. So on one count, at least, there were no worries.

His daughter Sughra was less sure of things. They lived in a three-story house with a view over almost the entire city. Sughra could not help noticing that whenever she went on the roof, there were fires raging everywhere. In the beginning, she could hear fire engines rushing past, their bells ringing, but this had now stopped. There were too many fires in too many places.

The nights had become particularly frightening. The sky was always lit by conflagrations like giants spitting out flames. Then there were the slogans which rent the air with terrifying frequency—*Allah-O-Akbar*; *Har, Har, Mahadev.*

Sughra never expressed her fears to her father, because he had declared confidently that there was no cause for anxiety. Everything was going to be fine. Since he was generally always right, she had initially felt reassured.

However, when the power and water supplies were suddenly cut off, she expressed her unease to her father and suggested apologetically that, for a few days at least, they should move to Sharifpura, a Muslim locality, to where many of the old residents had already moved. Mian sahib was adamant. "You're imagining things. Everything is going to be normal very soon."

He was wrong. Things went from bad to worse. Before long there was not a single Muslim family to be found in Mian Abdul Hai's locality. Then one day Mian sahib suffered a stroke and was laid up. His son Basharat, who used to spend most of his time playing self-devised games, now stayed glued to his father's bed.

All the shops in the area had been permanently boarded up. Dr. Ghulam Hussian's dispensary had been shut for weeks, and Sughra had noticed from the rooftop one day that the adjoining clinic of Dr. Goranditta Mall was also closed. Mian sahib's condition was getting worse day by day. Sughra was almost at the end of her wits. One day she took Basharat aside and said to him, "You've got to do something. I know it's not safe to go out, but we must get some help. Our father is very ill."

The boy went, but came back almost immediately. His face was pale with fear. He had seen a blood-drenched body lying in the street and a group of wild-looking men looting shops. Sughra took the terrified boy in her arms and said a silent prayer, thanking God for his safe return. However, she could not bear her father's suffering. His left side was now completely lifeless. His speech had been impaired, and he mostly communicated through gestures, all designed to reassure Sughra that soon all would be well.

It was the month of Ramadan and only two days to Id. Mian sahib was quite confident that the troubles would be over by then. He was again wrong. A canopy of smoke hung over the city, with fires burning everywhere. At night the silence was shattered by deafening explosions. Sughra and Basharat hadn't slept for days.

Two days passed. It was evening and the festival of Id was now only a day away. She remembered the excitement which used to grip the family on this occasion. She remembered standing on the rooftop, peering into the sky, looking for the Id moon and praying for the clouds to clear. But how different everything was today. The sky was covered in smoke and on distant roofs one could see people looking upward. Were they trying to catch sight of the new moon or were they watching the fires? she wondered.

She looked up and saw the thin sliver of the moon peeping through a small patch in the sky. She raised her hands in prayer, begging God to make her father well. Basharat, however, was upset that there would be no Id this year.

The night hadn't yet fallen. Sughra had moved her father's bed out of the room onto the veranda. She was sprinkling water on the floor to make it cool. Mian sahib was lying there quietly looking with vacant eyes at the sky where she had seen the moon. Sughra came and sat next to him. He motioned her to get closer. Then he raised his right arm slowly and put it on her head. Tears began to run from Sughra's eyes. Even Mian sahib looked moved. Then with great difficulty he said to her, "God is merciful. All will be well."

Forbidden Knowledge

Titles listed on the Catholic Church's Index of Forbidden Books (1515–1966)

Of Monarchy by Dante Alighieri, 1599
Excerpt: "The Church is the source neither of acting power nor of authority in the empire."

Essays by Michel de Montaigne, 1676
Excerpt: "There is no hostility that excels Christian hostility. Our zeal does wonders when it is seconding our leaning toward hatred, cruelty, ambition, avarice, detraction, rebellion."

Decline and Fall of the Roman Empire by Edward Gibbon, 1783
Excerpt: "Many a sober Christian would rather admit that a wafer is God than that God is a cruel and capricious tyrant."

Zoonomia by Erasmus Darwin, 1817
Excerpt: "Would it be too bold to imagine that all warm-blooded animals have arisen from one living filament?"

The Red and the Black by Stendhal, 1828
Excerpt: "My word, if I meet the God of the Christians, I am lost. He is a despot, and like all despots, full of ideas of vengeance."

Story of My Life by Giacomo Casanova, 1834
Excerpt: "I performed a great many ablutions on every part of her body, making her assume all sorts of positions, for she was perfectly docile, but as I was afraid of betraying myself, I felt more suffering than enjoyment."

All works by Honoré Balzac, 1841
Excerpt: "No man should marry until he has studied anatomy and dissected at least one woman."

Suddenly there was a knock on the door. Sughra's heart began to beat violently. She looked at Basharat, whose face had turned white like a sheet of paper. There was another knock. Mian sahib gestured to Sughra to answer it.

"Who can it be?" Sughra asked him.

Mian Abdul Hai tried to speak, but before he could do so, Basharat came running in. He was breathless. Taking Sughra aside, he whispered, "It's a Sikh."

Sughra screamed, "A Sikh! What does he want?"

"He wants me to open the door."

Sughra took Basharat in her arms and sat on her father's bed, looking at him desolately.

On Mian Abdul Hai's thin, lifeless lips, a faint smile appeared. "Go and open the door. It is Gurmukh Singh."

1252: Rome

INQUISITION

Law 2: At the commencement of his term of office, the head of state shall accuse of criminal conduct all heretics of both sexes, no matter by what name they appear on the rolls of citizens. And furthermore, that no heretical man or woman may dwell, sojourn, or maintain a bare subsistence in the country or any kind of jurisdiction or district belonging to it, whoever shall find the heretical man or woman shall boldly seize all their goods with impunity and freely carry them off, to belong to the remover with full right unless this kind of removing is restricted to persons designated by law.

Law 25: The head of state or ruler must force all the heretics whom he has in custody—provided he does so without killing them or breaking their arms or legs—as actual robbers and murderers of souls and thieves of the sacraments of God and the Christian faith, to confess their errors and accuse other heretics whom they know, and specify their motives. And those whom they have seduced, and those who have lodged them, as thieves and robbers of material goods, are made to accuse their accomplices and confess the crimes they have committed.

Law 37: In addition, the head of state or ruler of any city or district must delete or erase completely whatever in any statute or legal code is found to contradict or hinder in any way these regulations, statutes, or laws. And even in places outside his jurisdiction or district, these statutes, regulations, and laws shall be set forth if it seem good to the aforesaid diocesan or inquisitors.

Pope Innocent IV, *from "Ad Extirpanda." Innocent IV was elected to the papacy on June 25, 1243. In 1244, he fled Rome for Lyons, fearing the wrath of Emperor Frederick II, whom he had condemned and formally deposed for not recognizing the universal supremacy of the Church.*

"No, it's someone else," Basharat said.

Mian sahib turned to Sughra. "Open the door. It's him."

Sughra rose. She knew Gurmukh Singh. Her father had once done him a favor. He had been involved in a false legal suit and Mian sahib had acquitted him. That was a long time ago, but every year on the occasion of Id, he would come all the way from his village with a bag of homemade noodles. Mian sahib had told him several times, "Sardar sahib, you really are too kind. You shouldn't inconvenience yourself every year." But Gurmukh Singh would always reply, "Mian sahib, God has given you everything. This is only a small gift, which I bring every year in humble acknowledgement of the kindness you did me once. Even a hundred generations of mine would not be able to repay your favor. May God keep you happy."

Sughra was reassured. Why hadn't she thought of it in the first place? But why had Basharat said it was someone else? After all, he knew Gurmukh Singh's face from his annual visit.

Sughra went to the front door. There was another knock. Her heart missed a beat. "Who is it?" she asked in a faint voice.

Basharat whispered to her to look through a small hole in the door.

It wasn't Gurmukh Singh, who was a very old man. This was a young fellow. He knocked again. He was holding a bag in his hand, of the same kind Gurmukh Singh used to bring.

"Who are you?" she asked, a little more confident now.

"I am Sardar Gurmukh Singh's son, Santokh."

Sughra's fear had suddenly gone. "What brings you here today?" she asked politely.

"Where is Judge sahib?" he asked.

"He is not well," Sughra answered.

"Oh, I'm sorry," Santokh Singh said. Then he shifted his bag from one hand to the other. "These are homemade noodles." Then after a pause, "Sardarji is dead."

"Dead!"

"Yes, a month ago, but one of the last things he said to me was, 'For the last ten years on the occasion of Id I have always taken my small gift to Judge sahib. After I am gone, it will become your duty.' I gave him my word that I would not fail him. I am here today to honor the promise made to my father on his deathbed."

Sughra was so moved that tears came to her eyes. She opened the door a little. The young man pushed the bag toward her. "May God rest his soul," she said.

"Is Judge sahib not well?" he asked.

"No."

"What's wrong?"

"He had a stroke."

"Had my father been alive, it would have grieved him deeply. He never forgot Judge sahib's kindness until his last breath. He used to say, 'He is not a man, but a god.' May God keep him under his care. Please convey my respects to him."

He left before Sughra could make up her mind whether or not to ask him to get a doctor.

As Santokh Singh turned the corner, four men, their faces covered with their turbans, moved toward him. Two of them held burning oil torches, the others carried cans of kerosene oil and explosives. One of them asked Santokh, "Sardarji, have you completed your assignment?"

The young man nodded.

"Should we then proceed with ours?" he asked.

"If you like," he replied and walked away.

From "The Assignment." After the 1947 partition of British India, the Muslim playwright and short-story writer was compelled to move from Bombay to Karachi. One of his favorite hobbies was inventing rumors, once convincing friends that the Taj Mahal was moving to the United States. Salman Rushdie named him "the undisputed master of the modern Indian short story."

Celebrating Holy Week, Cordoba, 1998. Photograph by Stuart Franklin.

c. 58: Rome

JUMBLED ATOMS

Just so, don't think that the holy seats of the gods
Are found in any region of the world.
Our minds can hardly see, remote from sense,
The slender substance of their deities.
As they ever elude the touch and the strike of our hands,
They cannot touch a thing that we can touch.
A thing can't touch if it's not touchable.
Therefore their dwellings also must be different
From ours, and be as subtle as their bodies.
Further, to say that for man's sake the gods
Wished to prepare this glorious world, and therefore
It's only right to praise their handiwork
And think it will be deathless and eternal—
Shocking, that what the gods in their timeless wisdom
Founded for mankind to outlast the ages
You should ever shake from its base by any force,
Pound it with words and topple it—Memmius, to
Invent such errors and paste them one to the next
Is stupid. What gain can our grateful hearts bestow
Upon the blessed immortal gods, that they
Might take one step to act on our behalf?
What innovation after such long peace

Egyptian god Horus as a falcon, fourth century BC.

Can lure them on to wish to change their lives?
Only someone whom the old order thwarted
Takes joy in a new one; but if nothing irksome
Has ever befallen you down the beautiful ages,
What could enkindle a love for novelty?
Their lives, I suppose, lay sunk in sorrow and darkness
Until there dawned the birthday of the world?
And what did it hurt, that *we* had not been made?
Now whoever's been born, he ought to want to stay
Alive, so long as pleasures keep their charm.
But for him who's never tasted the love of life—
Never been on the roster—what harm, in not being born?
The model, moreover, first planted in their minds
For the very idea of man and the birth of the world,
Where did they get it? How could they see what to make?
How could they ever find out about first beginnings,
What those might make when you shuffle their order, if
Nature herself had given them no peek?
But many atoms jumbled in many ways,
Spurred on by blows through the endless stretch of time,
Are launched and driven along by their own weight
And come together and try all combinations,
Whatever their assemblies might create;
No wonder then, if into such arrangements
They happen also to fall, the tracks that would
Bring forth and still restore the universe.
But if I knew nothing of atoms, of what they were,
Still from the very ways of the heavens, from many
Other things I could name, I'd dare to assert
And prove that not for us and not by gods
Was this world made. There's too much wrong with it!

Lucretius, *from* On the Nature of Things. *Cicero once described Lucretius' poetry as "touched by flashes of genius." Lucretius had a deep contempt for the soothsayers and fortune-tellers, who stirred up religious fear; the first time he describes religion in his poem, it assumes the form of a monster in the sky. St. Jerome claimed that Lucretius was driven insane by a love potion and then committed suicide.*

ANSWERED PRAYER

Gibreel Farishta almost died.

He was filming at Kanya Kumari, standing on the very tip of Asia, taking part in a fight scene set at the point on Cape Comorin where it seems that three oceans are truly smashing into one another. Three sets of waves rolled in from the west east south and collided in a mighty clapping of watery hands just as Gibreel took a punch on the jaw, perfect timing, and he passed out on the spot, falling backward into tri-oceanic spume. He did not get up.

To begin with everybody blamed the giant English stuntman Eustace Brown, who had delivered the punch. He protested vehemently. Was he not the same fellow who had performed opposite Chief Minister N. T. Rama Rao in his many theological movie roles? Had he not perfected the art of making the old man look good in combat without hurting him? Had he ever complained that NTR never pulled *his* punches, so that he, Eustace, invariably ended up black and blue, having been beaten stupid by a little old guy whom he could've eaten for breakfast, on *toast*, and had he ever, even once, lost his temper? Well then? How could anyone think he would hurt the immortal Gibreel? They fired him anyway, and the police put him in the lockup just in case.

But it was not the punch that had flattened Gibreel. After the star had been flown into Bombay's Breach Candy Hospital in an air-force jet made available for the purpose, after exhaustive tests had come up with almost nothing, and while he lay unconscious, dying, with a blood count that had fallen from his normal 15 to a murderous 4.2, a hospital spokesman faced the national press on Breach Candy's wide white steps. "It is a freak mystery," he gave out. "Call it, if you so please, an act of God."

Gibreel Farishta had begun to hemorrhage all over his insides for no apparent reason and was quite simply bleeding to death inside his skin. At the worst moment the blood began to seep out through his rectum and penis, and it seemed that at any moment it might burst torrentially through his nose and ears and out of the corners of his eyes. For seven days he bled, and received transfusions, and every clotting agent known to medical science, including a concentrated form of rat poison, and although the treatment resulted in a marginal improvement, the doctors gave him up for lost.

The whole of India was at Gibreel's bedside. His condition was the lead item on every radio bulletin, it was the subject of hourly news flashes on the national television network, and the crowd that gathered in Warden Road was so large that the police had to disperse it with *lathi* charges and tear gas, which they used even though every one of the half-million mourners was already tearful and wailing. The prime minister cancelled her appointments and flew to visit him. Her son the airline pilot sat in Farishta's bedroom, holding the actor's hand. A mood of apprehension settled over the nation, because if God had unleashed such an act of retribution against his most celebrated incarnation, what did he have in store for the rest of the country? If Gibreel died, could India be far behind? In the mosques and temples of the nation, packed congregations prayed, not only for the life of the dying actor, but for the future, for themselves.

He recovered.

The recovery was as mysterious as the illness, and as rapid. It, too, was called (by hospital, journalists, friends) an act of the Supreme. A national holiday was declared; fireworks were set off up and down the land. But when Gibreel regained his strength, it became clear that he had changed—and to a startling degree—because he had lost his faith.

On the day he was discharged from hospital, he went under police escort through the immense crowd that had gathered to celebrate its own deliverance as well as his, climbed into his Mercedes, and told the driver to give all the pursuing vehicles the slip, which took seven hours and fifty-one minutes, and by the end

Adam relates the events of his life to Dante, illustration from *Paradise*, c. 1425.

of the maneuver he had worked out what had to be done. He got out of the limousine at the Taj hotel and without looking left or right went directly into the great dining room with its buffet table groaning under the weight of forbidden foods, and he loaded his plate with all of it—the pork sausages from Wiltshire and the cured York hams and the rashers of bacon from godknowswhere, with the gammon steaks of his unbelief and the pig's trotters of secularism; and then, standing there in the middle of the hall, while photographers popped up from nowhere, he began to eat as fast as possible, stuffing the dead pigs into his face so rapidly that bacon rashers hung out of the sides of his mouth.

During his illness he had spent every minute of consciousness calling upon God, every second of every minute. Ya Allah whose servant lies bleeding do not abandon me now after watching over me so long. Ya Allah show me some sign, some small mark of your favor, that I may find in myself the strength to cure my ills. O God most beneficent most merciful, be with me in this my time of need, my most grievous need. Then it occurred to him that he was being punished, and for a time that made it possible to suffer the pain, but after a time he got angry. Enough, God, his unspoken words demanded, why must I die when I have not killed—are you vengeance, or are you love? The anger with God carried him through another day, but then it faded, and in its place there came a terrible emp-

tiness, an isolation, as he realized he was talking to *thin air*, that there was nobody there at all, and then he felt more foolish than ever in his life, and he began to plead into the emptiness, ya Allah, just be there, damn it, just be. But he felt nothing, nothing nothing, and then one day he found that he no longer needed there to be anything to feel. On that day of metamorphosis, the illness changed and his recovery began. And to prove to himself the nonexistence of God, he now stood in the dining hall of the city's most famous hotel with pigs falling out of his face.

He looked up from his plate to find a woman watching him. Her hair was so fair that it was almost white, and her skin possessed the color and translucency of mountain ice. She laughed at him and turned away.

"Don't you get it?" he shouted after her, spewing sausage fragments from the corners of his mouth. "No thunderbolt. That's the point."

She came back to stand in front of him. "You're alive," she told him. "You got your life back. *That's* the point."

Salman Rushdie, *from* The Satanic Verses. *The Ayatollah Khomeini issued a fatwa against the Booker Prize–winning author in 1989 for the character in his novel modeled after Muhammad, whose faith in Allah is briefly shaken. A similar account about the Prophet is related in several expurgated verses of the Qur'an referred to as "the Satanic Verses." Rushdie published* Shalimar the Clown *in 2005 and* The Enchantress of Florence *in 2008.*

Colossal bronze statue of the Buddha Amitabha, Japan, 1252.

c. 1657: Paris

A WAGER

On contemplating our blindness and wretchedness, on observing the whole of the silent universe and humanity with no light abandoned to itself, lost in this nook of the universe not knowing who put us there, what we have come to achieve, or what will become of us when we die, incapable of all knowledge, I become frightened, like someone taken in his sleep to a terrifying, deserted island who wakes up with no knowledge of what has happened, and no means of escape. At that point I am astonished that we do not despair at so wretched a state. I see others around me whose nature is the same as mine, and I ask them if they are better informed than I am. They say they are not.

Then these wretched, lost people, having looked around and seen some agreeable enough objects, gave themselves to them and became attached to them. For my part I have not been able to find such an attachment, and considering how much more probable it is that there is something more that I cannot see, I have sought to find whether this God has not left some mark of himself.

If there is a God, he is infinitely beyond our comprehension, since, having neither parts nor limits, he bears no relation to ourselves. We are therefore incapable of knowing either what he is, or if he is. That being so, who will dare to undertake a resolution of this question? It cannot be us, who bear no relationship to him.

Let us therefore examine this point, and say God is, or is not. But toward which side will we lean? Reason cannot decide anything. There is an infinite chaos separating us. At the far end of this infinite distance a game is being played, and the coin will come down heads or tails. How will you wager? Reason cannot make you choose one way or the other; reason cannot make you defend either of the two choices.

So do not accuse those who have made a choice of being wrong, for you know nothing about it! "No, I will blame them not for having made this choice, but for having made any choice. For though the one who chooses heads and the other one are equally wrong, they are both wrong. The right thing is not to wager at all."

Yes, but you have to wager. It is not up to you—you are already committed. Which then will you choose? Let us see. Since you have to choose, let us see which interests you the least. You have two things to lose, the truth and the good, and two things to stake, your reason and will, your knowledge and beatitude. And your nature has two things to avoid, error and wretchedness. Your reason is not hurt more by choosing one rather than the other, since you do have to make the choice. That is one point disposed of. But your beatitude? Let us weigh up the gain and the loss by calling heads that God exists. Let us assess the two cases: if you win, you win everything; if you lose, you lose nothing. Wager that he exists then, without hesitating!

"This is wonderful. Yes, I must wager. But even so … Is there no way of seeing underneath the cards?" "Yes, scripture and the rest, etc." "Yes, but my hands are tied and I cannot speak a word. I am being forced to wager and I am not free; they will not let me go. And I am made in such a way that I cannot believe. So what do you want me to do?" "That is true. But at least realize that your inability to believe, since reason urges you to do so and yet you cannot, arises from your passions. So concentrate not on convincing yourself by increasing the number of proofs of God but on diminishing your passions. You want to find faith and you do not know the way? You want to cure yourself of unbelief and you ask for the remedies? Learn from those who have been bound like you and who now wager all they have. They are people who know the road you want to follow and have been cured of the affliction of which you want to be cured. Follow the way by which they began, by behaving just as if they believed, taking holy water, having masses said, etc. That will make you believe quite naturally and according to your animal reactions." "But that is what I am afraid of." "Why? What do you have to lose?"

The most beautiful thing we can experience is the mysterious. It is the source of all true art and science. He to whom the emotion is a stranger, who can no longer pause to wonder and stand wrapped in awe, is as good as dead—his eyes are closed. The insight into the mystery of life, coupled though it be with fear, has also given rise to religion. To know what is impenetrable to us really exists, manifesting itself as the highest wisdom and the most radiant beauty, which our dull faculties can comprehend only in their most primitive forms—this knowledge, this feeling is at the center of true religiousness.
—*Albert Einstein, 1930*

What harm will come to you from taking this course? You will be faithful, honest, humble, grateful, doing good, a sincere and true friend. It is of course true—you will not take part in corrupt pleasure, in glory, in the pleasures of high living. But will you not have others?

I tell you that you will win thereby in this life, and that at every step you take along this path you will see so much certainty of winning and so negligible a risk that you will realize in the end that you have wagered on something certain and infinite, for which you have paid nothing.

Blaise Pascal, *from* Pensées. *During what has been called his "worldly period" from 1651–1654, Pascal studied the weight and density of air and laid the foundations for the calculus of probability. On November 23, 1654, he experienced what he later called the "night of fire," an intense and mystical conversion that he believed to mark the beginning of a new life. His* Pensées *were unfinished at the time of his death in 1662.*

1513: Spain

LAY DOWN YOUR ARMS

On the part of the king, Don Fernando, and of Doña Juana, his daughter, queen of Castile and Leon, subduers of the barbarous nations, we their servants notify and make known to you as best we can that the Lord our God, living and eternal, created the heaven and the earth and one man and one woman—of whom you and we and all the men of the world were and are descendants. But on account of the multitude

> *If the Buddha or Confucius had been asked whether he believed in God, he would probably have winced slightly and explained—with great courtesy—that this was not an appropriate question. If anybody had asked Amos or Ezekiel if he was a "monotheist," who believed in only one God, he would have been equally perplexed.*
> *—Karen Armstrong, 2006*

which has sprung from this man and woman in the five thousand years since the world was created, it was necessary that some men should go one way and some another, and that they should be divided into many kingdoms and provinces, for in one alone they could not be sustained.

Of all these nations God our Lord gave charge to one man, called St. Peter, that he should be lord and superior of all the men in the world, that all should obey him, and that he should be the head of the whole human race, wherever men should live, and under whatever law, sect, or belief they should be—and he gave him the world for his kingdom and jurisdiction.

And he commanded him to place his seat in Rome as the spot most fitting to rule the world from, but also he permitted him to have his seat in any other part of the world and to judge and govern all Christians, Moors, Jews, Gentiles, and all other sects. This man was called pope, as if to say admirable great father and governor of men. The men who lived in

that time obeyed that St. Peter and took him for lord, king, and superior of the universe—so also they have regarded the others who after him have been elected to the pontificate, and so has it been continued even till now and will continue till the end of the world.

One of these pontiffs who succeeded that St. Peter as lord of the world in the dignity and seat which I have before mentioned made donation of these isles and terra firma to the aforesaid king and queen and to their successors, our lords, with all that there are in these territories.

So their highnesses are kings and lords of these islands and land of terra firma by virtue of this donation, and some islands—and indeed almost all those to whom this has been notified—have received and served their highnesses as lords and kings in the way that subjects ought to do—with good will, without any resistance, immediately, without delay—when they were informed of the aforesaid facts. And also they received and obeyed the priests whom their highnesses sent to preach to them and to teach them our holy faith, and all these—of their own free will, without any reward or condition—have become Christians and are so. And their highnesses have joyfully and benignantly received them and also have commanded them to be treated as their subjects and vassals, and you too are held and obliged to do the same. Wherefore, as best we can, we ask and require you that you consider what we have said to you and that you take the time necessary to understand and deliberate upon it—and that you acknowledge the Church as the ruler and superior of the whole world and the high priest called Pope—and in his name, the king and Queen Doña Juana our lords, in his place, as superiors and lords and kings of these islands and this terra firma by virtue of the said donation—and that you consent and give place that these religious fathers should declare and preach to you the aforesaid.

If you do so you will do well, and that which you are obliged to do to their highnesses, we in their name shall receive you in

Singing His Praises

Religious bands and a sampling of their albums, song titles, and lyrics

Genre	Band	Album	Song	Lyric
Christian Metal	STRYPER (Salvation Through Redemption, Yielding Peace, Encouragement, and Righteousness)	*To Hell with the Devil*	"Rock the Hell Out of You"	Why lose when you could win? Give God a try.
Muslim Punk	The Kominas	*Wild Nights in Guantanamo Bay*	"Sharia Law in the USA"	Suicide bomb the Gap.
Jewish Folk	Debbie Friedman	*The Alef Bet*	"The World of Your Dreams (Andy's Bar Mitzvah Song)"	I'm a latke, I'm a latke, and I'm waiting for Chanukah to come.
Christian Rap/Rock Crossover	DC Talk	*Jesus Freak*	"Word 2 the Father"	We're just two honks and a Negro servin' the Lord.
Muslim Hip Hop	Shaheed	*Scholar Warrior*	"Not My Myspace Friend"	I honor this song by puttin' the Prophet in it.
Hasidic Reggae	Matisyahu	*Shake off the Dust ... Arise*	"Struggla"	Three thousand years with no place to be / And they want me to give up my milk and honey.

all love and charity and shall leave you your wives and your children and your lands free without servitude, that you may do with them and with yourselves freely that which you like and think best. And they shall not compel you to turn Christians unless you yourselves when informed of the truth should wish to be converted to our holy Catholic faith, as almost all the inhabitants of the rest of the islands have done. And besides this, their highnesses award you many privileges and exemptions and will grant you many benefits.

But, if you do not do this and maliciously make delay in it, I certify to you that with the help of God we shall powerfully enter into your country and make war against you in all ways and manners that we can, and shall subject you to the yoke and obedience of the Church and of their highnesses. We shall take you and your wives and your children and shall make slaves of them, and as such shall sell and dispose of them as their highnesses may command. And we shall take away your goods and do you all the mischief and damage that we can—as to vassals who do not obey and refuse to receive their lord and resist and contradict him. And we protest that the deaths and losses which shall accrue from this are your fault and not that of their highnesses, or ours, nor of these cavaliers who come with us. And that we have said this to you, and made this Requisition, we request the notary here present to give us his testimony in writing, and we ask the rest who are present that they should be witnesses of this Requisition.

> **Juan López de Palacios Rubios**, *from* Requerimiento. *Conquistadores were required to carry a copy of this statement and read it aloud to the American natives they encountered. As a lawyer and jurist, Rubios found fault with the barbarous breaches of European civil society, among them promiscuity and domestic matriarchy.*

IRIS MURDOCH HEARS A CONFESSION

Guy said, "Hello, Anne."

"Hello, Guy."

"I'm glad you've come."

"I'm glad, too."

His voice was unexpectedly strong, a voice of authority. There was a silence. Guy was turning his head rhythmically to and fro and bending and stretching his fingers. Anne wondered if he was in pain.

"Won't you sit down? Come nearer. I want to see you."

Anne pulled a chair up beside the bed and sat down. She smiled at Guy.

He smiled with a strange, quick spasm. He said, "I'm so glad you've come, for Gertrude. You will stay till I go, and after too?"

"Yes, of course."

"She loves you, I think."

"Yes. I love her."

There was silence again. Anne breathed quietly, praying blankly, feeling an immense, tired quiet like a cloud rising up out of her. She did not feel able to make conversation, but there might be no need, perhaps it was all right just to sit there.

"Why did you leave the convent?" said Guy.

Anne was suddenly alert, electric with precision. "I changed my views about religion. It would have been a lie to stay."

"Maybe you should have hung on. Christian theology is changing so fast these days. The relieving troops would have arrived. You would have heard the sound of bagpipes."

"No theologian could have rescued me!"

"Lost your faith—?"

"That's not quite the phrase. Perhaps people don't all that often just *lose* their faith. I want to make a new kind of faith, privately for myself, and this can only be done out in the world."

"Inside you had to say what you didn't believe, even if you said nothing?"

"Yes."

"Do you still believe in a personal God?"

"Not in a personal God."

"Then in some sort of mysterious world spirit? Zeus, whoever you are."

"No, nothing of that sort. It's hard to explain. Perhaps I just can't make any more use of the word God."

"I've always hated God," said Guy.

"You mean the Old Man?"

"Yes."

"Did you ever have any Jewish religion? But of course your family were Christians."

"Scarcely. We knew about the Jewish festivals. There was a kind of nostalgia. It was odd. I knew about holiness."

"Isn't that religion?"

"What did you mean about a faith privately for yourself?"

"I suppose every faith is private. I just mean—it wouldn't have names and concepts, I would never describe it, but it would live and I would know it. I feel as if I've finished talking."

"I've often felt that," said Guy, "but it was an illusion. What will you do?"

"I don't know, some sort of social work, I'm not thinking about it yet."

"And Jesus, what about him?"

"What about him indeed."

"Will he be part of your new faith?"

"Yes," said Anne. "I—I think so—"

"My uncle David Schultz once told me that if at the world's end it turned out that Jesus was the Messiah, he would accept him. It's interesting to speculate on the alternative."

"Some of your family kept to the Jewish faith?"

"He was an uncle by marriage. But yes. You must ask Veronica Mount, she's the expert. I used to hate Jesus too."

"However could you? I can imagine hating God, but not Jesus."

"I mean the symbol not the man. One must pity the man. Judaism is a sober religion, teaching, prayer, no excesses. But Christianity is so soft, it's sentimental and magical, it denies death. It changes death into suffering, and suffering is always so interesting. There is pain, and then, hey presto, there is eternal life. That's what we all want, that our misery shall buy something, that we shall get something in return, something absolutely consoling. But it's a lie. There are final conclusions, one is shortly to be reached in this house. Eternal departures take place. Suffering has the shifting unreality of the human mind. A desire to suffer probably led you into that convent, perhaps it has led you out again. Death is real. But Christ doesn't really die. That can't be right."

"Right or wrong, it's the point."

"It's not *your* point."

"No—" Anne wanted to think about what he was saying, though his strained utterance distressed her. "I think—we want our vices to suffer—but not to go away."

"Yes. Yes. We want … because of the suffering … to be able to keep … everything … to be forgiven."

"That seems to you soft?"

"Yes."

They were silent again. Anne thought, I can say anything to this man.

Guy said, "You don't, I imagine, believe in the antireligious idea of life after death?"

"No. I agree it's antireligious. I mean—whatever it is—it's happening now and here." That's what I couldn't tell them in the convent, she thought.

"I wish I believed in the hereafter," said Guy. He had been looking away from her, twisting his hair with one restless hand, showing her his hawk-nosed profile. Now his eyes glittered at her. "Not for any vulgar reason of course. Not just to be let off this thing that's going to happen in the next few weeks. But—it's something I've always felt—"

"What?"

Circe, by Edgar Bertram Mackennal, 1893.

"I would like to be judged."

Anne reflected. "I wonder if it's a coherent idea? It seems to me a little like what you didn't care for about Christianity."

"I know exactly what you mean," said Guy. She had pleased him. He smiled a sweeter smile which softened the taut face. "It's romantic, sadomasochistic, a story idea, not what it seems—indeed—"

"Do you mean judgment as estimation, a clear account, or as punishment?"

"Oh both. I think one *craves* for both. To look over the recording angel's shoulder. And to have consequences. Consequences would prove something."

"What do you want proved? Gertrude said you were writing a book about punishment."

Guy frowned. "Did she? It's nothing yet. I mean—it's nothing, just a sketch."

"Can you tell me anything about it?"

"It's an impossible subject. If a Home Office official writes a book on punishment it's bound to be—oh you know—about deterrence and rehabilitation."

"And leaves out retribution, and that's what you want?"

"For myself, yes."

"Don't you think others may need it, want it, too?"

"Oh maybe, but I'm only interested in my own case. Like you."

From Nuns and Soldiers. *Murdoch reportedly wrote her twenty-six novels longhand, using a Mont Blanc fountain pen. After expressing an early interest in archaeology and painting, Murdoch turned toward philosophy, particularly the work of Ludwig Wittgenstein, whose theories informed her first novel,* Under the Net. *"We live in a fantasy world," Murdoch once said, "and the great task in life is to find reality."*

c. 620: Arabia

GOD SEES ALL

Everything in the heavens
and everything on earth glorifies God,
to whom belongs the dominion
and who deserves all praise;
and who has power over all things.
That is the one who created you all;
but some of you deny,
while some of you believe.
And God sees whatever you do.
God created the heavens
and the earth soundly,
and formed you all,
fashioning you expertly;
and the destination is to God.
God knows what is in
the heavens and the earth,
and knows what you conceal
and what you reveal.
And God knows what is contained in hearts.
Has no account come to you
of those who scoffed before?
They experienced the ill consequence
of what they were about,
suffering intense agony.
That is because their messengers
brought them clear explanations,
yet they said, "What?
Human beings directing us?"
And they scoffed and turned away,
though God was unaffected,
for God is absolutely independent,
worthy of all praise.

Those who scoff think
they'll never be resurrected:
say, "On the contrary—by my Lord,
you will surely be resurrected,
and then you will be told
about everything you did.
And that is easy for God."
So believe in God
and the messenger of God,
and the light that We sent down,
as God is aware of whatever you do.
The day God assembles you
for a day of gathering,
that will be a day of outdoing—
whoever believes in God
and acts with integrity,
God will efface their evils from them
and admit them to gardens
below which rivers flow,
to abide therein forever:
that is the great success.
As for those who scoffed
and repudiated Our signs,
they will be inmates of the fire,
where they will abide;
and what a miserable destination!

From the Qur'an. Islam holds that between 610 and 632 the archangel Gabriel commanded the Prophet Muhammad to convey the message of Allah to mankind. The revelation became a written text in 633. Because Arabic is the sacred language of Islam, the Qur'an is considered untranslatable, even though it has been rendered into nearly every other language.

1942: England

ELUDING THE DEVIL

My Dear Reverend Father Perrin,

What frightens me is the Church as a social structure. Not only on account of its blemishes, but from the very fact that it is something social. It is not that I am of a very individualistic temperament. I am afraid for the opposite reason. I am aware of very strong gregarious tendencies in myself. My natural disposition is to be very easily influenced—too much influenced—and above all by anything collective. I know that if at this moment

I never spoke with God,
Nor visited in heaven;
Yet certain am I of the spot
As if the chart were given.
                    —*Emily Dickinson, c. 1860*

I had before me a group of twenty young Germans singing Nazi songs in chorus, a part of my soul would instantly become Nazi. That is a very great weakness, but that is how I am. I think that it is useless to fight directly against natural weaknesses. One has to force oneself to act as though one did not have them in circumstances where a duty makes it imperative, and in the ordinary course of life one has to know these weaknesses, prudently take them into account, and strive to turn them to good purpose—for they are all capable of being put to some good purpose.

I am afraid of the Church patriotism existing in Catholic circles. By patriotism I mean the feeling one has for a terrestrial country. I am afraid of it because I fear to catch it. It is not that the Church appears to me to be unworthy of inspiring such a feeling. It is because I do not want any feeling of such a kind in myself. The word "want" is not accurate. I *know*, I feel quite certain, that any feeling of this kind, whatever its object, would be fatal for me.

There were some saints who approved of the Crusades or the Inquisition. I cannot help thinking that they were in the wrong. I cannot go against the light of conscience. If I think that on this point I see more clearly than they did, I who am so far below them, I must admit that in this matter they were blinded by something very powerful. This something was the Church seen as a social structure. If this social structure did them harm, what harm would it not do me, who is particularly susceptible to social influences and almost infinitely more feeble than they were?

Nothing ever said or written goes so far as the devil's words to Christ in St. Luke concerning the kingdoms of the world: "All this power will I give thee and the glory of it, for that is delivered unto me and to whomsoever I will I give it." It follows from this that the social is irremediably the domain of the devil. The flesh impels us to say *me* and the devil impels us to say *us*, or else to say like the dictators *I* with a collective signification. And, in conformity with his particular mission, the devil manufactures a false imitation of what is divine, an ersatz divinity.

By social I do not mean everything connected with citizenship, but only collective emotions.

I am well aware that the Church must inevitably be a social structure, otherwise it would not exist. But insofar as it is a social structure, it belongs to the Prince of this world. It is because it is an organ for the preservation and transmission of truth that there is an extreme danger for those who, like me, are excessively open to social influences. For in this way what is purest and what is most defiling look very much the same, and confused under the same words, make an almost undecomposable mixture.

Simone Weil, *from* Waiting for God. *At the age of five, Weil refused to eat sugar in a show of solidarity with French soldiers serving in World War I, who were without it. After being injured while training for the Spanish Civil War, she experienced the first of several mystical episodes that shaped her thinking. In 1942 she began to support the French Resistance but succumbed to overexertion and was committed to a sanatorium, where she died in 1943.*

Last Supper, by El Greco, c. 1567–70.

c. 500 BC: Nepal

SPIRITUAL THIRST

In the shade of the house, in the sunlight on the riverbank near the boats, in the shade of the sal-tree forest, in the shade of the banyan fig, Siddhartha grew up, the handsome son of the Brahmin, the young falcon, together with Govinda, his friend, the son of a Brahmin. Sunshine browned his pale shoulders on the riverbank, while bathing during the ritual ablutions, during the sacred offerings. Shadows flowed into his dark eyes in the mango grove when at play with other boys, while his mother sang, while the sacred offerings were made, while his father the scholar gave instruction, while the wise men conversed. Siddhartha had already been participating for quite some time in the discussions of the sages—with Govinda he practiced debating, with Govinda he practiced the art of concentration in the service of meditative absorption. Already he understood how to speak the Om without a sound, the word of words, soundlessly pronouncing it within while inhaling, soundlessly speaking it out while exhaling, his soul gathered in, composed, his brow surrounded by radiance, ringed with the glow of his clear-thinking mind. Already he understood; within the interior of his being he recognized Atman, indestructible, at one with the universe.

His father's heart skipped joyously for this son who was quick to learn, who was thirsty for knowledge; in him he saw growing a great sage and priest, a prince among the Brahmins.

Govinda knew this would be no ordinary Brahmin, no idle sacrificial official, no greedy merchant of magic formulas, no vain empty orator, no mean conniving priest, neither would he be a silly simple sheep in the herd of the many. No, nor did he, Govinda, want to be one among ten thousand Brahmins. He wanted to follow his beloved, his magnificent Siddhartha. And if ever Siddhartha were to become a god, if he were to arrive among the radiant, then Govinda wanted to follow him, as his friend, his companion, as his servant, his spearman, his shadow.

Heads of Zeus-Oromandes and a goddess, Turkey, first century BC.

Everyone loved Siddhartha in this way. He brought delight to everyone; to everyone he was a pleasure.

But he, Siddhartha, did not delight himself, he was no pleasure to himself. Ambling down the rosy paths of the fig garden, sitting in the bluish shade of the meditation grove, washing his limbs daily in the expiatory bath, making sacrifices in the deep shade of the mango forest with perfect decorum in all his gestures, beloved by all, a joy to all, in his own heart he still bore no joy. Dreams came to him and turbulent thoughts came flowing from the river water, sparkling from the night stars, melting from the sun's rays; dreams came to him and a restlessness of his soul rose in the smoke from the sacrifices, breathed from the verses of the Rig Veda, trickled down from the teachings of the old Brahmins.

Within himself Siddhartha had begun to nourish discontent. He had begun to feel that the love of his father and the love of his mother and even the love of his friend Govinda would not forever after delight him, soothe him, satisfy, and suffice him. He had begun to surmise that his venerable father and his other teachers, that these wise Brahmins had already conveyed the majority and the best part of their wisdom, that they had already poured out their plenty into his waiting vessel—and the vessel was not full, the mind was not satisfied, the soul was not calm, the heart not stilled. Ablutions were good, but they were water; they did not wash away sin, they did not quench spiritual thirst, they did not dissolve fear in the heart. Sacrificing to the gods and invoking them was excellent— but was this all? Did sacrifices bring happiness? And what was the nature of the gods? Was it really Prajapati who had created the world? Was it not the Atman, He, the Sole One, the All One? Were not the gods representations, created as you and I, subject to time, transitory? Was it therefore good, was it right, was it a meaningful and supreme act to sacrifice to the gods? To whom else was one to sacrifice, whom else was one to venerate, besides Him, the Only One, the Atman? And where was Atman to be found, where did He abide, where did His eternal heart beat, where else but within one's own I, deep inside, in what is indestructible, borne within every individual? But where, where was this innermost and ultimate I? The great sages taught that it was not flesh and bone, it was neither thought nor consciousness. Where, where then was it to be found? To press toward there, to penetrate to the I, to me, to the Atman—was there another path worth seeking? Alas, no one showed the way, no one knew it, not one's father, not the teachers or the sages, not the holy sacrificial hymns! The Brahmins and their sacred books knew everything, everything! They had seen to everything and more: the creation of the world, the origin of speech, food, inhalation, exhalation, the order of the senses, the deeds of the gods—they knew infinitely much—but was there value in knowing everything if one did not know the only thing that matters?

Certainly, many verses of the holy books, splendid verses, especially in the Upanishads of the Sama Veda, spoke of this, the innermost and ultimate. "Your soul is the entire world." So it is written there, and it is also written that when a person is asleep, in deep sleep, he enters into his innermost place and abides in Atman. Wondrous wisdom exists in these verses—all that the sages know is gathered here in magical words, pure as honey gathered by bees. No, this enormous quantity of knowledge, gathered and preserved here by countless generations of wise Brahmins was not to be despised. But where were the Brahmins, where the priests, the sages, or penitents who had succeeded in having this the deepest knowledge not only in their minds but also in their experience? Where was the initiate who could magically conjure intimacy with Atman from deep sleep into waking life, into every move, into every word and deed? Siddhartha knew many venerable Brahmins, his father best of all, the pure one, the scholar most highly revered. His father was admirable, his conduct calm and noble, his life pure, his words wise; fine, noble thoughts occupied his brow—but he, too, like so many who had acquired knowledge, did he live in bliss, was he at peace, was he not still a seeker, did he not

Among all nations, through the darkest polytheism glimmer some faint sparks of monotheism. —Immanuel Kant, 1781

thirst? Did he not return again and again, thirsting, to the holy sources, to drink, to sacrifice, to read the books, to engage in dialogue with other Brahmins? Why must he, who was blameless, wash sin away daily, take pains to purify himself every day, day after day after day? Did not Atman dwell inside him, did not the primal source flow within his own heart? It had to be found, the primal source within the individual I—one had to possess it oneself! Everything else was searching, sidestepping, going astray.

Such was Siddhartha's thinking, such was his thirst, such his suffering.

Often he would say these words from a section of the Chandogya Upanishad to himself: "Yea, of this Brahmin the name is Satyam—the True; he who knows this enters everyday into heaven." Often it seemed near, the heavenly world, but he had never quite reached it, never extinguished the ultimate thirst. And among all the wise and most sagacious men he knew and whose instruction he savored, among them all there was not one who had quite reached heaven, who had entirely quenched his eternal thirst.

Hermann Hesse, *from* Siddartha. *Considered the most widely read German author of the twentieth century, Hesse received the inspiration for his book about the quest for enlightenment while on a trip to Southeast Asia in 1911. He spent eleven years writing his longest and final novel,* The Glass Bead Game, *which was published in 1943. Three years later, he received the Nobel Prize for Literature.*

c. 1938: New York City

THE RISE AND FALL
OF JAMES BALDWIN

All the fears with which I had grown up, and which were now a part of me and controlled my vision of the world, rose up like a wall between the world and me, and drove me into the church.

As I look back, everything I did seems curiously deliberate, though it certainly did not seem deliberate then. For example, I did not join the church of which my father was

God never wrought miracle to convince atheism, because his ordinary works convince it. —*Francis Bacon, 1625*

a member and in which he preached. My best friend in school, who attended a different church, had already "surrendered his life to the Lord," and he was very anxious about my soul's salvation. (I wasn't, but any human attention was better than none.) One Saturday afternoon, he took me to his church. There were no services that day, and the church was empty, except for some women cleaning and some other women praying. My friend took me into the back room to meet his pastor—a woman. There she sat, in her robes, smiling, an extremely proud and handsome woman, with Africa, Europe, and the America of the American Indian blended in her face. She was perhaps forty-five or fifty at this time, and in our world she was a very celebrated woman. My friend was about to introduce me when she looked at me and smiled and said, "Whose little boy are you?" Now this, unbelievably, was precisely the phrase used by pimps and racketeers on the avenue when they suggested, both humorously and intensely, that I "hang out" with them. Perhaps part of the terror they had caused me to feel came from the fact that I unquestionably wanted to be *somebody's* little boy. I was so frightened, and at the mercy of so many conundrums, that

inevitably, that summer, *someone* would have taken me over; one doesn't, in Harlem, long remain standing on any auction block. It was my good luck—perhaps—that I found myself in the church racket instead of some other, and surrendered to a spiritual seduction long before I came to any carnal knowledge. For when the pastor asked me, with that marvelous smile, "Whose little boy are you?" my heart replied at once, "Why, yours."

The summer wore on, and things got worse. I became more guilty and more frightened, and kept all this bottled up inside me, and naturally, inescapably, one night, when this woman had finished preaching, everything came roaring, screaming, crying out, and I fell to the ground before the altar. It was the strangest sensation I have ever had in my life—up to that time, or since. I had not known that it was going to happen, or that it could happen. One moment I was on my feet, singing and clapping and at the same time working out in my head the plot of a play I was working on then; the next moment, with no transition, no sensation of falling, I was on my back, with the lights beating down into my face and all the vertical saints above me. I did not know what I was doing down so low, or how I had got there. And the anguish that filled me cannot be described. It moved in me like one of those floods that devastate counties, tearing everything down, tearing children from their parents and lovers from each other, and making everything an unrecognizable waste. All I really remember is the pain, the unspeakable pain; it was as though I were yelling up to heaven and heaven would not hear me. And if heaven would not hear me, if love could not descend from heaven—to wash me, to make me clean—then utter disaster was my portion. Yes, it does indeed mean something—something unspeakable—to be born, in a white country, an Anglo-Teutonic, antisexual country, black. You very soon, without knowing it, give up all hope of communion. Black people, mainly, look down or look up but do not look at each other, not at you—and white people, mainly, look away. And the universe is simply a

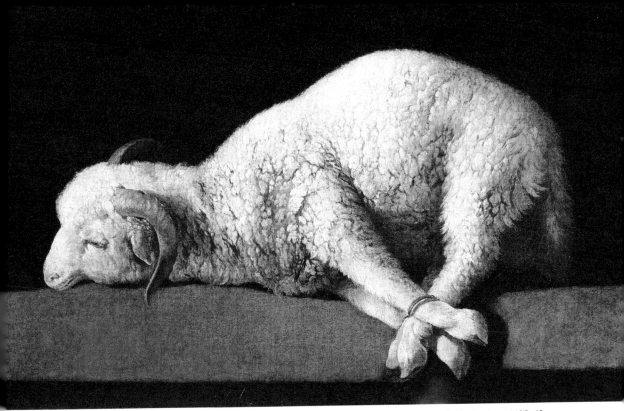

Agnus Dei, by Francisco de Zurbarán, c. 1635–40.

sounding drum; there is no way, no way whatever—so it seemed then and has sometimes seemed since—to get through a life, to love your wife and children, or your friends, or your mother and father, or to be loved. The universe, which is not merely the stars and the moon and the planets, flowers, grass, and trees, but *other people*, has evolved no terms for your existence, has made no room for you, and if love will not swing wide the gates, no other power will or can. And if one despairs—as who has not?—of human love, God's love alone is left. But God—and I felt this even then, so long ago, on that tremendous floor, unwillingly—is white. And if His love was so great, and if He loved all His children, why were we, the blacks, cast down so far? Why? In spite of all I said thereafter, I found no answer on the floor—not *that* answer, anyway—and I was on the floor all night. Over me, to bring me "through," the saints sang and rejoiced and prayed. And in the morning, when they raised me, they told me that I was "saved."

Well, indeed I was, in a way, for I was utterly drained and exhausted, and released, for the first time, from all my guilty torment. I was aware then only of my relief. For many years, I could not ask myself why human relief had to be achieved in a fashion at once so pagan and so desperate—in a fashion at once so unspeakably old and so unutterably new. And by the time I was able to ask myself this question, I was also able to see that the principles governing the rites and customs of the churches in which I grew up did not differ from the principles governing the rites and customs of other churches, white. The principles were blindness, loneliness, and terror, the first principle necessarily and actively cultivated in order to deny the two others. I would love to believe that the principles were faith, hope, and charity, but this is clearly not so for most Christians, or for what we call the Christian world.

I was saved. But at the same time, out of a deep adolescent cunning I do not pretend to understand, I realized immediately that I could not remain in the church merely as another worshipper. I would have to give myself something to do, in order not to be too bored and find myself among all the wretched unsaved of the avenue. And I don't doubt that I also intended to best my father on his own ground.

Anyway, very shortly after I joined the church, I became a preacher—a Young Minister—and I remained in the pulpit for more than three years. My youth quickly made me a much bigger drawing card than my father. I pushed this advantage ruthlessly, for it was the most effective means I had found of breaking his hold over me. That was the most frightening time of my life, and quite the most dishonest, and the resulting hysteria lent great passion to my sermons—for a while. I relished the attention and the relative

My heart is capable of every form,
A cloister for the monk, a fane for idols,
A pasture for gazelles, the pilgrim's Kaaba,
The Tables of the Torah, the Qur'an.
Love is the faith I hold: wherever turn
His camels, still the one true faith is mine.
—Ibn al-Arabi, c. 1200

immunity from punishment that my new status gave me, and I relished above all the sudden right to privacy. It had to be recognized, after all, that I was still a schoolboy, with my schoolwork to do, and I was also expected to prepare at least one sermon a week. During what we may call my heyday, I preached much more often than that. This meant that there were hours and even whole days when I could not be interrupted—not even by my father. I had immobilized him. It took rather more time for me to realize that I had also immobilized myself, and had escaped from nothing whatever.

The church was very exciting. It took a long time for me to disengage myself from this excitement, and on the blindest, most visceral level, I never really have, and never will. There is no music like that music, no drama like the drama of the saints rejoicing, the sinners moaning, the tambourines racing, and all those voices coming together and crying holy unto the Lord. There is still, for me, no pathos quite like the pathos of those multicolored, worn, somehow triumphant and transfigured faces, speaking from the depths of a visible, tangible, continuing despair of the goodness of the Lord.

I have never seen anything to equal the fire and excitement that sometimes, without warning, fill a church, causing the church, as Leadbelly and so many others have testified, to "rock." Nothing that has happened to me since equals the power and the glory that I sometimes felt when in the middle of a sermon I knew that I was somehow, by some miracle, really carrying, as they said, "the Word"—when the church and I were one. Their pain and their joy were mine, and mine were theirs—they surrendered their pain and joy to me, I surrendered mine to them—and their cries of "Amen!" and "Hallelujah!" and "Yes, Lord!" and "Praise His name!" and "Preach it, brother!" sustained and whipped on my solos until we all became equal, wringing wet, singing and dancing, in anguish and rejoicing, at the foot of the altar. It was, for a long time, in spite of—or, not inconceivably, because of—the shabbiness of my motives, my only sustenance, my meat and drink. I rushed home from school, to the church, to the altar, to be alone there, to commune with Jesus, my dearest Friend, who would never fail me, who knew all the secrets of my heart. Perhaps He did, but I didn't, and the bargain we struck, actually, down there at the foot of the cross, was that He would never let me find out.

He failed His bargain. He was a much better Man than I took Him for. It happened, as things do, imperceptibly, in many ways at once. I date it—the slow crumbling of my faith, the pulverization of my fortress—from the time, about a year after I had begun to preach, when I began to read again. I justified this desire by the fact that I was still in school, and I began, fatally, with Dostoevsky. By this time, I was in a high school that was predominantly Jewish. This meant that I was surrounded by people who were by definition beyond any hope of salvation, who laughed at the tracts and leaflets I brought to school, and who pointed out that the Gospels had been written long after the death of Christ. This might not have been so distressing if it had not forced me to read the tracts and leaflets myself, for they were indeed—unless one believed their message already—impossible to believe. I remember feeling dimly that there was a kind of blackmail in it. People, I felt, ought to love the Lord *because* they loved Him, and not because they were afraid of going to hell. I was forced, reluctantly, to realize that the Bible itself had been written by men and translated by men out of languages I could not read, and I was already, without quite admitting it to myself, terribly involved with the effort of putting words on paper. Of course, I had the rebuttal ready: these men had all been operating under divine inspiration. *Had* they? *All* of them? And I also knew by now, alas, far more about divine inspiration than I dared admit, for I knew how I worked myself up into my own visions, and how frequently—indeed, incessantly—the visions God granted to me differed from the visions He granted to my father. I did not understand the dreams I had at night, but I knew that they were not holy. For that matter, I knew that my waking hours were far from holy. I spent most of my time in a state of repentance for things I had vividly desired to do but had not done. The fact that I was dealing with Jews brought the whole question of color, which I had been desperately avoiding, into the terrified center of my mind. I realized that the Bible had been written by white men. I knew that, according to many Christians, I was a descendant of Ham, who had been cursed, and that I was therefore predestined to be a slave. This had nothing to do with anything I was, or contained, or could become; my fate had been sealed forever, from the beginning of time. And it seemed, indeed, when one looked out over Christendom, that this was what Christendom effectively believed. It was certainly the way it behaved.

From The Fire Next Time. *After preaching at the Fireside Pentecostal Church and moving to Greenwich Village to live as a bohemian, Baldwin in 1948 left for Paris, where one year later he wrote his breakthrough essay, "Everybody's Protest Novel." Between 1953 and 1956, the novelist, essayist, poet, and playwright published* Go Tell It on the Mountain, Notes of a Native Son, *and* Giovanni's Room.

A scene from *The Seventh Seal*, directed by Ingmar Bergman, 1957.

CHURCH & STATE
IN AMERICA

by Elisabeth Sifton

In Germany in 1799, just eleven years after the Federalist Papers appeared in America, the Protestant theologian Friedrich Schleiermacher wrote a marvelous book entitled *On Religion: Speeches to Its Cultured Despisers.* He observed, in his high-spirited opening lines, that for a long time "faith has not been every man's affair," that only a "few have discerned religion itself, while millions, in various ways, have been satisfied to juggle with its trappings. Now, especially, the life of cultivated people is far from anything that might have even a resemblance to religion." Teasing his sophisticated audience for their hostility to the subject—"I know how well you have succeeded in making your earthly life so rich and varied that you no longer stand in need of an eternity … You are agreed, I know, that nothing new, nothing convincing can any more be said on this matter"—he nonetheless plunged in.

Schleiermacher knew little of religion in the New World, but his comments hit very near the mark for America, then and now. And although our Founding Fathers didn't know his sermons (which weren't translated into English for almost a century), they might well have recognized some of the issues as Schleiermacher saw them. All these modern pioneers approached the church-state conundrum with a brilliant intellectual clarity and emotional, spiritual depth that was characteristic of their times. Those early years of our republic were years when religion's place in society was explored profoundly

---

Elisabeth Sifton was a book editor and publisher for more than forty years. She is the author of The Serenity Prayer: Faith and Politics in Times of Peace and War.

Buddha displays his powers to his family by levitating, Thai mural, eighteenth century.

on both sides of the Atlantic—in contrast to the loud but superficial rhetoric dominating the debate today—and we would do well to recall the terms they used and to consider the issues in the light of that epoch.

Let me first state my dubious credentials for writing on this subject. I think of myself as a Christian or, to use W. H. Auden's impeccable response to the question as to whether he was one, "Well, I'm trying to be." I grew up in the precincts of an interdenominational Protestant seminary, and though I was christened and confirmed as an Episcopalian, I attended many

The strength of a country is the strength of its religious convictions.
—Calvin Coolidge, c. 1925

kinds of church service in my youth; I learned from my elders and betters that it was best to speak with courtesy to or about other Christians and non-Christians whatever their sect (I didn't yet know how rare this was). I'm still a devout reader of the Gospels but now almost never go to church, having developed an allergy to the pious self-congratulatory tone that permeates so many of them. So I live as a skeptic and doubter, my view of churches afforded from both the familiar inside and the disaffected outside. Still, I hope I understand the wisdom of the words spoken by the man who brings his ailing son to be healed by Jesus and is instructed to believe. "Lord, I believe," he answers, "help thou my unbelief." Plenty of Americans find themselves in this in-between territory.

In college, as a student of the French and Scottish Enlightenments, I was enraptured by the ideas advanced by Descartes, Hume [*Edinburgh*, page 47], Locke, Voltaire [*Ferney*, page 109], Rousseau, Diderot—ideas which I was certain had changed the world for the better. I became a lifelong, fervent enthusiast for the Enlightenment program of ridding human society of superstition and fear, evils that from the points of view of these writers had been most powerfully propagated over the centuries by the church, with the strength of sword and gallows behind it, with royal armies, prisons, and laws supporting the *ecclesia*. These men wanted, instead, to get people to trust in their own judgment and the workings of their own minds.

Now, is there an inevitable contradiction between those great Enlightenment aims to advance knowledge and understanding and the enlightening goals of true religion? I don't think so, any more than Schleiermacher did, or John Adams, James Madison, and Thomas Jefferson [*Monticello*, page 88]. Eighteenth-century deists as our Founding Fathers were, they claimed to believe in an almighty being that had created the natural world, while they rejected the notions of "revealed religion." Their deism gave them an honorable position from which to deal with their conventionally devout fellow citizens, the depth of whose spiritual sentiments they respected.

When the architects of our nation insisted that "All men are created equal," they knew that adherence to this philosophical idea, respected in all religions, would require considerable political energy and skill to maintain in a modern polity. It had never been done before. They risked their lives for their revolutionary beliefs and, more than almost any group in human history, gave them embodied meaning. Their superb affirmation of the sovereignty of the people was and is thrilling; likewise their insistence that the nation's executive, legislative, and judicial authorities should do their work—divided and balanced, so as to check against any aggregation of dictatorial power—only with the consent of the governed. I judge the United States Constitution, which gave structure and detail to these controversial ideas, and which of course also insists on religious freedom and prohibits the government from establishing a state church, as the Enlightenment's greatest public document.

The robust lucidity with which our Founders handled church-state issues has, however, been horribly mauled of late, as debates between believers and nonbelievers over power, money, and meaning have turned both fatuous and ugly; opinions violently clash about the proper relation between our government and our religious institutions, and about the appropriate significance of reason and science in our lives—and whether they conflict or can coexist with religious belief. These disputes boil up into a battle royal about the very nature of our state and civil society. Meanwhile, superstition and fear are fed from new, sometimes secular, sources.

Yet that religion was woven into America's national life from the start we all know well. We treasure the heartwarming foundational image of John Winthrop's city on a hill, which President Reagan glorified by calling it a "shining" city on a hill. The theocracy of the Massachusetts Bay Colony was in fact harsh and unpretty, but the Puritans did conceive of their New World community as one directed by God's word, and so religious commitment conjoined with our Founders' Enlightenment faith in reason—creating the peculiar American culture that is both more religious and more secular than many other nations.

By 1776, however, a century and a half after the landing at Plymouth Rock, what do we find? George Washington went to church infrequently and rarely took Communion. Benjamin Franklin was suspicious of all organized religion. John Adams wrote to Jefferson in 1815, "The question before the human race is, whether the God of nature shall govern the world by his own laws, or whether priests and kings shall rule it by fictitious miracles?" James Madison believed that an established religion—a church whose doctrines were guaranteed and enforced by state law—did harm both to religion and to free government, and he found it abhorrent to imagine God being twisted to fit political expediency: this was, he said, to throw religion to the wolves.

The dangers in the other direction were even greater, to his mind. "What influence in fact have ecclesiastical establishments had on civil society?" Madison asked in 1785. "In some instances they have been seen to erect a spiritual tyranny on the ruins of the civil authority; in many instances they have been seen upholding the thrones of political tyranny; in no

A scene from *There Will Be Blood*, directed by Paul Thomas Anderson, 2007.

Houses of the Holy

Second Temple *Jerusalem, Israel*
Faith: Judaism
Built: 515 BC
History: Decimated by Roman forces under Titus in 70, leaving only western retaining wall, now known as the Wailing Wall
Current use: Wall has replaced Temple as primary worship site, where devotees typically slip written prayers among cracks in wall's stones

Umayyad Mosque *Damascus, Syria*
Faith: Islam
Built: c. 710
History: Supposed resting site of enshrined head of St. John the Baptist, worshipped by both Muslims and Christians
Current use: Symbol of religious tolerance, host to first papal mosque visit

Borobudur *Yogyakarta, Indonesia*
Faith: Buddhism
Built: c. 814
History: Hidden for nearly 800 years in volcanic ash and overgrowth; rediscovered in early nineteenth century
Current use: Buddhist observances such as annual peace prayer and rituals of Waisak, a holiday celebrating the Buddha

Sun Temple *Konarak, India*
Faith: Hinduism
Built: c. 1250
Size: 857 ft. x 540 ft.
History: Idol of the sun god Surya once levitated here by means of magnetic system incorporated into temple's architecture, according to one legend
Current use: Thriving tourist site, host to yearly festival of classic sacred Hindu dance, whose poses are depicted in carvings on temple's walls

Lakewood Church Central Campus *Houston, Texas*
Faith: Nondenominational Christianity
Built: 1975 as the Summit sports center; 2005 renovation for church use
History: Former home of the Houston Rockets; now houses U.S.'s largest congregation
Current use: Televised weekly services; classes such as Dancercise and Managing Your Finances God's Way; events such as concerts, fashion shows, and Girls Night Out at the Movies

instance have they been seen the guardians of the liberties of the people. Rulers who wished to subvert the public liberty may have found an established clergy convenient auxiliaries. A just government instituted to secure and perpetuate it needs them not." Nearly fifty years later, having experienced these issues firsthand as president (1809–1817), Madison remained steadfast in a letter written to Reverend Jasper Adams in 1832:

> It may not be easy, in every possible case, to trace the line of separation between the rights of religion and the civil authority with such distinctness as to avoid collisions and doubts on unessential points. The tendency to a usurpation on one side or the other or to a corrupting coalition or alliance between them will be best guarded against by entire abstinence of the government from interference in any way whatever, beyond the necessity of preserving public order, and protecting each sect against trespasses on its legal rights by others.

In his sustained political opposition to even a hint of an established church, Madison was joined by his great collaborator Thomas Jefferson. Jefferson had another worry on this point: he hated the very idea of enforced uniformity of opinion, or coerced belief, and he rightly associated church-state alliances with it. In 1782, he wrote in *Notes on Virginia*:

> Truth can stand by itself. Subject opinion to coercion: whom will you make your inquisitors? Fallible men, men governed by bad passions, by private as well as public reasons. And why subject it to coercion? To produce uniformity. But is uniformity of opinion desirable? No more than of face and stature … Difference of opinion is advantageous in religion … Is uniformity attainable? Millions of innocent men, women, and children, since the introduction of Christianity, have been burnt, tortured, fined, imprisoned: yet we have not advanced one inch toward uniformity.

What has been the effect of coercion? To make one half the world fools, and the other half hypocrites. To support roguery and error all over the earth.

Recognizing the disastrous effects of enforced uniformity of opinion has been an admirable constant of the American political character. To my mind the finest modern expression of it can be found in Justice Robert Jackson's 1943 opinion—written when wartime pressures to conform to America's patriotic ideal were predictably strong—that struck down a law requiring the uniform recitation of the Pledge of Allegiance in schools (West Virginia State Board of Education v. Barnette); this passage from it ends with one of the greatest sentences in all of American jurisprudence:

Compulsory unification of opinion achieves only the unanimity of the graveyard. There is no mysticism in the American concept of the state or of the nature or origin of its authority. We set up government by consent of the governed, and the Bill of Rights denies those in power any legal opportunity to coerce that consent … If there is any fixed star in our constitutional constellation, it is that no official, high or petty, can prescribe what shall be orthodox in politics, nationalism, religion, or other matters of opinion or force citizens to confess by word or act their faith therein.

This noble refusal to be pushed around in matters spiritual and political is not respected by those who currently insist on a different version of the foundational story. Many pious people now claim that the first Americans were all God-fearing Christians who wanted their new nation to be ruled by God—and a high proportion of these people also happen to dislike the secular democratic liberties expressed and expanded in the Progressive Era, New Deal, New Frontier, and Great Society.

One of the cleverest exponents of this position is Justice Antonin Scalia, known also for his vehement "originalism" in matters of constitutional law. Blithely misinterpreting two centuries of post-Enlightenment political philosophy, Justice Scalia asserts that the consensus of Western thought has been until recently "that government—however you want to limit that concept—derives its moral authority from God. Not just of Christian or religious thought, but of secular thought regarding the powers of the state. That consensus has been upset, I think, by the emergence of democracy." The devilish secularism of modern democracy must, then, be defeated. As he puts it:

The reaction of people of faith to this tendency of democracy to obscure the divine authority behind government should not be resignation to it, but the resolution to combat it as effectively as possible. We have done that in this country (and continental Europe has not) by preserving in our public life many visible reminders that—in the words of a Supreme Court opinion from the 1940s—"we are a religious people, whose institutions presuppose a supreme being."

Never mind that the opinion he quotes was Justice William O. Douglas' in 1952 (*Zorach* v. *Clauson*). Douglas didn't even try to support his vacuous assertion, but Scalia can't (could never) prove his even more expansive notion of divine authority guiding the work of our democratic institutions, so he takes diversionary action. Look, he says, at "In God We Trust" on our coins, "the opening of sessions of our legislatures with a prayer" and of our Supreme Court sessions with "God save the United States and this Honorable Court," "one nation, under God" in our Pledge of Allegiance, and so on. (Never mind also that the Pledge was composed only in 1892 by a secular socialist, and the "one nation, under God" phrase added only in 1954.)

I'd like to think Scalia knows that these polite deistic references to the Almighty, which have been sprinkled around the American political landscape for hundreds of years, are hardly proof of a foundational theocracy. Most Americans—including energetic Christians like President Theodore Roosevelt, who opposed putting "In God We Trust" on specie—do not believe the federal government is divinely ordained and dislike the reverberant public God talk. As a Baptist pastor in Alabama wrote some years ago, "Giving lip service to God does not advance faith, it cheapens it. It takes the language of faith and reduces it to mere political rhetoric. Language that has the power to heal and mend should never be treated so callously."

Leaving aside these rhetorical flourishes, Scalia and those who agree with him disregard the dangers the Founders warned against: the tendency of religious groups to corruption and folly when granted political power, their likely insistence on uniformity of opinion, and the subversion of public liberty consequent upon both. But in a political climate that encourages views like his, we have had to endure the increased clout of religious groups that once scorned electoral politics and now are emboldened to use them to gain power and impose uniformity of

opinion on a whole range of social and political issues—gay marriage, stem-cell research, affirmative action, modern evolutionary biology and paleontology, any limitations on executive power. As Garry Wills has observed, their success has depended on a strange alliance of many small fringe organizations far from the center of American mainstream politics but encircling our national life and threatening to strangle it. These include Protestant fundamentalists, conservatives in the Catholic Church, ultra-Orthodox Jewish communities, and secular, sometimes quite violent reactionaries who join them to assault the foundational beliefs of the American nation, kidnap doctrine, and lobby for laws they like, believing they must do this whenever God gives them the opportunity.

Secular media are tempted to presume that these right-wing voices represent the views of "American religion" today, which is manifestly untrue. But what do they know? They don't report on the many sensible clergy and congregants who deplore absolutism, who try to obey the inner counsels and outer

Pakistani troops at prayer, Kashmir, 1999. Photograph by Steve McCurry.

practices of their religious commitments, live at peace with their neighbors, and honor the republic. Worse, the ultrasecular denizens of our media-driven world ignore the evidence of what one might call the spiritual temperament among rational people whether of the left, right, or center. They do not seem to grasp that making the daily effort to obey virtually impossible spiritual commands, to live in hope even under the most tragic or evil circumstances, and to do this as a "discipline of the heart"—that this practice, as Buddhists call it, is what distinguishes the genuine religious life. Among devout people of whatever sect or group, the real index of faith is measured not in the frequency of public declarations of religious allegiance, or belief in God, or trust in this or that set of historic events or "fictitious miracles" (as Adams called them), but in continual spiritual exercise, in daily contrition, in daily recommitment to what you hope is a true, decent way of life.

All the world's religions have devised different forms of private and public worship to encourage these disciplines of the heart, tell different stories about different foundational leaders, and have committed different sins and errors, of course. But they share an understanding of the effort—all the more real for its innerness. As Schleiermacher said, "Religion … in its own original, characteristic form, is not accustomed to appear openly, but is only seen in secret by those who love it." Respectful deists like the Founders knew this.

Since religious commitment is bound to affect a person's professional, political, and public behavior, one can't convincingly argue that it should be partitioned off as a private matter that has nothing to do with a person's public conduct, as dogmatic secularists and atheists nowadays insist. Alas, many stout defenders of the principles of secular government, including some otherwise very smart judges, resort to this dead-end logic—keep religion private, don't let it into public life, make the Founders' wall between church and state into a wall between private religion and public politics.

But the Founders, with their stronger grasp on what religion actually is, wisely did not make this extreme demand, although they understood perfectly well that the republic must defend against religion's absolute claims intruding into what is necessarily the proximate, compromised life of politics.

For the unfortunate contemporary dumbing down of the church-state debate, blame must be apportioned on all sides: not just on the sclerotic pedantry you find in modern legal squabbles on the subject, but also on pious loudmouths who favor public pledges about their faith-based commitments, and on agnostics and atheists who hold a general disregard

Mankind was never so happily inspired as when it made a cathedral.
—Robert Louis Stevenson, 1878

of religion in America's modern culture and who are proud of their hostility to the life of faith. The nuanced difficulties of reconciling religious conduct with good citizenry in a secular republic, difficulties the Founders recognized from the start, will never be resolved if the impermeable-wall standard, now so favored, is used insensitively.

And in the great American tradition, the difficulties are magnified by money. Many noisy people who insist on the inevitable conflict between the realms of reason, science, and secular government on the one hand and those of religion on the other have a vested worldly commitment—financial, bureaucratic, social— in keeping up the divide. On the faith side, we have a bewildering, broad array of voices, among them the antimodern, antirational pastors who claim they read the Bible as literal truth (to be honest, I don't actually believe they do) and who are manifestly hostile to modern civil rights and modern science (though they have their Black-Berrys and take their flu shots, I notice). You'd think, among these last especially, given their claim to adhere to an old-fashioned sense of the holy, they'd be the first to acknowledge that

America as we live and breathe it—in malls, office buildings, supermarkets, and banks; on the television screen, the Internet, and highway billboards; in stadiums and on the street—America is just astonishingly given over to the worship of Mammon. Mammon!

There was a time when prophetic voices could be heard in the land warning their flocks to keep a distance from greed, corruption, and vanity—the regrettable hallmarks, they thought, of collective life in the West's rational, freedom-loving capitalist democracies. They fought against what they considered America's evils and dangers: ethnic and racial fault lines, indifference

He who is unable to live in society, or who has no need because he is sufficient for himself, must be either a beast or a god.
—Aristotle, c. 350 BC

to the safety and welfare of workers, lack of democracy in the industrial workplace, a politics that worsened class conflict instead of lessening it, disregard of the world beyond our borders—and all these aggravating the threat of war. There are still such people in the American churches, but all too few clergy or indeed politicians bring these indictments up to date. Worse, instead of calling out for repudiation of the unbridled capitalist interests that define, shape, color, and fill America's public spaces, these religious leaders mostly welcome them, bowing down to the gods of secular culture, to trendy styles of commerce and entertainment, and to the market. Zealous hypocritical megapastors are not alone in having capitulated to Mammon, because after all their huge megacongregations love them for it—for the busy self-help centers and community social halls made over into feel-good pseudopsychotherapeutic rallying points for visiting politicians and snake-oil salesmen, for the churches' transformation into power bases with their own revenue streams.

But while high-minded secular liberals denounce the bloated God shouters for their divisive anger, they don't always themselves renounce our common submersion in the shallow waters of America's money-soaked culture. Nor do they see that the small-minded, mega-ambitious scientists and neoatheists who attack *all* churches and deride *all* religions for their destructive irrationality, are also profiting from the inane superficialities and hypocrisies of "public opinion," and that this is just as dangerous to the well-being of our republic.

When Daniel Dennett, Sam Harris, Richard Dawkins, Christopher Hitchens, and other neoatheists speak of "religion," what do they think they're talking about? Their critiques, varied as they may be, come nowhere near the wisdom or complexity of the Founders' skepticism about ecclesiastical "trappings," as Schleiermacher called them, and they disregard the deep wellsprings of human feeling that churches are supposed to channel, as Schleiermacher understood. Hope, fear, transcendent meaning, joy, suffering, terror, and love don't seem to figure in their assessments. Well, it's easy to demonstrate the mere irrationality of "belief in God" when you reduce the idea of spiritual life to fatuous, banal insignificance. (I might add that their one-dimensional, simplistic ideas about scientific inquiry also pervert the respectful, awe-filled language of true science and reason—but that's another story.)

As the world careens along new highways of communication and trade, as manifest inequalities in the financial, economic, and labor markets increase, as toxic brews of racist and ethnic hostility simmer or boil over, you might hope for some depth and nuance. You might want to hear the voices of people, whether atheists or believers, representing the large majority of Americans who have welcomed modern science, cared about social justice, honored the life of the spirit, and tried to resolve, not intensify, the tensions between state, society, and church, to adjust, not destroy the ligaments connecting religion and modern science. But, like the pastors, too many of America's political leaders seem undone—as much perhaps by their own complicity in the unforeseen victories of greed and aggression as by the callous disregard of the commonweal and the unleashing of local and international violence all over the globe. There are striking exceptions, of course, like the surprising victor in the 2008 presidential election, but public discourse in America continues to be rancorous and trifling, despite President Obama's contrary example.

All the more reason for both good government and good religion to work for a renewal of the republic's best, most benign energies. That would require secular, agnostic, and atheist voices, together with religious ones, to adjust their vocabulary and tone to the requirements of the public square. Our vulgar mass culture won't encourage this, naturally, but why surrender ourselves to the lowest common denominator? Good governance never does. And were pastors, priests, and rabbis to step back a bit—back from what has become for some of them either chauvinistic drum beating or cynical poll counting or an anxious search for cultural "relevance"—and instead offer their flocks a separate place and time to reconsider, say, the imperishable, eternal spiritual values of humility, silence, and principled, practiced nonviolence, they would purify their own bloodied discourse, remove it from hectic public argument where it doesn't belong, and offer a countervailing force to our media's triviality and our society's implausible loyalty to outmoded, only half-understood imperial grandeurs.

We should never forget— the Founders never forgot— that the most dangerous, most deluded ventures have been those animated by religious zeal, and zealous belief in the virtues of America's secular way of life may count as one of these reckless imperial religions. American churches could teach us about this instead of demonstrating it, help us battle our moral and spiritual weaknesses— our hubris, vanity, and complacency—instead of indulging them. That task, like the task of governing our unruly, complicated nation, needs plenty of hard-headed, realistic political smarts, and it absolutely requires a level, courteous tone of voice. We must learn how to talk to one another.

Mammon, by George Frederick Watts, 1885.

The Sacred Grove, by Arnold Böcklin, 1882.

THE COURTESY OF GOD

by Garret Keizer

The devil you say

These days what the Epistle of James says about believing in God—that the devils believe in him too, ergo beware of taking too much credit for your credos—is often on my mind. God may or may not be in his heaven, but on any given week he is likely to be enthroned at the top of that great chain of being known as the *New York Times* Best Sellers List. Like James and the devil, I am not impressed.

By that I do not mean that I consider myself beyond the God debate or beyond those of my fellow mortals who find it compelling. In fact, if there is any unifying notion in what you are about to read, it is my deep distrust of any human being who fancies himself "beyond" just about anything, be it money, jealousy (of best-selling authors, for instance), using a turn signal, or putting on a tie. I would never buy a book whose title began with *Beyond*, though I

Garret Keizer is a contributing editor to Harper's Magazine. *His next book,* The Unwanted Sound of Everything We Want, *will be published in the spring by Public Affairs Books.*

have known a few beyond-good-and-evil types who weren't beyond stealing one.

If I am unimpressed with the God debate it is less for wanting to seem aloof than for needing to start with easier questions. Lacking the credentials, say, that entitle any expert on a nanolayer of slime covering a pebble called earth to give us the complete skinny on absolute being, a hubris beside which the nitwit ruling of a Kansas school board seems cautiously understated, I want questions better suited to my pay grade. Never mind does God exist—does the God debate exist?

I am not sure it does, or if it does, what it signifies besides a consumer culture's endless obsession with buying the right accessories, the insignia most favored by one's defined target group, the Jesus-fish trunk magnet or the Darwin fish with legs, or maybe a badge betokening higher evolution in the form of a chromium squirrel. The self-appointed champions of faith and reason doth protest too much, methinks.

The God Delusion author Richard Dawkins, for instance, argues that the practice of prayer is like talking to an imaginary friend, a textbook example of "begging the question"—in this case the question Dawkins' book is dedicated to answering—a rhetorical fallacy most of the sixteen and seventeen year olds I used to teach grasped without much trouble, though getting them to spell non sequitur was a tougher slog. If this is the best "reason" can say for itself, God help us.

On the other hand, what leap of faith matches the breathtaking courage, to say nothing of the oxymoronic splendor, of the so-called atheistic humanist? To believe not only that millions of human beings have been deluded for thousands of years (and about a point of some consequence) but also that such specimens of humanity as Bach, Montaigne, Gandhi, John Coltrane, and Martin Luther King Jr. have been *supremely* deluded, and then to offer as a saving alternative to this delusional nonsense—drumroll, please, if only to drown out the irreverent guffaws—*humanism*! What is

a virgin birth to that? *Credibile est, quia ineptum est,* "It is believable because it is ridiculous," said fiery old Tertullian. No atheist and no humanist either, he had what it takes to be both.

Perhaps "the God debate" is an oxymoron, too. Simone Weil [*England*, page 170], working in the tradition of the *theologia negativa*, which holds that God is better defined by an *is not* than an *is*, suggested that atheists and theists were merely affirming different aspects of the same ineffable truth. Believers will balk at this; atheists are rarely pleased. Camus liked Weil, true, but then I've never been convinced Camus was an atheist. Camus was more of a wistful agnostic, a type I tend to trust: not beyond "losing their faith" but not beyond feeling sad about it

However much I die in sin,
God lives and his great mercy will
forgive me if remorse bites in.
                    —*François Villon, 1462*

either, the sort of people who don't need to be water boarded to tell you which movie they *really* want to see.

Camus and Weil rate high in my hagiography, but the soul I'd rather meet if there's such a place as heaven and if the auditing is sloppy enough to let me in is the father of Simone Weil's friend Simone Deitz. At table Mr. Deitz would gently provoke the Catholic-leaning and habitually undernourished Weil to religious disputations so that in the passion of her arguments she would not notice him slipping extra pieces of steak onto her plate. Like another, considerably more famous Jew, he couldn't seem to get beyond the idea that a young girl should eat. ("Little maid, arise," says the wonder-working rabbi of Nazareth to Jairus' comatose daughter, followed by a gag order and the recommendation of a light snack.)

That's what's missing most for me in the God debate: Mr. Deitz, *his* style of religious argument, his motive for it too. His pity and discretion. Convinced enough to write whole books, are God's mightiest defenders convinced enough of his existence to give their lives toward establishing such a world as would make it easier to believe in divine benevolence? If celebrity atheists are really serious about debunking an idea that has given countless people some kind of handhold in the midst of horror and dread, might they devote at least a share of their royalties to treat the despair of those bereaved by the irresistible lucidity of their arguments? If religion is the opiate of the people, and if you love the people, then you

My Lord is both the Muslim Allah and the Hindu Gosain, and thus I have settled the dispute between the Hindu and the Muslim.
—Guru Arjan, c. 1580

must have a strong drug to offer when you tell them "Just say no." Roosevelt believed in a New Deal but he also repealed Prohibition. His faith was not beyond pity.

Autumn in New York

The secularism championed by the infidels and vilified by the elect—that, too, is a discussion I can't quite follow. Secular is not the opposite of sacred. Discussing God over cocktails while children die in drone attacks—that is the opposite of sacred, to say nothing of its relation to such fond ideas as human evolution.

I see the secular life of humanity as the self-effacing courtesy of God. "The marvelous courtesy and homeliness of our Father," wrote Julian of Norwich, a fourteenth-century Englishwoman mystic who found me at a time when I needed her most. The God of Genesis [*Moriah*, page 111] puts man and woman (naked and utterly unencumbered by moral conundrums) in a garden, not a temple. In the heavenly city of Revelation there is no temple either, an absence the author makes a point of noting. Interesting, no, that front and back the Christian Bible makes the implicit declaration that the best of all possible worlds is what most of us would call secular.

Having presided as an Episcopal priest at so many funerals—none of them strictly

"secular"—I find it easy to imagine my own. In addition to "We Gather Together to Ask the Lord's Blessing," as sung for generations by my dissenting ancestors, I would like the hymn "Autumn in New York," as sung by Billie Holiday. In this I am not beyond tradition. My religion has always pictured heaven in the image of that most secular of all enterprises: a city.

Like many of the Hebrew prophets before him (Isaiah being a notable exception), Jesus was a country boy, so it's no surprise that he got riled whenever he came near the pillars of power. But the religion that calls him Christ caught on as an urban phenomenon. Ephesians, Corinthians, Romans, Thessalonians, all those Pauline epistles bear witness to the spread of the new religion in urban centers. It was in the country where the pagans held out the longest, hardly atheists to be sure—if the religious illiteracy of our times is revealed in anything, it's in the use of "pagan" as a synonym for "irreligious"—but deeply suspicious of the city and its secular enthusiasms.

I lack the natural religiosity of the true pagan. Except by the sea (but never far from a port), it is in urban centers where I feel God most powerfully, in the bustling secular that I glimpse heaven. The New England countryside where I live is full of the majesty of creation, yes, but its spiritual life often feels too Druidical for my tastes: chthonic powers and wind whistling in the hollow trees, Wiccan high priestesses stuffing their turkeys with wacky tobacky.

If so-called secularism has any drawback it is that it is not secular enough. The trouble lies with that little *ism*—not unlike the sad caboose of *ianity* coupled to the name of Christ. Given what we are, both suffixes are probably necessary. We need our little dogmas, and pity lets us have them. I know a novelist who tried for a while to write pseudonymously. The stories were all that mattered, he said. "People need an author," his publisher finally told him. If what we call the secular is the courtesy of God, religion is God's concession to those of us who need an author.

If the easy categorization rings false, it probably should. Lately I've been reading the published diary of a nineteenth-century clergyman named Francis Kilvert. In describing his pastoral rounds through the Welsh countryside—even when he makes no mention of God at all—his every utterance seems suffused with a sense of the divine, as if God were seeing the world through him. Shall we call Kilvert secular? Shall we say he reads like Meister Eckhart writing under a pseudonym?

An epicurean physician who occasionally dined with Dr. Johnson once said that he wished he was a Jew so that he could savor

Page of a handwritten score from Mass in B Minor, by Johann Sebastian Bach, c. 1738.

pork with the additional relish of sinning. There are some days when I wish I was an atheist so that I could feel Divinity's love of the secular with the additional relish of having no name for what I felt, only knowing that, as Billie says of autumn in New York, "It's good to live it again."

The devil redux

If anything makes me nervous about people who abandon or abstract their belief in God, it's what they begin to believe instead. They will tell you it is humanity or science; if only that were true. Historically what they have tended to believe in is evil.

Pink Ganesha, by Ton Leenarts, 1988.

By that I do not mean that they embrace evil, that man without God must perforce become a fiend. History shows us fiends of all creedal stripes, not a few of the worst with their hands fervently clasped in prayer. I mean rather that man without God has a marked historical tendency to feel the fiend breathing down his neck. The telltale heart of a "Godless society" is not a commercialized Christmas or a decommissioned Sabbath but an overblown Halloween.

Among those historical observations that we might call "sublimely interesting," one of my favorites is the fact that the great age of witch hunting was the late Renaissance. It is Shakespeare's monarch and patron King James I who writes *Daemonologie* (1597), a treatise on witchcraft that the Church Fathers of a thousand years before would have found laughable. (Along the same lines, St. Augustine would never have said that Jesus Christ was his "favorite philosopher," if only for fear of demeaning Jesus.) In his classic intellectual history *The Seventeenth Century Background,* Basil Willey contends that as God became more remote to the early modern European imagination, the devil loomed larger. Still a medieval man at heart, Dante gives us a Satan about as compelling as a hamster; Milton's is a pre-Romantic hero who speaks in pentameter verse. When George W. Bush gave his famous "Axis of Evil" speech, many people heard his language as "medieval." To me he looked and sounded more like a Renaissance man, right down to the detail of his vice president standing like a Medici pope at his side.

The more "primitive" the Christianity, the less prominent the devil. Judaism, which Christians of the past and present fancy themselves beyond, is so primitive it hardly pays any attention to him at all. Golems, okay, but a master of metaphysical evil? "With such a son-in-law, I should need a Satan?" For the fourth- and fifth-century Christian hermits known as the desert fathers, the devil was real enough, but seems to have been something on the order of crabgrass or computer spam—nasty to be sure but perfectly manageable if you kept after it. According to patristic scholars Norman Russell and Benedicta Ward, one reason the hermits took to the desert had to do with their belief that the devils had taken flight from the cities to escape the sound of the Bible being read aloud there. In other words, the hermits were essentially on a mopping-up operation. Victory was already behind them.

Even the fantastic eschatology of the biblical Book of Revelation is entirely anticlimactic on this score. The beast appears and is immediately bound and cast into the lake of fire. I've known small-town exterminators to have a harder time with mice. Compare this confidence—and in the case of the desert fathers, their humor—with the fetishistic treatment of evil in American cinema, with the great Satan of the mullahs and the post-9/11 invocations of the dark side. Read the Modernist but equally Manichaean manifestos that damned tonal music as the spawn of the fascist beast, or the inquisitorial proclamations that if you like to read sonnets by dead white men you might as well go the whole nine yards and buy yourself a slave.

Then tell me a cheerful story, will you, about all the things we have evolved beyond.

May the Force take a hike

That said, I am more at ease with atheists than with sophisticated theists. I mean those people who say that God is far too big to care about their little woes, usually meaning that they are far too smart to fall for any such baloney. They are beyond anthropomorphism. They can spell anthropomorphism. For them God is sort of like a force—"whatever it was Einstein meant when he spoke of God," as if they have a prayer of ever knowing. It is a most peculiar smugness. If I say that the source of all being is best likened to the force that assigns my sorry butt a number every time I step onto a bathroom scale, I deserve to live in the twenty-first century; if I say that this source is better likened to Albert Einstein [*Princeton*, page 25], disheveled lover of elegant equations and gamey women, I am not fit to forgo saying grace in respectable company.

A deity who is "too big" to care for the minutiae of my secular life is as preposterous to me as a deity who rigs the raffle at St. Elizabeth's so

I do not feel obliged to believe that the same God who has endowed us with sense, reason, and intellect has intended us to forgo their use.
—*Galileo, 1615*

the parish can keep the car—and his proponents twice as vain in that they lack the forgivable inducement of the car. I would like to know what difference there is between John D. Rockefeller, who said God had made him rich, and his dot-com descendent, who says that a less anthropomorphic paradigm would make him believe. Actually, I do know the difference. The first looks out over Lake Michigan and wonders if God might be pleased to have a University of Chicago; the second parks his Beemer in the same place and takes a sanctified trot along the shore.

The sophisticated would not have prayed for my former altar girl Laney, though it was hard, seeing her rearranged in the ICU, to know exactly what to pray. For mercy, I guess. The jeep had dragged her for a ways, and she was not wearing a seat belt when it did. She was one of the most angelic presences I've ever known, handing me the communion bread, playing with the younger children after church, shining a light and a flashlight too for her uncles when they worked on their trucks, dancing with gravity on the balance beam. Later on she had a serious boyfriend, a job as a physical therapist, a life to call her own. She was studying the Japanese art of reiki, she told me on one of her less frequent visits to church, which was "like what Jesus did when he healed people with his touch." Hers was the first funeral I was asked to do after I had stopped doing funerals. I bit my lip as I stood at the pulpit I had left only months before, angry at God and man, probably as sorry for myself as for the devastated family, the mother wearing that beatific expression I have learned over the years to recognize as the pity of some prescribing family physician, which these days must needs be combined with the courage to beard the FDA. At least as long ago as the seventeenth century, physicians were known for their atheism; Sir Thomas Browne offered his *Religio Medici* as a corrective. Here is my corrective: let those of us who believe what the devils believe never disdain the science that gave us drugs, or the physician whose only religion is the easing of pain.

As for Laney, she was no sure proof of God, and her disappearance proves nothing about God, but God feels a little less present to me because she is no longer in the world. My soul feels a little more tired. Little maid, pray for me.

Notice the quick slide to self-reference: the mark of religion at its lowest common denominator, blessme, blessme, blessme, like that scoundrel Jacob in the Bible, or whyme, whyme, whyme, like that complainer Job. *Why Laney?* Perhaps Orwell was thinking of Jacob when he said that the best explanation for anti-Semitism was to be found in the Old Testament. More than Camus and Weil put together, I love Orwell, but on that score he can take a hike, and may the Force be with him as he goes out the door.

I believe in the God of Jacob more than in the God of Stephen Hawking, though I believe not a little in the holiness of Stephen Hawking. I believe in the God of John Brown. To those who would tell me that I am but a short step away from saying I believe in the God of Osama bin Laden, I strenuously object. One *half* of a short step.

That is really the crux of the matter, isn't it: what we talk about when we talk about God, at least in the context of what Americans with

characteristic solipsism refer to as "our post-9/11 world"—with atheists telling us, "This is where religion inevitably leads," and radio evangelists telling us, "This is where religion based on the Qur'an [*Arabia*, page 168] instead of the inspired Word of God inevitably leads," and liberal apologists for monotheism telling us, "Come, come, ladies and gentlemen, we are surely beyond all that." What 9/11 told us, what the death of Laney told me, is that we are beyond nothing, neither the childish question nor the primal cry, and least of all that desperate conjunction of the two, whether uttered by a Muslim zealot prostrate beneath the shadow of American might or a New York accountant racing down the doomed tower stairs: *What must I do to be saved?*

Credo

Which leaves the matter of why I've opted for the answers that I have, none of which places my faith beyond criticism or reproach. It turns out I believe in God for some of the same reasons that I believe in evolution, because I accept the testimony of estimable witnesses. "If everybody jumped off a cliff would you do that too?" If the right people did, I might.

But science is not like that, you will tell me; it allows you to look at the evidence and draw your own conclusions. Yes it does, and thanks for the reminder, but I am lying through my teeth if I say that it makes perfect sense to me that you have this amoeba and then, after billions of years and any number of extraordinarily fortuitous mutations, you have Marilyn Monroe singing "Happy Birthday, Mr. President." As if that weren't enough, you have a creature capable of recalling the scene with more emotions than there were candles on the cake: nostalgia and cynicism, poignancy and lust, an atavistic prick of what the Neanderthals felt when they buried their dead with a sprinkling of red ochre. Many happy returns, Jack. Sing on, Norma Jean. Tell me one more time, Mr. Darwin.

I suppose I should add that I also find it hard to believe that a chimp at a typewriter will eventually produce *War and Peace*. I think

Heretics and Blasphemers

	Name	Socrates
	Accused in	399 BC: Athens
Profession		Philosopher, vagrant
Charged with		Refusing to worship the city's gods, corrupting the youth
Further Infractions		Disturbing the city's peace
Accusers		Meletus, Anytus, and Lycon (members of the Patriot Party)
Sentenced to		Death by hemlock
Legacy		Foundation for Western philosophy

	Name	Jesus Christ
	Accused in	33: Jerusalem
Profession		Itinerant preacher, unemployed carpenter
Charged with		Claiming to be the Son of God and King of the Jews
Further Infractions		Claiming to have the power to destroy the temple
Accuser		Caiaphas, head of Sanhedrin Council
Sentenced to		Death by crucifixion
Legacy		Christianity

	Name	Arius
	Accused in	325: Constantinople
Profession		Priest
Charged with		Claiming that Jesus was not equal with God
Further Infractions		Writing songs for sailors, travelers, and millers in which his claims were demonstrated
Accuser		Council of Nicea
Sentenced to		Excommunication, works burned by Emperor Constantine
Legacy		None

	Name	Galileo
	Accused in	1633: Rome
Profession		Astronomer, mathematician, physicist
Charged with		Upholding Copernicus' heliocentric view of the universe
Further Infractions		None
Accuser		Pope Urban VIII
Sentenced to		Recantation of theories, house arrest for life
Legacy		Foundation for modern physics

	Name	Sarmad
	Accused in	1661: Delhi
Profession		Mystic, poet
Charged with		Denying ascension of the Prophet, proclaiming faith in Hindu gods
Further Infractions		Walking naked in the streets in violation of Islamic law
Accuser		Mughal Emperor Aurangzeb
Sentenced to		Death by beheading
Legacy		Sufi Sainthood

	Name	Salman Rushdie
	Accused in	1989: Iran
Profession		Author
Charged with		Writing *The Satanic Verses*
Further Infractions		Altering the Prophet's dictation, misusing sacred names
Accuser		Ayatollah Ruhollah Khomeini
Sentenced to		Death by unspecified means (called for by the Ayatollah in a fatwa)
Legacy		Knighthood

a chimp at a typewriter will eventually produce a gun and blow out his brains. Futility can be endured for only so long. Tolstoy understood that, which is perhaps another reason, besides the bulk of his tome, that we use *War and Peace* in the example. A chimp at a typewriter is what I often feel like, with the additional and bitter relish that, unlike the chimp, I want to produce *War and Peace*, or something like it, and I suspect that no matter how many trillions of years I had, I never could. So, like any animal in existential distress, I emit a cry—and for reasons the animal itself may not fully understand.

I'm getting warmer, which is to say closer to the flush of embarrassment that comes over us when we cut through the cant and actually

All service ranks the same with God—
With God, whose puppets, best and worst,
Are we: there is no last nor first.
          —*Robert Browning, 1841*

say which movie we really want to see, which one gets us crying every time.

When everything else falls away, my Calvinist upbringing, my prissy love of English church architecture, my sense of connection to Johns Donne [*London*, page 115] and Brown, my contrarian orthodoxy, the please-never-die faces of those who have helped me believe in supernatural love, this is all that remains: I called and He heard. "Out of the depths have I called to thee, O Lord"—as have others who called without any requiting consolation, not even that of knowing for certain that calling in this way was a joke. "*Eli, Eli, lama sabachthani?*" [My God, My God, why have you forsaken me?] He belongs to them more than me.

In positioning my faith like this, and not in a proposition more arguable, I leave myself with little defense against the charges of infantilism, autosuggestion, lunacy itself. Yet among those who would gleefully sign the papers for my committal are individuals who will tell you that it's possible for a capitalist society to produce a healthcare system in which making

many people well can and will take precedence over making a few people rich. They have their magical thinking, I have mine.

For the record mine is not a restatement of that old platitude about there being "no atheists in the foxholes." Given the godforsaken cast of most battlefields, I should not be surprised to learn that there are *nothing but* atheists in the foxholes. It is only that some of the atheists manage to pray.

That is what I did when I began this essay. I knew that one of my reasons for taking it on was that I needed the money, and that most of the others, including some I might have regarded as nobler, were probably just as base. I did not feel that God, being God and the God of Jacob to boot, needed to be told my motives, or that I necessarily needed to be forgiven for them. Interviewing applicants for a temporary job blowing the shofar, some rabbis are said to have asked each of three finalists what he was thinking during his audition. "I thought of the Blessed One calling creation into being," said the first. "I thought of the Law given on Mount Sinai," said the second. Sheepishly the third confessed, "I thought that I have six daughters, and they all need dowries." The rabbis didn't need to go beyond that. They hired the third, they slipped the man a little steak, though I'm not sure if that was because they pitied his predicament or admired his nerve.

No, if I prayed, it was mainly because I was deeply skeptical, not of God but of the value of talking about God. "We need more cooks, not more cookbooks," reads the epigraph on a well-known cookbook, and after so many years of imparting recipes from behind a pulpit I find myself wishing I'd spent more time in front of a stove. Still there was the matter of a dowry, and thus the need of a job. So I prayed I could pull it off, I prayed for mercy, I prayed that I would write something capable of gently unsettling every single human being who troubled to read it. In a word I prayed for the chimp. Of course I am in no position to tell anyone whether God exists. But perhaps you are in a position to tell me whether God answers prayers.

A scene from *Simon of the Desert*, directed by Luis Buñuel, 1965.

THE ORIGINAL SIN

by Francine Prose

But I suffer not a woman to teach, nor to usurp authority over the man, but to be in silence.

—St. Paul

Hardly anyone noticed this summer when former president Jimmy Carter explained why he had decided to leave the Baptist Church. However "painful and difficult," wrote Carter in an essay that appeared in the *Guardian*, his break with the denomination to which he had belonged for sixty years had begun to seem like the only possible response to past opinions expressed and codified by the Southern Baptist Convention. "It was an unavoidable decision when the convention's leaders, quoting a few carefully selected Bible verses and claiming that Eve was created second to Adam and responsible for original sin, ordained that women must be 'subservient' to their husbands and prohibited from serving as deacons, pastors, or chaplains in the military service. This was in conflict with my belief—confirmed in the

Francine Prose is a novelist, essayist, and author of nonfiction. Her books include Goldengrove *and* Reading Like a Writer. *Her latest work is* Anne Frank: The Book, The Life, The Afterlife.

holy scriptures—that we are all equal in the eyes of God."

Considerably more attention was generated some months earlier by another story about how religion conceives and enforces its view of a woman's place. The horrific attack on two Afghan girls en route to school—the young women were severely disfigured by acid allegedly thrown by Taliban fighters—was widely reported and discussed. Obviously, the assault was more brutal, shocking, and newsworthy than an elderly white guy's regretful decision to separate himself from the misguided

We have just enough religion to make us hate, but not enough to make us love one another.
—Jonathan Swift, 1706

pronouncements of some other elderly white guys. And just as clearly, the Taliban's plans for women far exceed the darkest imaginings of the Southern Baptists, whose tenets—"a wife is to submit herself graciously to the servant leadership of her husband"—seem genial and reassuringly vague when compared to the restrictions that the Taliban impose, and seek to impose, on women, regulations that narrow the parameters of daily life down to a space in which anyone, male or female, would suffocate. Under Taliban rule Afghan women cannot work, attend school, leave home without a male chaperone, or ride in a taxi. Minor infractions, such as showing an ankle, are punished by public whippings. More serious violations, such as adultery, are capital crimes for which the sentence is death by hanging or stoning.

The acid attack on the schoolgirls offered graphic and persuasive confirmation of one reason why we have gone to war, or in any case one reason we've been given: according to some, once we defeat the Taliban, every Afghan girl can go to school. That's the outcome everyone wants, though it is less often mentioned that literacy rates among Afghan women were appallingly low long before the Taliban, back in the 1980s when we were still arming the mujahideen—including many future Taliban warriors—to fight against the Russians. The Taliban's demonic and demonizing attitude toward women represents merely the most current extreme manifestation of the grotesque misogyny fostered throughout history by religion and patriarchal tribal culture. Both the Taliban and the Southern Baptists employ the "lessons" of biology and scripture to "prove" women's inferiority, a view of our gender unlikely to be eliminated by another air strike or drone-missile deployment, or by the polite demurrals of a former president.

Sensible, decent Jimmy Carter got it right again. "This view that women are somehow inferior to men is not restricted to one religion or belief. It is widespread. Women are prevented from playing a full and equal role in many faiths. Nor, tragically, does its influence stop at the walls of the church, mosque, synagogue, or temple. This discrimination, unjustifiably attributed to a higher authority, has provided a reason or excuse for the deprivation of women's equal rights across the world for centuries. The male interpretations of religious texts and the way they interact with and reinforce traditional practices justify some of the most pervasive, persistent, flagrant, and damaging examples of human-rights abuses."

Like countless theologians, clerics, and believers, Carter distinguishes between the ideas expressed by the founders of those faiths and the distortions and biases of those who organized and spread the religion. But how much comfort, finally, can women take in knowing that it wasn't God, Jesus, or the Prophet but some later rabbi, Church Father, or caliph who banned them from praying during their menstrual periods, who forbid them to enter a mosque or feel the sun on their faces, who ruled that their husbands could beat them for disobedience, and who first suggested that each and every one of them was a living reminder of the permanent harm that Eve had done humankind?

Almost as soon as anyone (mostly women, for obvious reasons) started noticing or asking how the world's religions viewed their female adherents, women—and I would assume some men—either had to face it or not, make excuses or not, question their faith or not. During the 1970s, feminists called attention to any number of ancient fertility-mother cults. But though pre-Christian cultures had goddesses, and priestesses in their temples, Greek and Roman myths are essentially crime blotters recording rapes, near rapes, and metamorphoses into animals or plants to avoid or atone for being raped. There is no word for *heroine* in Homeric Greek.

Judaism did little to challenge men's most primitive suspicions of and prejudices against women. The Old Testament abounds with stories of women sold and traded like cattle, of marriageable girls held hostage in return for years of hard labor by their suitors. Of course there are also stories of women who defy male authority, such as Queen Esther, who dared approach the king without being asked, and Deborah, who accompanied the Israelites into battle. But according to Leviticus, only sons may partake of the meat of the sacred burnt offering, and after childbirth, women must arrange for sacrifice— a lamb or, in the absence of a lamb, two turtle doves or young pigeons—to end their term of "uncleanness," a week if they've given birth to a son, two weeks if it's a girl. Each month, after her period, a woman must undergo a strenuous head-to-toe purification. Measures are taken, as in Islam, to protect men from temptation. Some observant Jewish wives must shave their heads, lest the sight of a ringlet cause a man to lose all self-control. Many Jewish men begin their day with a prayer thanking God for not having been born female. For the last decades of her life, my mother, a scientist and a doctor, attended High Holy Day services at a Greenwich Village synagogue with a separate women's section up in the balcony, farther from the action—presumably so that her white hair and frail shoulders would not distract a man from the serious business of prayer.

However radical the changes that Jesus and his disciples made to Old Testament theology, they did little to modify or improve

Horned witch, France, eighteenth century.

the patriarchs' most neurotic anxieties and destructive biases against women. Uta Ranke-Heinemann's scholarly and wry *Eunuchs for the Kingdom of Heaven* catalogues the jaw-dropping and (if one can maintain a sense of humor about sexual hatred and vilification) hilarious insults that the Church Fathers, among them St. Augustine and Thomas Aquinas, routinely leveled at women. In one unsettling chapter, Ranke-Heinemann—a Catholic theologian and the first woman to hold a distinguished chair in theology at the University of Essen, from which she was fired in 1987 for suggesting that the Virgin Birth was a matter of faith and not a biological fact—discusses the prohibitions that have resulted from the Church's solemn responsibility to keep inferior beings from assuming the privileges or rightful duties of their betters.

According to the *Apostolic Constitutions*, a fourth-century compilation from older writings on church liturgy and canon law, if Jesus wanted women to hold ecclesiastical office, he would have found and appointed a woman disciple; after all, there were plenty of women around. And if the man was the head of the household, the existence of a female priest in the house would mean that the body was ruling the head—and how unnatural would that be? "In keeping with the will of their spiritual lords, women in church had to be quiet, so quiet that they could only move their lips without making a sound."

Long before Muhammad, St. Ambrose forbade women to teach in church and John Chrysostom suggested that women be veiled in public. One early Christian philosopher after another (quite a few of them saints, such as St. Jerome) emphasized the fact that woman's only purpose on earth, indeed her only route to salvation, was to provide her husband with children. For anything else that was necessary, for work or companionship, advice or entertainment, he would sensibly and naturally choose another man. In St. Augustine's essay "On Marriage and Concupiscence," the author of *Confessions* sounds remarkably like the Southern Bap-

World War I National Savings Committee poster, c. 1916.

tist Convention. "Nor can it be doubted that it is more consonant with the order of nature that men should bear rule over women, than women over men. It is with this principle in view that the apostle says, 'The head of the woman is the man,' and 'Wives, submit yourselves unto your own husbands.'"

The Church Fathers devoted considerable energy to debating the question of whether sex with a beautiful woman was more or less sinful than sex with an ugly one, as well as the subject of whether or not Adam and Eve had intercourse in Paradise before the fall of man. By contrast, there was little disagreement about whose fault *that* was. Whom would the serpent choose to tempt—the man who had named the animals or his foolish wife? Poor Eve: one bite of fruit, and centuries of blame for every small or severe pain that measures our distance from Eden.

Ranke-Heinemann tracks much of this back to the body-hating, pleasure-despising strain introduced into the early church by the Essenes and Gnostics. Later, the early and medieval saints and theologians would show little interest in concealing their horror of sex and the body. According to one thought often attributed to Thomas Aquinas, any variation on the so-called missionary position was as sinful as having intercourse with one's own mother.

The debate over sex with the beautiful versus sex with the ugly had its twisted roots in the belief that there was an almost mathematical ratio between pleasure and sin. The greater the pleasure, the worse the evil. Apparently, too, there also was considerable worry about ejaculation as something that drains and weakens the male, a dangerous process in general and particularly in the presence of the predatory woman who, unlike her mate, doesn't lose in sex a life-sustaining fluid. The rabbinic admonition to think of a woman as "a pitcher of filth with its mouth full of blood" was echoed in the work of the twelfth-century theologian Petrus Cantor. "Consider that the most lovely woman has come into being from a foul-smelling drop of semen; then consider her midpoint, how she is a container of filth; and after that consider her end, when she will be food for worms."

To ask which came first—fear of women or fear of sex—is one of those chicken-and-egg questions more suited to Zen meditation than logical inquiry. In any case, religion is an aid to those who suffer from either, or both, terrors. Orthodox Judaism assumes the disgustingness of female bodily fluids, especially

Kill a man, and you are an assassin. Kill millions of men, and you are a conqueror. Kill everyone, and you are a god.
—*Jean Rostand, 1939*

those that accompany every child's entrance into the world. Christianity saw no reason to challenge the Old Testament ban on sex with menstruating women, a prohibition which also appears in the Qur'an. But it's more than a physical thing. What's at issue here is not merely a horror of the other but an awareness of the way that horror can augment one's sense of self, an acknowledgement of how the conviction of God-granted superiority can be a source of comfort and self-esteem. What man wouldn't have more confidence moving through the world with a submissive wife or wives shuffling like ducklings behind him? Conversely, any indication that the woman is catching up to walk alongside or, worse yet, ahead, inspires even in decent men a frenzy of maddened, injurious activity, as if one's own masculinity and the fragile social structure that masculinity has created will survive or shatter depending on whether or not a man continues to win that race. Such fears must feed the perpetual worry that one is sharing his bed with an enemy, an inferior, a repellent but necessary specimen of an alien species. And how useful religion is in helping us sort all that out! Every modern society—from Puritan New England to France under Napoleon, from Nazi Germany to Eisenhower-era

America—has understood the importance, the necessity, of keeping women in their place.

To automatically hate and fear anything or anyone different from ourselves and to want to feel smarter and worthier than an entire race or gender are two of the least admirable and most regrettable aspects of human nature. So it does seem peculiar that religion, with its emphasis on self-perfection through prayer and the help of God, should so rarely include intolerance among the roster of sins for which we wish to be forgiven, or to avoid altogether. Strange, but not so very strange, when we consider that religions are not merely belief systems but social institutions whose leaders have always understood how effectively fear, hate, and the assurance of racial, national, or sexual superiority—and sex—can be used to define and control a society.

God created man and, finding him not sufficiently alone, gave him a companion to make him feel his solitude more keenly.
—Paul Valéry, c. 1942

Ages before Freud, it was understood that the power of sex was a potential agent of destabilization and chaos. Consider the story of Paris and Helen of Troy, or Tristan and Isolde. Unruly erotic attraction is a major reason why people break rules, sometimes with tragic results. The theologians were right about one thing: follow your desires, and things start to fall apart. How much simpler it is to tell a community of celibate monks when to go to sleep and get up, and what to do every minute in between, than it is to rein in a teenage boy who wants to go visit his girlfriend. Some politicians have long understood that regimenting sexuality is a time-tested way of maintaining moral authority. And the fear of women and of everything that women represent—the fear of life, of sex, of fecundity, of birth and rebirth and renewal—fosters the kind of death worship that in turn fosters more wars, more killing, more repression, and more pointless misery.

Like every means of social control, faith-based misogyny has its cost, and women have been made to pay an unequal fraction of the price. Let me quote Jimmy Carter one last time, for the exactitude with which he connects the dots between the ideology of the Southern Baptist Convention and the mistreatment of women worldwide. "At its most repugnant, the belief that women must be subjugated to the wishes of men excuses slavery, violence, forced prostitution, genital mutilation, and national laws that omit rape as a crime. But it also costs millions of girls and women control over their own bodies and lives, and continues to deny them fair access to education, health, employment, and influence within their own communities."

Lately, there have been some signs of progress, shifts perhaps more visible to the optimist than to the impatient. One sees chadors being shed by female protestors in the streets of Tehran; lending cooperatives and trade schools have been established to help Muslim women hold jobs outside the family compound. Women appear more often in Protestant and Jewish pulpits. There's no doubt that many women's lives are better than they were a century, even a half century, ago. Women can vote and own property. Abortion has been legalized in many countries, at least for the moment. But organized religion, and the anxieties and terrors it encourages and employs as a means of social control, have fought—and continue to fight—these positive changes, every step of the way. Despite the small steps forward, life continues to worsen for, among others, Afghan women, whose rights were limited this year by the Shiite Personal Status Law, which restricts women's rights to inherit or divorce and legalizes marriage to minors. Daily, all over the world, there are mutilations and murders and beatings, all in the name of God. Women and men everywhere are still being made to suffer in a continual retelling of that old Bible story of headstrong, impossible Eve, who was the first person to step out of line and question what she had been told.

The Vision Legend of the Fourteenth Century, by Luc Olivier Merson, c. 1872.

SECULAR REVIVAL

by Warren Breckman

I n the late 1790s, the poet François-René de Chateaubriand languished in his London exile. He had journeyed to America at the beginning of the decade in hopes that the New World sun would burn off the lingering clouds of his morose childhood in the dank and gloomy family castle in Brittany but had returned to Europe, summoned by the call to arms against the French revolutionaries. After suffering a wound, he retreated to England. As he recalled in his *Memoirs*, in the summer of 1798 he had just dodged an engagement with one Charlotte Ives that would have "buried" him "in an English county," leading the life of a "hunting gentleman," when a letter from his sister Julie interrupted his navel-gazing. "My dear," wrote Julie from Saint-Servan, "we have just lost the best of mothers: I grieve to inform

Warren Breckman teaches history at the University of Pennsylvania and is the coexecutive editor of Journal of the History of Ideas. *His most recent book is the forthcoming* Adventures of the Symbolic: Postmarxism and Democratic Theory.

you of this fatal blow. When you cease to be the object of our solicitude, we shall have ceased to live. If you knew how many tears your errors had caused our venerable mother to shed, how deplorable they appear to all who think and profess not only piety but reason—if you knew this, perhaps it would help to open your eyes, to induce you to give up writing."

Chateaubriand's "error" was his first published book, a lengthy essay voicing the combative hostility toward organized religion that had become stock-in-trade for French advocates of enlightenment in the twilight years of the eighteenth century. Cast into despair by

I am a sort of collector of religions—and the curious thing is that I find I can believe in them all. —George Bernard Shaw, 1907

this account of the torment he had caused his dying mother, written by a sister who herself had died by the time it reached him, Chateaubriand went back to navel-gazing with a vengeance. He underwent a conversion. "I became a Christian. I did not yield, I admit, to any mighty supernatural illumination. My conviction came out of my heart. I wept and I believed." Instead of yielding to Julie's plea to cease writing, he resolved to expiate his sin by composing another work, a religious one. The poet's most famous book, *The Genius of Christianity*, appeared fortuitously just days after Napoleon mended relations with Pope Pius VII in 1802. Perhaps because he was all too familiar with the withering power of skepticism, Chateaubriand did not deign to meet the critics of religion on their chosen battlefield by arguing *rationally* for the doctrinal truth of Catholicism. Instead he tried to bring the rationalists to tears. He poured his literary gifts into sumptuous descriptions of the power and beauty of ritual and the sensual and emotional satisfactions of faith. Madame Fortunée Hamelin expressed a common response to Chateaubriand's book when she exclaimed, "What, this is Christianity? But it is delicious!"

What a contrast to Sigmund Freud's depiction of religion as the universal obsessional neurosis of humanity. Religion, conceded Freud, has performed vital functions within civilization, offering us an imaginary compensation for our helplessness in the face of nature through fantasies of a controlling intelligence and an illusion of our capacity to summon that power through rituals and prayer. Above all, Freud saw religion as a mechanism of repression, channeling instinctual drives into socially acceptable forms. Chateaubriand's lush Catholicism does not at all fit this notion of religion as the ultimate form of renunciation, but Freud's portrayal of the austere and sublime legalism of Mosaic Judaism certainly does. Ultimately, however, Freud and Chateaubriand may not have disagreed entirely on the essence of religion. Freud was, shall we say, too Freudian not to recognize that human instincts will have their due. Renunciation only works if it actually satisfies the instincts it represses, even if the paths to satisfaction may be unexpected and devious.

If one wishes to see Freud's identity papers marking him as a latter-day citizen of the Enlightenment, look no further than his 1927 book *The Future of an Illusion*. There he predicts that people will finally see the falsity of the "fairy tales" of religion. Intelligence will then triumph over the life of the instincts, and psychoanalysis will offer the key to finally releasing humanity from its mind-forged manacles. Yet it may be that the truly Freudian insight belongs to the imaginary interlocutor whom Freud creates to present the counter argument. "You emerge as an enthusiast," charges Freud's fictive opponent. "If you want to expel religion from our European civilization, you can only do it by means of another system of doctrines; and such a system would from the outset take over all the psychological characteristics of religion—the same sanctity, rigidity, and intolerance, the same prohibition of thought—for its own defense."

One standard image of the nonbelieving secularist is of a hedonistic immoralist—as Fyodor Dostoevsky feared, if God is dead, everything is permitted. But to the contrary, it may be that secularism does not escape the dynamic that Freud believed is the motor of religion: the repression of instinct followed by a sublimation into other satisfactions—in other words, precisely the process that turns religion into an obsessional neurosis. Even among champions of the secular worldview, we sometimes find worries that secularism lacks magic and emotional depth, that it is a hyperrationalist creed that preserves the internal compulsions of religion without its animating beliefs or its consoling message of cosmic meaning and personal redemption. Frequently, the counsel of the secularist is to be brave, buck up, and face the world as a heroic pessimist. Defenders of religion are all too ready to claim that secularism offers at best a wizened form of experience and sensation. Such a view has us moderns living within a purely immanent world, blocked from any relation to a truly transcendent sphere. In such a world, the colors are a shade paler, the sounds a tone flatter than in a world touched by the divine. A host of religiously minded writers would warn that where our belief in the transcendent has vanished, we seek impoverished substitute sources of transport: in artistic experience, sport, love, or at the extreme, drugs. There will be many secularists, myself among them, who believe that the emotional and sensory scale is not so irretrievably tilted in favor of religious experience. And I would challenge secularists to reaffirm the depth and authenticity of their nonreligious experience. Nonetheless, it may be that the fundamental austerity of the secularist worldview helps account for religion's obstinate refusal to go away.

That religion remains a vital force in the contemporary world seems an obvious enough observation in 2009. However, it contradicts one of the master narratives of twentieth-century thought. Psychoanalysis was just one species of a widespread conviction among twentieth-century western European and American intellectuals that in the modern world religion would steadily retreat and secular reason would triumph. Adherents of this belief could draw legitimacy from science's evident conquest of domains formerly claimed by faith. They could point to a distinguished pedigree, including the heroes of the scientific revolution, the *philosophes* of the Enlightenment, and a pantheon of nineteenth-century giants, including Karl Marx [*Kreuznach*, page 60], Charles Darwin, Friedrich Nietzsche [*Sils-Maria*, page 142], Émile Durkheim, and Max Weber [*Heidelberg*, page 118]. Contrary to Nietzsche's famous declaration, God may not have been dead, but He certainly observed the dominant philosophical debates of the twentieth century from the margins. That was as true of Oxford

I never could understand how a man could be of two religions at once.
                    —*John Henry Newman, 1864*

logicians carving into received belief like a roast at High Table as it was of Parisian existentialists urging us to shoulder responsibility for a godless world. Among social scientists and historians, it became a veritable article of faith that organized religion's presence in public life was dwindling and faith was becoming more and more a matter of private conscience. In the sweeping liberal imagination of mid-century American social science, secularization was virtually synonymous with modernization. Insofar as historians studied religion, it was almost invariably inserted into a narrative of decline. Political scientists routinely described the modern ideologies—communism and fascism, or even the liberal belief in progress—as ersatz secular religions, and that description took for granted that the real thing had left the stage of history. The theology departments of many American universities discretely evolved into religious studies, a rainbow coalition that acknowledged religion as an anthropological, historical, and social fact without compelling anyone to take oaths. Within academia, outward professions of faith, insistence on the persistent power of religion, or explicit calls for religion to play a public role seemed not just awkward infractions against scholarly politeness but also violations of the taken-for-granted normal order of modern reality.

Measured against so many trends in the intellectual history of the twentieth century, the return of religion to the halls of academe must be considered a sea change in the intellectual life of America and Europe. Religion is in. Across the spectrum of the humanities and social sciences, scholars are studying religious phenomena, and there is a new willingness to open a dialogue between philosophy and theology. This does not necessarily mean that scholars themselves have had a conversion on the road to Damascus. With the exception of evangelical universities

A religious war is like killing someone over who has the better imaginary friend.
—Larry Beinhart, 2008

and the occasional individual faculty member, universities remain staunchly secular zones. I would dare say that for most professional scholars, religion reclaims their attention not because faith reasserts its ancestral claim but because the secularist narrative has gotten snagged in contradictions and complexities. Among these snags must count the weakening of confidence in the oppositional terms that structured the secular worldview: irrational versus rational, faith versus knowledge, and the most basic dichotomy, religious versus secular. It is unlikely that diminishing confidence among secularist intellectuals would have occurred had it not coincided with the robust return of religion in cultures around the globe. Quite simply, the world has refused to cooperate with the expectations and divinations of the secularists.

Western Europe is more or less the only region of the world that witnesses low reported levels of individual belief. Not surprisingly, western Europeans frequently look on with dismay and incomprehension at America, where broad swaths of life never ceased to be religious. In America, secularists never denied that believers would remain, but they did expect their num-

bers to decline and the holdouts to settle into a private style of faith. The first assumption is obviously contradicted by the roughly 92 percent of Americans who currently profess belief in God or a universal spirit. Then, too, there are the growing numbers of Americans who describe themselves as "spiritual," a nebulous term that could mean almost anything, and clearly an ongoing trend.

As to the second assumption, far from retreating into the private sphere, religion in America has reasserted its public role. This has been a crucial dimension of the political landscape of America since the early 1980s, when the Moral Majority burst onto the scene. In the ensuing decades, we have seen Christian fundamentalists exert an extraordinary influence on the Republican Party, while grassroots fundamentalist activists have gained power in local politics and school districts. Public education has been a particular target, because from the 1940s to the 1960s, American public schools were the objects of a vigorous secularizing effort that had prohibited religious exercises and Bible reading. Recent years have witnessed repeated efforts to roll back these measures, bring prayer back into the schools, and offset the teaching of Darwinian evolution with instruction in creationism. George W. Bush supported these campaigns in various ways, including his controversial faith-based initiatives, which allowed religious organizations to compete for government money without a strict separation between their religious activities and their social-service programs.

The reinvigoration of religion's public role has not been the sole preserve of the Christian Right. Progressive movements have drawn heavily on religious themes, most prominently the civil-rights movement. Barack Obama's eloquence is often leavened by biblical resonances, and his message of hope taps the veins of religious yearning and expectation that marble the bedrock of American oratory. Moreover, even though Obama has reversed some of Bush's religiously driven policies, such as the restriction on human embryonic stem-cell research, he has

Pregame prayers at Billy Ryan High School, Texas, 2003. Photograph by Gueorgui Pinkhassov.

continued Bush's willingness to partner with faith-based social organizations. What separates the two administrations is Obama's promise to refuse to endorse employment discrimination based on faith within religious organizations receiving taxpayer dollars. This in turn signals one of the most important departures of the new administration, namely Obama's much stronger emphasis on the inclusiveness of America as a land of faith. "We know that our patchwork heritage is a strength, not a weakness," he said in his inaugural address. "We are a nation of Christians and Muslims, Jews, and Hindus—and nonbelievers."

Obama speaks in the tongue of America's civil religion, and here "religion" means more than just a metaphor for love of flag and country. True to Obama's claim, Christianity may have provided the predominant frame in this country, but it is remarkable that the American civil religion seems capable of drawing all the major faiths into its ambit. Indeed, it seems that America is a machine for generating faith—

studies have found that immigrants of all faith traditions often become more, not less religious as they steep in the melting pot. That is, perhaps, not as surprising as it might sound. Alexis de Tocqueville [*United States*, page 29], after all, had already described the potent link between religion and democracy in America. To this day it is difficult to overlook the paradox that in a land that prides itself on the constitutional separation of church and state, religion nonetheless provides crucial ligaments that tie many people to their civic identity. (Witness a 2006 survey that suggested that Americans consider atheists the least trusted minority in American society. In light of that, Obama's inclusion of nonbelievers was not incidental.)

Almost anywhere one looks across the globe, there is ample evidence of the strengthening of individual belief. That includes, most obviously, the intensification of faith throughout the Islamic world, but it would also have to include the spread of evangelical Protestantism, a worldwide phenomenon described by

John Micklethwait and Adrian Wooldridge in their recent book *God Is Back: How the Global Revival of Faith Is Changing the World*. Yet the truly striking phenomenon is the reassertion of the public role of religion, a phenomenon that ties together the intensification of personal faith and a host of economic and geopolitical factors. Again, the most conspicuous example is Islam. Militant Islam exploded into world awareness with the Iranian Revolution in 1979. In the late 1970s, the mujahideen began to wage guerilla war against the Soviet-backed Afghan government and then against the USSR itself. That in turn prepared for the ascendancy of the Taliban theocracy in Afghanistan. So long as the parameters of the Cold War remained in place, the emergence of Islamic militancy could be and was folded into the struggle between America and the Soviet Union. Only after the collapse of the USSR did militant Islam emerge as a perceived global threat. Only then could the great ideological polarization of the Cold War be supplanted by the image of a world torn between an epochal conflict between Judeo-Christian and Islamic cultures, the so-called clash of civilizations.

Militant Islam so commanded world attention even before 9/11 that it is easy to forget the many other instances of the return of religion to public life. Examples abound. In what seems to be a vindication of Islam's tolerant tradition, we see the peaceful growth of political Islam within Turkey, a democracy that has been aggressively secularist since its founding by Atatürk in 1923. With the collapse of Yugoslavia, religious-ethnic identities emerged with a vengeance in the Balkans in the 1990s, and here too the Muslims occupied the position of a basically tolerant and peace-seeking minority. In the overthrow of communism, Christianity frequently played a conspicuous role. This was particularly strong in Poland, where the Solidarity movement drew on Catholic social teaching, and the native-born Pope John Paul II became a moral polestar for the opponents of Communism. Then, too, there were the powerful currents of Liberation Theology that swept through Latin America during the 1970s and 1980s, currents, incidentally, that John Paul II opposed because of their openness to Marxism. In Israel, after the triumphant 1967 Six-Day

Decree establishing freedom of worship, French engraving, 1799.

LIBERTÉ des CULTES.

War, the moderate religious political parties became more militantly messianic in their belief that settling the territories Israel had captured from Egypt, Jordan, and Syria was a fulfillment of God's will that Israel once again reach to its biblical borders.

Surveying this global landscape of renewed public religion in 1999, Peter Berger, one of the greatest living sociologists of religion, concluded, "the assumption that we live in a secularized world is false. The world today, with some exceptions … is as furiously religious as it ever was, and in some places more so than ever." Reading that, our brow knits in discontent, and we pause to ask, really? Just as furiously? Undoubtedly, the predictions of a Sigmund Freud have not come to pass; and the ironclad identification of modernization with the decline of religion looks more like a metaphysical belief than an accurate description of reality. Nonetheless, whatever complications secularism has encountered in both its own self-understanding and its ability to account for sociopolitical developments, it is misguided to turn the tables and portray secularism as the illusion and religion as the reality of our world.

The emergence of modern secularism over the last several hundred years has been truly epoch-making, and it has reshaped our entire world. Even in regions of the world where religious revival has taken virulent forms, fundamentalists encounter champions of secularism. Where secularists are absent, it is only because they have been imprisoned, killed, or driven out. Where religion once sealed off the limits of the thinkable, in the modern era a new epoch cracked open these closed boundaries. For unprecedented millions around the world, fundamentalist belief has become more and more one possible choice among several. The actual clash that defines our world is not between allegedly Judeo-Christian and Islamic civilizations, but between *closed* and *open* worldviews. It is not a clash between civilizations. It is a clash within them, among their members and among the possibilities existing within these specific cultures. An open worldview is capacious enough to embrace both religious belief and outright nonbelief. Here, the secularist worldview actually intersects with the examples of moderation and tolerance found in all the great faith traditions.

Yet, insofar as this is possible, it is only on the grounds prepared by secularism. For secularism emerged historically as the only mode humans have found to successfully and peacefully manage the tensions of diverse belief systems within a pluralistic framework.

To understand this point, we need for a moment to set aside our discussion of secularism as a worldview based on nonbelief and instead consider secularism from another angle, namely the institutional development of the secular sphere. And to do this, we need to recall the long history of the distinction between the *religious* and the *secular* within the Christian tradition. This is a distinction as old as Christianity itself.

Jesus Christ himself counseled, "Render unto Caesar the things which are Caesar's, and unto God the things that are God's." St. Augustine enshrined this division as a philosophical principle when he separated the city of God from the earthly city, and drew a sharp line between the sacred history contained in the Bible and the secular history of the affairs of men. Medieval Christian thinkers distinguished between the spiritual and the temporal, medieval lawyers distinguished between ecclesiastical and temporal powers. These two powers were meant to operate together in a harmonious and complementary way, though in actuality the Middle Ages witnessed almost continual competition between the Pope and the worldly monarchs. Ironically, secularism has its origins in this Christian idea of the *saeculum*. Of course, the original Christian concept of the secular had nothing to do with nonbelief, but with a division of human reality into two distinct regions. Moreover, in the medieval imagination, the division between the ecclesiastical and temporal powers was unmistakably superseded by the higher power of God. Yet the seed was planted for the development of the modern idea of a secular state and society.

The modern democracies of Europe and the Americas all, in some way, preserve this division between the secular and the religious. But a funny thing happened on the way to modernity. The relationship between secularism and religiosity got reversed. Where religion and the all-encompassing reality of God defined the boundaries of the medieval secular domain, in modern democratic societies the secular envelops the religious. The secular sphere now sets the appropriate boundaries of religion within public life. Of course, it is a basic dimension of this modern arrangement that the state does not meddle in matters of private conviction, but make no mistake: it is of fundamental concern to the state that it retains the right to define the

I daresay anything can be made holy by being sincerely worshipped.
—Iris Murdoch, 1990

relationship between private belief and public life. Insofar as believers bring their beliefs into the public realm, they have to operate on the terms of this secular arrangement.

It is important to appreciate the magnitude of this fact. Historically, comprehensive belief systems have been, as the phrase implies, totalizing in their claims to righteousness and the imperative to organize spiritual, social, and political life around their truth. By contrast, recognition of the value of pluralism and tolerance in the democratic public sphere means these "liberal" values must already have penetrated into the heart of the comprehensive doctrine itself, challenging its totalizing impulse and relativizing it in relation to competing general claims. Even those who fight for a more public role of religion within liberal democratic societies do so as secularists. This point is made forcefully whenever liberal societies encounter people whose religious doctrines have not been transformed in this way, a lesson that liberal democracies have learned anew since 9/11.

So we can define secularization as a specific pattern of transformation and differentiation in

the relationship between religious and ecclesiastical institutions on the one side and secular institutional spheres such as the state, economy, science, art, entertainment, health, and welfare on the other side. To describe secularization in this fashion does not obligate us to identify it with the decline of religion, but rather with a way of organizing the social and political life of a specific community. Moreover, it opens the possibility for a more nuanced understanding of the relationship between secularism and religion in different cultures. After all, the division between the secular and the religious may have originated in Latin Christendom, but it has spread across the globe, exported first in the age of European expansionism and then later as an ideal of liberal democracy. And as it has taken root in new settings, the differentiation between secular and religious spheres has taken on local color, depending on the specifics of the religious tradition and the social dynamics at play. Instead of presenting us with an image of insurmountable clashes between civilizations or irreconcilable conflicts between belief and nonbelief, this view suggests a world filled with various concrete examples of complicated negotiations between different spheres of human life and belief.

Of course, these negotiations are not always easy, as we see when anti-abortionists disregard the civil law and picket clinics or even murder doctors in the name of protecting life. And we must acknowledge those cases where the negotiations have become severely imperiled, as in present-day Pakistan, which teeters on the brink of all-out religious civil war. Or broken down altogether as theocracy triumphs and forcibly absorbs the secular sphere back into religion, as in Taliban Afghanistan, with its marauding religious police and its brutal enforcement of Sharia law. Terrifying as these examples are, the violent rejection of secularism is the exception that proves the rule. Fundamentalism in the modern world is a reactionary formation that would be unimaginable without the presence of its enemy—and that presence conditions the reaction. Contradicting the image of a clash of civilizations, radical Islam perceives its enemy not only to be infidel Americans, but also tolerant Muslims who advocate a modern secular organization of religious life.

What is the future of secularism? As we have seen, this worldview and its belief that religion was on the decline have experienced a number of severe setbacks in recent decades. The weakening of the secularization model that incubated in western culture from at least the eighteenth-century Enlightenment through to the twentieth century is indeed a remarkable fact in the intellectual landscape of the present. Ultimately, however, the emergence of modern secularism, including outright atheism, is itself a far more extraordinary event. After all, from the earliest evidence of human symbolic activity—art, song, dance, and ritual—dating back at least fifty thousand years, there is evidence of religion: conceptions of an afterlife, of deities, and of the human desire to summon these supernatural powers. Measured against this vast stretch of time, the strictly naturalist conception of the world is a brand new creature. It may have begun to stir as long ago as three, four, five, or six hundred years—exact chronology is not the really important point. To an ear tuned to the long duration of human history, the claim that the cosmos is godless still rings with bold novelty.

The predictions of the radical secularizers may have proven overly exuberant when measured against the tenacity of belief and the complexity of the present world. And the

Superheroes

Name: Gitche Manitou
Group Affiliation: Algonquins
Feats of Strength: Designed the world, generated life
Manifestations: All earthly phenomena

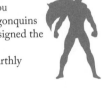

Name: Allah
Group Affiliation: Muslims
Feats of Strength: Revealed the Qur'an, the Torah, and the Gospels
Manifestations: None

Name: Morrígan (trio of deities)
Group Affiliation: Celts
Feats of Strength: Determined men's births and deaths
Manifestations: Crow, Washer at the Ford

Name: Zeus
Group Affiliation: Greeks
Feats of Strength: Ruled gods and men, stopped the moon from shining
Manifestations: Swan, bull, shower of gold

Name: Yu the Great
Group Affiliation: Daoists
Feats of Strength: Made land arable, regulated water flow
Manifestation: Bear

Name: Shiva
Group Affiliation: Hindus
Feats of Strength: Destroyed universe in order to recreate it
Manifestations: Three-eyed man, beggar, naked ascetic

Name: uMvelinqangi
Group Affiliation: Zulus
Feats of Strength: Ruled over dark forces
Manifestations: Thunder, earthquakes

Name: Yahweh
Group Affiliation: Jews
Feats of Strength: Razed Sodom and Gomorrah, saved the Israelites
Manifestations: Pillar of fire, burning bush

polemics of best-selling atheist authors like Richard Dawkins and Christopher Hitchens may seem to vindicate Freud's imaginary opponent's warning that religion could only be replaced by another doctrine, one equally marked by sanctity, rigidity, and intolerance. Yet if the human past was fully intertwined with religion, the future is long and open. As far as the eye can see, it is a future indelibly stamped by the great turning point when nonbelief entered the world. In considering these prospects, let us transpose onto the grandest metaphysical scale Chairman Mao's response when he was asked about the impact of the French Revolution: "Too soon to tell."

Basmalah, invocation of Allah which begins nearly every sura of the Qur'an and translates to "In the name of God, the Benevolent, the Merciful."

Secularism is undoubtedly suffering through a crisis of confidence. Perhaps, though, this presents an opportunity to reinvigorate the secularist vision. Outspoken atheists such as Hitchens and Dawkins may allow nonbelievers to do some cheerleading, but they are not likely to reenergize the radically secular worldview. After all, their arguments are familiar; they have been enumerated many times already. They are, as Freud's fictive opponent feared, likely to breed intolerance. Better to recognize that both the history of religion and the secular story are not lacking in examples of intolerance, but neither is one or the other short on acts of charity and hospitality, right up to and including love across the borders. Besides, it is not clear that anyone stops believing because of the better argument.

The secularizers should worry less about converting believers and more about reinvigorating secularism's own potential for deep meaning and rich experience. From at least Chateaubriand's time, savvy defenders of the faith have known that they will not win an argument on the basis of reason alone. So they have largely ceded that ground to secularists. But in common with the Romantic Chateaubriand, defenders of faith have insisted that religion holds a lock on the power to satisfy people's need for emotional fulfillment. Secularists have been all too willing to allow believers to monopolize the language of sublimity, ecstasy, deep meaning, mystery, and transcendence. It is time to insist on the authenticity and meaningfulness of the secularist's transports, reveries, epiphanies, and, if you will, transcendent experiences. Secularists have allowed themselves to be portrayed as heroic pessimists, cold rationalists, immoralists, or callow hedonists. Time now to reaffirm the drama and pathos of the secularist adventure. If Chateaubriand wanted us to weep at Catholic Mass, then it is time for secularists to get dewy-eyed when, for instance, they read the resounding final words of Darwin's *Origin of Species*. "There is grandeur in this view of life, with its several powers, having been originally breathed into a few forms or into one; and that, whilst this planet has gone cycling on according to the fixed law of gravity, from so simple a beginning, endless forms most beautiful and most wonderful have been, and are being, evolved."

We should put aside the language of a clash. The reinvigoration of secularist values need not involve an attack on religion, any more than the reassertion of religion need involve an attack on nonbelief. Indeed, in a pluralist situation, secularists can worry about the order of their own house, without concerning themselves overly much with their neighbors. But this is the important point: religion and nonreligion can coexist in this way when and only when they both already stand firmly within a relationship defined by secularization. The moment that secularized relationship ceases to be the case, we would all have cause to worry, believers and nonbelievers alike.

CONVERSATIONS

SØREN KIERKEGAARD  BERTRAND RUSSELL

Fear and Trembling, 1843

Human Society in Ethics and Politics, 1954

Faith is the highest passion in a human being. Many in every generation may not come that far, but none comes further. Whether there are also many who do not discover it in our own age I leave open. I can only refer to my own experience, that of one who makes no secret of the fact that he has far to go, yet without therefore wishing to deceive either himself or what is great by reducing this latter to a triviality, to a children's disease which one must hope to get over as soon as possible. But life has tasks enough, even for one who fails to come as far as faith, and when he loves these honestly life won't be a waste either, even if it can never compare with that of those who had a sense of the highest and grasped it. But anyone who comes to faith (whether he be greatly talented or simple-minded makes no difference) won't remain at a standstill there. Indeed, he would be shocked if anyone said this to him. Just as the lover would be indignant if someone said he had come to a standstill in his love, for he would reply, "I'm by no means standing still in my love, for I have my life in it." And yet he too doesn't come any further, not to anything else. For when he finds that out he has another explanation.

We may define "faith" as a firm belief in something for which there is no evidence. Where there is evidence, no one speaks of "faith." We do not speak of faith that two and two are four or that the earth is round. We only speak of faith when we wish to substitute emotion for evidence. The substitution of emotion for evidence is apt to lead to strife, since different groups substitute different emotions. Christians have faith in the Resurrection, communists have faith in Marx's Theory of Value. Neither faith can be defended rationally, and each therefore is defended by propaganda and, if necessary, by war. The two are equal in this respect. If you think it immensely important that people should believe something which cannot be rationally defended, it makes no difference what the something is. Where you control the government, you teach the something to the immature minds of children and you burn or prohibit books which teach the contrary. Where you do not control the government, you will, if you are strong enough, build up armed forces with a view to conquest. All this is an inevitable consequence of any strongly held faith unless, like the Quakers, you are content to remain forever a tiny minority.

JOHN MILTON REINHOLD NIEBUHR

Paradise Lost, 1667

Th' Apostate, and more haughty thus replied:
That we were form'd then, say'st thou? and the
      work
Of secondary hands, by task transfer'd
From Father to his Son? Strange point, and new!
Doctrine which we would know whence learn'd:
      who saw
When this creation was? Remember'st thou
Thy making, while the Maker gave thee being?
We know no time when we were not as now;
Know none before us, self-begot, self-raised
By our own quick'ning pow'r, when fatal course
Had circled his full orb, the birth mature
Of this our native Heav'n, ethereal sons.
Our puissance is our own; our own right hand
Shall teach us highest deeds, by proof to try
Who is our equal: then thou shalt behold
Whether by supplication we intend
Address, and to begirt th'almighty throne
Beseeching or besieging. This report,
These tidings, carry to th'Anointed King;
And fly, ere evil intercept thy flight.

"The Christian Church in a Secular Age," 1937

Every form of modern secularism contains an implicit or explicit self-glorification and deification. Humanistic rationalism, forgetting that human reason as well as human physical existence is a derived, dependent, created, and finite reality, makes it into a principle of interpretation of the meaning of life; and believes that its gradual extension is the guarantee of the ultimate destruction of evil in history. It mistakes the image of God in man for God Himself. It does not realize that the freedom by which man is endowed in his rational nature is the occasion for his sin as well as the ground of morality. It does not understand that by this reason nature's harmless will to live is transmuted into a sinful will to power. It is by this reason that men make pretentious claims for their partial and relative insights, falsely identifying them with absolute truth. Thus rationalism always involves itself in two descending scales of self-deification. What begins as the deification of humanity in abstract terms ends as the deification of a particular type of man, who supposedly possesses ultimate insights.

RALPH WALDO EMERSON  G. K. CHESTERON

"Address to the Harvard Divinity School," 1838

The Everlasting Man, 1925

Jesus Christ belonged to the true race of prophets. He saw with open eye the mystery of the soul. Drawn by its severe harmony, ravished with its beauty, he lived in it, and had his being there. Alone in all history, he estimated the greatness of man. One man was true to what is in you and me. He saw that God incarnates himself in man and evermore goes forth anew to take possession of his world. He said, in this jubilee of sublime emotion, "I am divine. Through me, God acts; through me, speaks. Would you see God, see me; or, see thee, when thou also thinkest as I now think." But what a distortion did his doctrine and memory suffer in the same, in the next, and the following ages! There is no doctrine of the reason which will bear to be taught by the understanding. The understanding caught this high chant from the poet's lips, and said, in the next age, "This was Jehovah come down out of heaven. I will kill you, if you say he was a man." The idioms of his language and the figures of his rhetoric have usurped the place of his truth, and churches are not built on his principles, but on his tropes. Christianity became a mythos, as the poetic teaching of Greece and Egypt before. He spoke of miracles, for he felt that man's life was a miracle, and all that man doth, and he knew that this daily miracle shines as the character ascends. But the word Miracle, as pronounced by Christian churches, gives a false impression; it is Monster. It is not one with the blowing clover and the falling rain.

We have all heard people say a hundred times over, for they seem never to tire of saying it, that the Jesus of the New Testament is indeed a most merciful and humane lover of humanity, but that the Church has hidden this human character in repellent dogmas and stiffened it with ecclesiastical terrors till it has taken on an inhuman character. This is very nearly the reverse of the truth. The truth is that it is the image of Christ in the churches that is almost entirely mild and merciful. It is the image of Christ in the Gospels that is a good many other things as well. The figure in the Gospels does indeed utter in words of almost heart-breaking beauty his pity for our broken hearts. But they are very far from being the only sort of words that he utters. Nevertheless they are almost the only kind of words that the Church in its popular imagery ever represents him as uttering.

There is something appalling, something that makes the blood run cold, in the idea of having a statue of Christ in wrath. There is something insupportable even to the imagination in the idea of turning the corner of a street or coming out in the spaces of a marketplace, to meet the petrifying petrifaction of *that* figure as it turned upon a generation of vipers, or that face as it looked at the face of a hypocrite. The Church can reasonably be justified therefore if she turns the most merciful face or aspect toward men; but it is certainly the most merciful aspect that she does turn.

Reconsideration:

"The Grand Inquisitor" *by Fyodor Dostoevsky*

FREEDOM BY NECESSITY

by Terry Eagleton

First published in tsarist Russia in 1880, *The Brothers Karamazov* is Fyodor Dostoevsky's metaphysical masterpiece, a novel alive with rumors of damnation and intimations of immortality. Sigmund Freud believed that the book betrayed darkly enigmatic, even criminal tendencies in Dostoevsky, while a Russian neologism—*Karamazovshchina*—came to denote the depravity, violence, and psychological deviation which the work explores. Like much of Dostoevsky's fiction, his final novel combines the tragic with the grotesque, moments of mystical ecstasy with episodes of savage farce. His characters seem to occupy a permanent state of pathological anguish or morbid sensitivity: ruined gentlefolk, buffoonish landowners, and socially paranoid clerks reap a perverse delight from being insulted or humiliated.

His extraordinary novels, among them *Crime and Punishment* (1866), *The Idiot* (1869), and *Demons* (1872), present a society that is sunk in feudal poverty but gripped by avant-garde ideas, awash with anarchism and nihilism, God-fearers and God-deniers. As one who felt the lure of Russian Orthodox Christianity, Dostoevsky set his face firmly against radical politics and liberal secularism; like many a modernist, he was as politically conservative as he was artistically audacious. Yet his imagination was haunted by rebels and parricides, by the damned and debauched, as much as by the saints and scripture. Perhaps dissoluteness is merely a crooked way to heaven. Perhaps the devil understands more about God in his own fashion than the stuff-shirted prig.

The Brothers Karamazov is not only a meditation on grace and sinfulness, hell and salvation. It is also a whodunit. Enormously complex and running to nearly one thousand pages in some editions, the novel revolves around the murder of the landowner Fyodor Karamazov; and the whole action—packed into a mere four days—provides the highly wrought drama of the finest of detective stories. On this slim narrative foundation rests an enormous, unwieldy superstructure of social commentary, religious meditation, and philosophical rumination. Fyodor's sons, the titular brothers, occasionally teeter on the

Terry Eagleton is a cultural critic and the author of more than forty books, including Literary Theory, The Illusions of Postmodernism, *and most recently,* Reason, Faith, and Revolution: Reflections on the God Debate. On Evil *is forthcoming from Yale University Press.*

"After Raphael Part 2," by Victoria Hall, 2005.

brink of madness and spiritual ruin, each exhibiting contempt for petty-bourgeois morality. The violent and sexually dissolute Dmitri, a half-sensual, half-childlike moral ruffian, is rent by Oedipal rage. Alexei, the youngest brother, equally disdains the moral middle ground but in the direction of the angelic rather than the demonic. The rationalist middle brother, Ivan, appears to reject God out of hand, engaging in a lively debate with the Devil, who appears as a shabby-genteel figure wearing a pair of unfashionable checkered trousers.

The most extraordinary set piece in the novel is "The Grand Inquisitor." Ivan shares the tale of the Grand Inquisitor and Jesus with Alexei, as part of a continuing dialogue between the brothers on the question of religious faith. Their discussions are dramatic,

Forgive, O Lord, my little jokes on Thee
And I'll forgive Thy great big one on me.
—Robert Frost, 1962

strategic affairs rather than straightforward philosophical arguments. We are not therefore to mistake this marvelously rich narrative simply as a reflection of Dostoevsky's own views. Like Marlowe's narrative in *Heart of Darkness*, it is a story within a story. We do not know how accurately it reflects Ivan's own beliefs, or how far it is influenced by its conversational occasion. During the episode, we are allowed no direct access to his consciousness. Instead, we are given a story which has no existence apart from this particular act of telling, which Ivan himself airily dismisses at one point as "just the muddled poem of a muddled student." Perhaps he is just trying to get a rise out of his brother, who finds the fable more or less incomprehensible. Is he just out to shake Alexei's faith? The complex, devious form of the episode, in other words, alerts us to the fact that we are in the presence of literature, not philosophy or theology. The Grand Inquisitor indicts Christ, which does not seem characteristic of the re-

ligiously inclined Dostoevsky. On the other hand, the Inquisitor's low view of the common herd sounds close enough to his author's own opinions. There is nothing in this great chapter we are allowed to take straight. The truth is not to be bought so cheaply.

"The Grand Inquisitor" is simple enough in plot: Jesus returns to earth, imprudent enough to choose as his point of reentry the city of Seville during the Spanish Inquisition. The near-ninety-year-old Grand Inquisitor orders his guards to seize the Savior, intent on having him burnt the next day in the public square as "the vilest of heretics," and enters into Jesus' prison cell to explain why. What follows is either one of the craftiest apologies for religious despotism ever written or a scathing satire of such autocracy. Why has Jesus, the Inquisitor demands, bound the intolerable burden of absolute freedom on poor, feeble, depraved humanity? How dare he and his Father profess their eternal love for men and women while dangling before their eyes impossible ideals? Better, surely, to offer people what they clamor for most—the bread of the earth—rather than some ethereal bread of heaven. The terrible truth is that human beings cannot bear the burden of freedom. "There is nothing more seductive for man than the freedom of his conscience," the Inquisitor explains to Jesus, "but there is nothing more tormenting either. And so, instead of a firm foundation for appeasing human conscience once and for all, you chose everything that was unusual, enigmatic, and indefinite, you chose everything that was beyond men's strength." Man yearns for nothing more than to surrender his frightful liberty to some benign ruler, who will care for his bodily needs and relieve him of the spiritual suffering known as the will to choose.

The only relief, the Inquisitor suggests, is the Church. "Better that you enslave us, but feed us," is the people's cry; the Church in its wisdom responds to this plea with the three sacred consolations of "miracle, mystery, and authority." Unlike the ruthlessly intellectual Ivan, the common people want to worship, not understand,

and the Church's traditional combination of miracle working, a cloak of mystery and enigma, and an authority which appeals to no purely rational foundation, graciously allows them veneration. The Grand Inquisitor understands, as he is sure God does not, just how weak and wretched human beings are. His love consists of protecting them in their frailty, not sadistically rubbing their noses in it. When the Grand Inquisitor ends his denunciation, Jesus says nothing. Instead, he leans forward and kisses the old man on the lips. The Inquisitor does not have Jesus put to death after all. Instead, he sends him away, demanding he never return.

Unlike most atheists and agnostics—in fact, unlike most devout believers—Dostoevsky grasps that God is the source of human freedom, not the obstacle to it. God's love, as Thomas Aquinas argues, is what allows us to be ourselves, as the care of a wise parent allows us to flourish as autonomous beings. Paradoxically, it is our dependence on God which liberates us. Dostoevsky has no patience for the lurid adolescent fantasy of God as a Big Daddy who is out to spoil our secret pleasures, a kind of celestial bully or Bill O'Reilly in the sky. We have good psychological reasons for cherishing that fantasy, chronic masochists that we are. Freud knew well the gratification we reap from the pummeling that our merciless, vindictive superego doles out to us. It is just that we have to unlearn this infantile view of God and come to see him as friend, lover, fellow sufferer, and counsel for the defense. And this we are notably reluctant to do. It is far more convenient to view him as an irascible old bastard who, like some pampered rock star, needs to be endlessly placated and cajoled. That way we can enjoy the Oedipal delights of rebelling against him.

The Grand Inquisitor is also right to see that God is overwhelming, for in the Old Testament, Yahweh manifests as a fearsome fire who is terrible to look upon, a sublime abyss that defeats all representation. What the Inquisitor fails to grasp is that what is sublimely overwhelming about God is his love. He is a holy terror who destroys only in order to renew, uncompromis-

ing in his mercy and forgiveness. His passion for his creatures has the intransigence of all purely unconditional things. God does not have, as many Gnostics comfortably imagined, a creative face and a destructive one. The scandal is that the two faces are one and the same.

Freedom, too, has two faces. It is both gift and curse, poison and cure, self-achievement and self-undoing. The lives of free creatures are both precarious and exhilarating, which is more than can be said for goldfish. The historical animal, unlike the natural one, is perpetually at risk, "condemned to be free," says Sartre. "We live in freedom by necessity," Auden adds. We drag our liberty behind us like a ball and chain. But while human beings can abuse their freedom, they are not truly human without it. The greatest compliment ever paid to humanity is the doctrine of hell. If we are free to reject the very source of

As you know, God is generally on the side of the big squadrons against the small ones.
—Comte de Bussy-Rabutin, 1677

our freedom, spit in the face of our Creator, then we must be mighty indeed. And if the Creator has humbled himself in this way, willing his own vulnerability, then he is perhaps not as controlling as he is rumored to be. The thought, however, is as alarming as it is agreeable, which is why the Grand Inquisitor can see nothing better to do with freedom than to yield it up instantly to another, like a soccer player desperate to pass the ball he has just received.

This act of renunciation, we may note, is not quite the same as the belief that the highest form of freedom is the voluntary ceding of it. For the Inquisitor, who has the demeaning view of humanity typical of the conservative, men and women should abandon their liberty because it is a curse. By contrast, for a certain kind of tragic protagonist, freedom is to be surrendered precisely because it is our dearest possession. If we can freely give it away, grapple our destiny deliberately, then we are invulnerable indeed. In the very act of submitting to a higher authority, we reveal a power that transcends it. There is something of this paradox in the crucifixion of Christ, as Jesus' loving acceptance of the Father's will lays the ground for his resurrection. Only by embracing humiliation and death, without thinking of them as stepping stones to glory, is he able to transfigure weakness into power. Yet this paradox may also be the devil's most subtle temptation. It was for those Nazis who found a deeper kind of freedom, one far superior to the paltry liberal variety, in submitting themselves to the Führer and Fatherland. There is a thin line between the SS commandant and the martyr who voluntarily gives up his or her body to be burnt for the sake of others.

Americans typically think of the positive aspects of idealism, whereas the Inquisitor attends to its destructive consequences. For a European like myself, the idealism of the

Men are not flattered by being shown that there has been a difference of purpose between the Almighty and them.
—*Abraham Lincoln, 1865*

United States, which is also, ironically, one of the most materialistic civilizations history has ever produced, is a constant source of wonderment. Americans must affirm rather than deny, hope rather than lament, be winners rather than losers, eternally aspire rather than cravenly submit. In this Faustian world of ceaseless striving, negativity constitutes a thought crime. With a victory of mind over matter worthy of Christian Science, there are no limits to the human will.

This blasphemous ideology, summarized in the common American lie that you can do anything you set your mind to, fails to acknowledge the frailty and finitude of the human, which is where the Inquisitor knows better. Also unlike the Inquisitor, this boundless optimism fails to acknowledge what one might call the terrorism of the ideal. Ideals are essential, but like the "law" for St. Paul, they can do no more than

show you where you went wrong, but they cannot reveal to you how to go right. This is why Paul calls the law cursed. Ideals have the stiff-necked implacability of the Freudian superego, a faculty which encourages us to aspire beyond our powers, fail miserably, and then lapse into self-loathing. Idealism is the accomplice of violence and despair, not an antidote to them. The neoconservative desire to drag a barbaric world into the light of civilization is on display at Guantanamo Bay.

It is against this high-minded fury, this self-destructive cycle, that the Inquisitor seeks to protect the common people. If we do not expect too much of others, we will not fall into postures of tragic despondency when they inevitably fall short. Cynicism or nihilism is the other face of idealism. Realism is the only sure foundation for the moral life. What we share most with our fellow human beings *is* our fleshly weakness. Any solidarity based not on this, but on some community of noble purpose, is likely to prove fragile. Solidarity of weakness is mutual forgiveness, and forgiveness represents the ultimate form of realism since, in order to be authentic, it must reckon with the full horror of the offense in the act of setting it aside. As Freud was aware, man's more sublime impulses must be rooted in his baser ones, and will not flourish otherwise. What we creatures have in common, in the end, is the unadorned body, which is what is most universal about us but also what is most vulnerably precarious and particular. This is why the concentration-camp victim, stripped of all specific culture and history, is prototypically human in his or her very dispossession. The real alternative to the idealist is the loser. The message of the New Testament is that it is above all the losers, whores, serial adulterers, colonial collaborators, and scum of the earth, not the pious and well-behaved, who will inherit the kingdom. It is notable that Jesus does not even ask these shady characters to repent before he consorts with them, a striking and scandalous innovation in Judaic practice.

The Grand Inquisitor's theology goes awry because he does not see that the dangerous freedom God bequeaths to men and women is, among other things, freedom from the law. Which is why Jesus says, "My yoke is easy, and my burden is light." It is the legalistic Scribes and Pharisees, so he claims, who bind intolerably heavy burdens on the backs of the poor. Jesus' greatest demands on the other hand are love and mercy. With these simple requests, he shows that God is not Big Daddy, not a restrictive and withholding adversary. In the Old Testament, the Hebrew word for "adversary" is Satan, and God begins to look like Satan for those who conceive of him as a fearsome Mega Power, and who think that they can bargain their way into his favor by doing all the right things. According to Jesus, God has already forgiven them—what they need to do is let him love them. This is exceedingly hard. It is far more pleasurable to hug one's chains.

The Grand Inquisitor ranks among those who regard God as their adversary. He believes that like a brutal despot, God loads on men and women more than they can bear; the burden he loads on them is known not as tithe or tax but freedom. However, this overlooks God's own solidarity with human weakness, which is known as Jesus. On Calvary, God proves feeble and fleshly even unto death. His only signifier is the tortured body of one who spoke out for love and justice and was done to death by the state. Only if one can look on this terrible failure and still live can one lay a foundation for anything more edifying. Only by being entombed in the earth can one reach for the sky. It is in the place of excrement, as Yeats reminds us, that love has pitched his mansion. Any moral idealism that refuses this truth is just so much ideology.

Dostoevsky must have known that the Jesus of the New Testament rejects the Inquisitor's own sharp distinction between earthly and heavenly bread. Salvation for Matthew's gospel is not a "religious" or ethereal affair; it is a matter of feeding the hungry and visiting the sick. In true Judaic spirit, the teaching is ethical to core. It is the materialistically minded who like their religion to be otherworldly, in compensation for their own this-worldly crassness. It is not surprising that a material girl like Madonna should be attending classes on mysticism at the

Portrait of Domenican monk Girolamo Savonarola, by Fra Bartolomeo, c. 1495.

Kabbalah Center in Los Angeles. How else can she escape for a moment from her agents, minders, managers, hair stylists, and the rest? Surely salvation cannot lie in anything as prosaic as a cup of water and a crust of bread. The Grand Inquisitor is a thoroughly worldly type, objecting to what he sees as cruelly unrealistic spiritual demands. What he does not see is that God is a unique kind of superego, one who loves and accepts failure rather than simply rewarding success. Nothing could be more worldly wise than that.

Sources

p. 21, Caen Onfray, Michel. *The Atheist's Manifesto.* Translated by Jeremy Leggart. New York: Arcade Publishing, 2007. Copyright © 2007, 2008 by Arcade Publishing, Inc. Used with permission of Arcade Publishing, Inc.

p. 23, Galilee *The New Testament.* New Revised Standard Version. http://bible.oremus.org/?passage=Matthew+5-6.

p. 25, Princeton Einstein, Albert. "Science and Religion." From *The Agnostic Reader.* Edited by S. T. Joshi. Copyright © 2007 by S. T. Joshi. Used with permission of Prometheus Books.

p. 29, United States Tocqueville, Alexis de. *Democracy in America.* Translated by Henry Reeve, Esq. New York: Edward Walker, 1850.

p. 31, Algeria Ibn Khaldun. *The Muqaddimah.* Translated by Franz Rosenthal. Princeton, NJ: Princeton University Press, 1981.

p. 32, Greece *The Homeric Hymns.* Translated by Jules Cashford. London: Penguin Books Ltd, 2003. Copyright © 2003 by Jules Cashford. Used with the permission of Sinclair-Stevenson Agency.

p. 33, Étrépigny Jean Meslier. *Testament: Memoir of the Thoughts and Sentiments of Jean Meslier.* Translated by Michael Shreve. Amherst, NY: Prometheus Books, 2009. Copyright © 2009 by Michael Shreve. Used with permission of Prometheus Books.

p. 35, Connecticut Edwards, Jonathan. *Selected Sermons of Jonathan Edwards.* New York & London: The MacMillan Company, 1904.

p. 37, France ben Yedaiah, Isaac. From *The Medieval Reader.* Edited by Norman F. Cantor. New York: HarperCollins, 1995.

p. 38, Kraków Lenin, Vladimir Ilich. *Religion.* London: Lawrence & Wishart, Ltd. Used with permission of Lawrence & Wishart, Ltd.

p. 40, Athens Critias. Untitled. Translated by R. G. Bury, revised by J. Garret. http://www.wku.edu/~jan.garrett/302/critias.htm. Used with permission of J. Garret.

p. 42, Como Straparola, Gianfrancesco. *The Italian Novelists.* Translated by Thomas Roscoe. London & New York: Frederick Warne and Co.

p. 46, Brooklyn Whitman, Walt. *Leaves of Grass.* New York: The Modern Library, 1921.

p. 47, Edinburgh Hume, David. *The Natural History of Religion.* Stanford, CA: Stanford University Press, 1965.

p. 48, Brittany Zola, Emile. *The Attack on the Mill and Other Stories.* Translated by Douglas Parmée. London, New York & Toronto: Oxford University Press, 1984. Copyright © 1984 by Douglas Parmée. Used with permission of Oxford University Press.

p. 53, Wittenberg Luther, Martin. *Complete Works Volume 31: Career of the Reformer I.* Edited by Harold J. Grimm and Helmut T. Lehmann. Philadelphia: Muhlenberg Press, 1957. Copyright © 1957 by Fortress Press. Used with permission of Augsburg Fortress.

p. 55, Argentina Borges, Jorge Luis. "The Gospel According to Mark." From *Collected Fictions.* Translated by Andrew Hurley. New York: Penguin Books USA, 1998. Copyright © 1998 by Maria Kodama. Translation Copyright © 1998 by Penguin Putnam Inc. Used with permission of Viking Penguin, a division of Penguin Books (USA) Inc.

p. 57, Japan Nichiren. *Sources of Japanese Tradition.* Compiled by Ryusaku Tsunoda, Wm. Theodore de Bary, and Donald Keene. New York: Columbia University Press, 1960. Copyright © 1958 by Columbia University Press, New York. Used with permission of Columbia University Press.

p. 59, Moscow Marina Tsvetaeva. "God (3)," translated by Paul Geary, from *Women in Praise of the Sacred.* Edited by Jane Hirshfield. New York: HarperCollins, 1994. Copyright © 1994 by Jane Hirshfield. Used with permission of HarperCollins.

p. 60, Kreuznach Marx, Karl. Introduction to *A Contribution to the Critique of Hegel's "Philosophy of Right."* New York & Cambridge: Cambridge University Press, 1970. Copyright © 1970 by Cambridge University Press. Used with permission of Cambridge University Press.

p. 61, Tennessee O'Connor, Flannery. *Wise Blood.* New York: Farrar, Straus and Giroux, 1985. Copyright © 1949, 1952, 1962 by Flannery O' Connor. Used with permisssion of Farrar, Straus and Grioux, LLC.

p. 63, Rouen *Jeanne d'Arc: being the story of her life, her achievements, and her death, as attested on oath and set forth in the original documents.* Edited by T. Douglas Murray. New York: McClure Phillips & Co., 1902.

p. 65, Rome St. Jerome. *Select Letters.* Translated by F. A. Wright. Cambridge, MA: Harvard University Press. Copyright © 1933 by the President and Fellows of Harvard College. Used with permission of the publishers and the Trustees of the Loeb Classical Library. The Loeb Classical Library® is a registered trademark of the President and Fellows of Harvard College.

p. 66, Weimar Goethe, Johann Wolfgang von. *Faust, part I.* Translated by Randall Jarrell. New York: Farrar, Straus and Giroux. Copyright © 1959, 1961, 1965, 1973, 1976 by Mary von Scharder Jarrell. Used with permission of Farrar, Straus and Giroux LLC.

p. 68, England Hazlitt, William. *Literary Remains of the Late William Hazlitt.* New York & London: Saunders and Otley, 1836.

p. 69, Shiraz Hafiz. *The Gift: Poems by Hafiz, The Great Sufi Master.* Translated by Daniel Ladinsky. New York: Penguin Books, 1999. Copyright © 1999 by Daniel Ladinsky. Used with permission of Daniel Ladinsky.

p. 70, Iowa City Robinson, Marilynne. "Darwinism." From *The Death of Adam.* New York: Picador, 1998. Copyright © 1998 by Marilynne Robinson. Used with permission of Houghton Mifflin Harcourt Publishing Company. All rights reserved.

p. 75, Rio de Janeiro Guillermoprieto, Alma. *The Heart That Bleeds.* New York: Vintage Books, 1995. Copyright © 1993 by Alma Guillermoprieto. Used with permission of Alfred A. Knopf, a division of Random House, Inc.

p. 78, Poland Singer, Isaac Bashevis. *The Slave.* Translated by Isaac Bashevis Singer and Cecil Hemley. New York: Farrar, Straus And Cudahy, 1962. Copyright © 1962 by Isaac Bashevis Singer. Used with permission of Farrar, Straus and Giroux, LLC.

p. 81, China Wang Wei. "Stone Gate Temple in the Blue Field Mountains," translated by William Barnstone. From *Laughing Lost in the Mountains: Poems of Wang Wei.* Translations by Tony Barnstone, William Barnstone, and Xu Haixin. Lebanon, NH: University Press of New England, 1991. Copyright © 1991 by Univeristy Press of New England. Used with permission of University Press of New England.

p. 82, Constantinople Comnena, Anna. *The Alexiad.* Translated by E. R. A. Sewter, revised by Peter Frankopan. London: Penguin Books Ltd, 2003. Copyright © 1969 by E. R. A. Sewter. Used with permission of Penguin Books Ltd.

p. 84, Edinburgh James, William. *The Varieties of Religious Experience: A Study in Human Nature.* New York, Bombay, and Calcutta: Longmans, Green, and Co., 1911.

p. 86, Ávila St. Teresa. *The Life of Saint Teresa by Herself.* Translated by J. M. Cohen. London: Penguin Books Ltd, 1957. Copyright © 1957 by J. M. Cohen. Used with permission of Penguin Books Ltd.

p. 86, Antioch Julian. *The Works of the Emperor Julian: Volume III.* Translated by Wilmer C. Wright. Cambridge, MA: Harvard University Press, 1923. Copyright © 1923 by the President and Fellows of Harvard College. Used with permission of the publishers and the Trustees of the Loeb Classical Library. The Loeb Classical Library® is a registered trademark of the President and Fellows of Harvard College.

p. 88, Monticello Jefferson, Thomas. *The Life and Selected Writings of Thomas Jefferson.* New York: The Modern Library, 1993.

p. 89, Egypt Plutarch. *Plutarch's Lives, Volume 2.* Translated by John Dryden, edited by Arthur Hugh Clough. New York: The Modern Library, 2001.

p. 91, Warsaw Kolitz, Zvi. *Yosl Rakover Talks to God.* Translated by Carol Brown Janeway. New York: Pantheon Books, 1999. Copyright © 1999 by Carol Brown Janeway. Used with permission of Pantheon Books, a division of Random House, Inc.

p. 93, Lydia Herodotus. *The Histories.* Translated by Aubrey de Sélincourt. Middlesex: Penguin Books Ltd, 1996. Copyright © 1954 by Aubrey de Sélincourt. Revised edition copyright © 1996 by John Marincola. Used with permission of Penguin Books Ltd.

p. 93, Indiana The Religious Society of Friends. *A Declaration of Some of the Fundamental Principles of Christian Truth.* Richmond, IN: Nicholson & Bro., 1887.

p. 95, Saragossa *The Song of Roland.* Translated by W. S. Merwin. From *Medieval Epics.* New York: The Modern Library, 1963. Copyright © 1963, 1991 by W. S. Merwin. Used with permission of The Wylie Agency LLC.

p. 96, Sumer Enheduanna. "The Hymn to Inanna." From *Women in Praise of the Sacred.* Edited by Jane Hirshfield. New York: HarperCollins, 1994. Copyright © 1994 by Jane Hirshfield. Used with permission of HarperCollins. All rights reserved.

p. 98, Mt. Judge Updike, John. *Rabbit, Run.* New York: Ballantine Books, 1960. Copyright © 1960 and renewed 1988 by John Updike. Used with permission of Alfred A. Knopf, a division of Random House, Inc.

p. 101, Thebes Euripides. *The Bacchae.* Translated by Philip Vellacott. London: Penguin Books Ltd, 1973. Copyright © 1954 by Philip Vellacott. Used with permission of Penguin Books Ltd.

p. 104, United States Johnson, James Weldon. *The Autobiography of an Ex-Colored Man.* From *Three Negro Classics.* New York: Avon Books, 1965.

p. 106, China Xunzi. *Basic Writings of Mo Tzu, Hsün Tzu, and Han Fei Tzu.* Translated by Burton Watson. New York: Columbia University Press, 1964. Copyright © 1963, 1964 by Columbia University Press. Used with permission of Columbia University Press.

p. 107, Chang'an Han Yu. "Memorial on the Bone of Buddha." From *Anthology of Chinese Literature, Vol. I.* Edited by Cyril Birch. New York: Grove Press, Inc., 1965. Copyright © 1965 by Grove Press, Inc. Used with permission of Grove/Atlantic, Inc.

p. 109, Ferney Voltaire. *A Philosophical Dictionary, volume the second.* London: W. Dugdale, 1843.

p. 110, Syria Ibn Munqidh, Usama. *The Book of Contemplation: Islam and the Crusades.* Translated by Paul M. Cobb. London: Penguin Books Ltd, 2008. Copyright © 2008 by Paul M. Cobb. Used with permission of Penguin Books Ltd.

p. 111, Moriah *The Old Testament.* New Revised Standard Version. http://bible.oremus.org/?passage=Genesis+22.

p. 112, Nunavut Igjugârjuk with Penny Petrone. *Northern Voices: Inuit Writing in English.* Toronto, Buffalo, London: University of Toronto Press, 2002.

p. 113, Dublin Joyce, James. *A Portrait of the Artist as a Young Man.* New York: B. W. Huebsch, Inc., 1922.

p. 115, London Donne, John. "Hymn to God, My God, in my Sickness." Poetry Foundation, http://www.poetryfoundation.org/archive/poem.html?id=173370

p. 116, Utah Krakauer, Jon. *Under the Banner of Heaven.* New York: Anchor Books, 2004. Copyright © 2003 by Jon Krakauer. Used with permission of Doubleday, a division of Random House, Inc.

p. 118, Heidelberg Weber, Max. *The Protestant Ethic and the Spirit of Capitalism.* Translated by Talcott Parsons. New York: Dover, 2003. Copyright © 1958 by Charles Scribner's Sons. Used with permission of Scribner, a division of Simon & Schuster, Inc.

p. 120, Judaea Josephus. *The Essential Writings.* Translated and edited by Paul L. Maier. Grand Rapids, MI: Kregel Publications, 1988. Copyright © 1988 by Kregel Publications, a division of Kregel, Inc. Used with permission of Kregel Publications, a division of Kregel, Inc.

p. 122, Paris Herzl, Theodor. *A Jewish State.* New York: Federation of American Zionists, 1917.

p. 123, Hindustan Babur. *Babur Nama: Journal of Emperor Babur.* Translated by Annette Susannah Beveridge. Abridged and edited by Dilip Hiro. New Delhi: Penguin Books India, 2006. Copyright © 2006 by Penguin Books India. Used with permission of David Higham Associates.

p. 124, England Hopkins, Gerard Manley. *Poems of Gerard Manley Hopkins.* Mt. Vernon, NY: Peter Pauper Press, 1949.

p. 125, Tel Aviv Roth, Philip. *The Counterlife.* New York: Vintage Books, 1996. Copyright © 1986 by Philip Roth. Used with perission of Farrar, Straus and Giroux LLC.

p. 129, Kars Pamuk, Orhan. *Snow.* Translated by Maureen Freely. New York: Alfred A. Knopf, 2004. Copyright © 2004 by Alfred A. Knopf, a division of Random House, Inc. Used with permission of Alfred A. Knopf, a division of Random House, Inc.

p. 134, Yasnaya Polyana Tolstoy, Leo. *Confession.* Translated by David Patterson. New York and London: W. W. Norton & Company, 1996. Copyright © 1983 by David Patterson. Used with permission of W. W. Norton & Company, Inc.

p. 136, Bithynia Pliny the Younger. *The Letters of the Younger Pliny.* Translated by John Delaware Lewis. London: Kegan Paul, Trench, Trubner, & Co., Ltd, 1890.

p. 136, Boston Wheatley, Phillis. *Memoir and Poems of Phillis Wheatley, a Native African and a Slave.* Boston: Geo. W. Light, 1834.

p. 138, Dayton, TN Mencken, H. L. *The Baltimore Evening Sun,* July 11, 1925. From *A Religious Orgy in Tennessee: A Reporter's Account of the Scopes Monkey Trial.* Hoboken, NJ: Melville House Publishing, 2006. Copyright © 1925 by The Baltimore Sun. Used with permission of The Baltimore Sun.

p. 141, Neyshabur Attar, Farid ud-Din. *The Conference of the Birds.* Translated by Afkham Darbandi and Dick Davis. London: Penguin Books Ltd, 1984. Copyright © 1984 by Afkham Darbandi and Dick Davis. Used with permission of Penguin Group Ltd.

p. 142, Sils-Maria Nietzsche, Friedrich. *The Gay Science.* Translated by Walter Kaufmann. New York: Vintage Books, 1974. Copyright © 1974 by Random House, Inc. Used with permission of Random House, Inc.

p. 143, Seattle McCarthy, Mary. *Memories of a Catholic Girlhood.* New York and San Diego, CA: Harcourt, Inc., 1957.

p. 146, Kiev *Harvard Studies and Notes in Philology and Literature: Volume 12—Russian Primary Chronicles.* By Samuel H. Cross. Edited and translated by Serge A. Zenkovsky. Cambridge, MA: Harvard University Press, 1930. Copyright © 1930 by The President and Fellows of Harvard College. Used with permission of Harvard University Press.

p. 148, Washington, DC Lincoln, Abraham. *Complete Works: Volume Two.* New York: The Century Company, 1907.

p. 150, Buffalo Grove, NY Red Jacket. "Red Jacket on the Religion of the White Man and the Red." From *The World's Famous Orations.* Edited by William Jennings Bryan. New York and London: Funk and Wagnalls Company, 1906.

p. 152, Utopia More, Thomas. *Utopia.* Translated by Paul Turner. New York: Penguin Books, 2003. Copyright © 1961, 2003 by Paul Turner. Used with permission of Penguin Books Ltd.

p. 154, Amritsar Manto, Saadat Hasan. *Mottled Dawn.* New Delhi: Penguin Books India, 1997. Copyright © 1997 by Penguin Books India. Used with permission of Penguin Books India.

p. 156, Rome Pope Innocent IV. *Ad Extirpanda.* Translated by David Renaker. *The Atheist Seventeenth Century Website.* http://userwww.sfsu.edu/~draker/history/Ad_Extirpanda.html.

p. 158, Rome Lucretius. *On The Nature of Things: De rerum natura.* Translated by Anthony M. Esolen. Baltimore and London: The Johns Hopkins University Press, 1995. Copyright © 1995 by The Johns Hopkins University Press. Used with permission of The Johns Hopkins University Press.

p. 160, Bombay Rushdie, Salman. *The Satanic Verses.* New York: Picador, 1988. Copyright © 1988 by Salman Rushdie. Used with permission of Viking Penguin, a division of Penguin Group (USA) Inc.

p. 162, Paris Pascal, Blaise. *Pensées and Other Writings.* Translated by Honor Levi. New York: Oxford University Press, Inc., 1999. Copyright © 1995 by Honor Levi. Used with permission of Oxford University Press, Inc.

p. 164, Spain de Palacios Rubios, Juan Lopez. "The Requerimiento." From *The Spanish Conquest in America: And Its Relation to the History of Slavery and to the Government of Colonies,* by Arthur Helps. New York: Harper & Brothers Publishers, 1856.

p. 166, London Murdoch, Iris. *Nuns and Soldiers.* New York and London: Penguin Books, 1980. Copyright © 1980 by Iris Murdoch. Used with permission of Viking Penguin, a division of Penguin Group (USA) Inc.

p. 168, Arabia *The Qur'an.* Translated by Thomas Cleary. Starlatch Press, 2004. Copyright © 2004 by Thomas Cleary.

p. 170, England Weil, Simone. *Waiting for God.* Translated by Emma Craufurd. New York: HarperCollins, 2001. Copyright © 1951, renewed 1979 by G. P. Putnam's Sons. Used with permission of G. P. Putnam's Sons, a division of Penguin Group (USA) Inc.

p. 171, Nepal Hesse, Hermann. *Siddhartha.* Translated by Rika Lesser. New York: Barnes & Noble Classics, 2007. Copyright © 2007 by Rika Lesser. Used with permission of Barnes & Noble, Inc. All rights reserved.

Statement of Ownership, Management, and Circulation 1. Publication title: Lapham's Quarterly. 2. Publication number: 025-071. 3. Filing date: 10/01/2009. 4. Issue frequency: Quarterly. 5. Number of issues published annually: 4. 6. Annual subscription price: $60.00. 7. Complete mailing address of known office of publication: 33 Irving Place, 8th Floor, New York, NY 10003. 8. Complete mailing address of headquarters or general business office of Publisher: 33 Irving Place, 8th Floor, New York, NY 10003. 9. Full names and complete mailing addresses of Publisher, Editor, and Executive Editor. Publisher: Louisa D. Kearney, 33 Irving Place, 8th Floor, New York, NY 10003. Editor: Lewis H. Lapham: 33 Irving Place, 8th Floor, New York, NY 10003. Executive Editor: Kira Brunner Don: 33 Irving Place, 8th Floor, New York, NY 10003.10. Owner. Full Name: American Agora Foundation, Inc.: 33 Irving Place, 8th Floor, New York, NY 10003.11. Known bondholders, mortgagees, and other security holders owning or holding 1 percent or more of total amount of bonds, mortgages, or other securities: none. 12. Tax Status: Has not changed during preceding 12 months. 13. Publishing title: *Lapham's Quarterly*. 14. Issue date for circulation data below: Fall 2009. 15. Extent and nature of circulation: Average number of copies each issue during preceding 12 months. A. Total number of copies (net press run): 41,970. B. Paid circulation (by mail and outside the mail): (1) Mailed outside-county paid subscriptions stated on PS Form 3541: 15,099. (2) Mailed in-county paid subscriptions stated on PS Form 3541: none. (3) Paid distribution outside the mails including sales through dealers and carriers, street vendors, counter sales, and other paid distribution outside USPS: 10,394. (4) Paid distribution by other classes of mail through the USPS: none. C. Total paid distribution: 25,493. D. Free or nominal rate distribution (by mail and outside the mail): (1) Free or nominal rate outside-county copies included on PS Form 3541: 73. (2) Free or nominal rate in-county copies included on PS Form 3541: none. (3) Free or nominal rate copies mailed at other classes through the USPS: none. (4) Free or nominal rate distribution outside the mail (carriers or other means): 465. E. Total free or nominal rate distribution: 538. F. Total distribution: 26,031. G. Copies not distributed: 15,939. H. Total: 41,970. I. Percent paid: 97.9%. Extent and nature of circulation: Number of copies of single issue published nearest to filing date. A. Total number of copies (net press run): 41,061. B. Paid circulation (by mail and outside the mail): (1) Mailed outside-county paid subscriptions stated on PS Form 3541: 16,797. (2) Mailed in-county paid subscriptions stated on PS Form 3541: none. (3) Paid distribution outside the mails including sales through dealers and carriers, street vendors, counter sales, and other paid distribution outside USPS: 9,158. (4) Paid distribution by other classes of mail through the USPS: none. C. Total paid distribution: 25,955. D. Free or nominal rate distribution (by mail and outside the mail): (1) Free or nominal rate outside-county copies included on PS Form 3541: 78. (2) Free or nominal rate in-county copies included on PS Form 3541: none. (3) Free or nominal rate copies mailed at other classes through the USPS: none. (4) Free or nominal rate distribution outside the mail (carriers or other means): 489. E. Total free or nominal rate distribution: 567. F. Total distribution: 26,522. G. Copies not distributed: 14,539. H. Total: 41,061. I. Percent paid: 97.9%. 16. Publication of statement of ownership will be printed in the Winter 2010 issue of this publication. 17. Signature and title of Editor, Publisher, Business Manager, or Owner: Louisa D. Kearney, Publisher. Date: September 24, 2009. I certify that all information furnished on this form is true and complete. I understand that anyone who furnishes false or misleading information on this form or who omits material or information requested on the form may be subject to criminal sanctions (including fines and imprisonment) and/or civil sanctions (including civil penalties). United States Postal Service.

LAPHAM'S
Q U A R T E R L Y

Televangelist Jimmy Swaggart preaching at Nassau Coliseum, 1987. Photograph by Steve McCurry.